LES

THE AUTOBIOGRAPHY OF LESTER PIGGOTT

Happy Birthday '96

love

Alison & David

xxx

LESTER

THE AUTOBIOGRAPHY
OF LESTER PIGGOTT

CORGI BOOKS

LESTER: THE AUTOBIOGRAPHY OF LESTER PIGGOTT
A CORGI BOOK : 0 552 14443 6

Originally published in Great Britain by Partridge Press,
a division of Transworld Publishers Ltd

PRINTING HISTORY
Partridge Press edition published 1995
Corgi edition published 1996

Set in 10/11pt Linotype Sabon by
Phoenix Typesetting, Ilkley, West Yorkshire

Corgi books are published by Transworld Publishers Ltd,
61-63 Uxbridge Road, London W5 5SA,
in Australia by Transworld Publishers (Australia) Pty Ltd,
15-25 Helles Avenue, Moorebank, NSW 2170
and in New Zealand by Transworld Publishers (NZ) Ltd,
3 William Pickering Drive, Albany, Auckland.

Reproduced, printed and bound in Great Britain by
Cox & Wyman Ltd, Reading, Berks.

To the memory
of my mother and father

Contents

Prologue
A Tenth Derby Winner

By Derby Day 1996 it was over eighteen months since I had ridden in a race in Britain, and nine months since I had announced in September 1995 that I would not be returning to the saddle.

Back in 1985, after announcing my 'first' retirement, I had embarked on a farewell tour before having what I thought would be my last domestic ride at Nottingham in October. Ten years later, having made my comeback in 1990 and carried on riding in Britain until November 1994, I was not inclined to make any great fuss about quitting again. You can't retire twice.

But my withdrawal from the front line did not mean that I could not still be involved in racing at the highest level, and the 1996 Vodafone Derby brought me one of my greatest thrills in the shape of a handsome bay colt trained by my son-in-law William Haggas, who in 1989 had married my elder daughter Maureen.

Shaamit had run just twice as a two-year-old, winning at Doncaster second time out, but we'd always thought very highly of him, and early in 1996 William was seriously contemplating entering the colt in the Derby. It was an expensive business, as Shaamit had not been among the initial entries for the race, and to put him in at the supplementary stage in April would cost his owner Khalifa Dasmal £8,000.

Having had some experience of riding in the Derby, I was asked by William to put Shaamit through his paces before the decision was made, and took the colt up the Waterhall gallop at Newmarket. My nine Derby winners had shown me that the quality a horse most needs for the race is balance, and after that gallop I assured William that Shaamit, clearly a colt of great quality, would not fail on that score. He'd got what it takes, and had to have a go.

A series of setbacks meant that Shaamit went to Epsom on 8 June without a previous run that season, but he made light of his inexperience by showing a tremendous turn of foot in the straight to go clear and hold off Dushyantor to win by a length and a quarter. It was a great family triumph, and to have played a part, however small, in Shaamit's preparation was a huge thrill. It really felt like my tenth Derby winner.

Shaamit's victory delivered the perfect end to a great Derby week for me, as four days before the race the Epsom executive had staged the official opening of the Piggott Gates, through which the Derby runners would exit from the parade ring to the racecourse. These gates display portraits – by artist Roy Miller – of my nine Derby winners as well as other famous horses I rode to victory at Epsom, and to be thus enshrined was a very great honour.

One of the most significant names from my riding past, however, was missing from the distinguished line-up commemorated on those gates. Brandy . . .

I

Born not made

Brandy, a half-tamed bay New Forest pony, was my first love. Though small, she was a real handful, and given half a chance would run away with whoever was on her back. Both my parents regularly rode her in the attempt to teach her some manners, but as soon as she had me on her again she'd take off, bolting for what felt like miles before running out of puff. Despite my tender age, being carted never bothered me: I suppose I must have relished the feeling of speed even then, and when I fell off her – which I did frequently – I always climbed back on immediately.

Brandy was the perfect schoolmistress for my earliest lessons in riding (though my parents occasionally thought differently), and we regularly took part in local gymkhanas, held during the wartime years to raise money for the Red Cross. A feature of these events was celebrity races, in several of which the recalcitrant Brandy was persuaded to scoot home clear of her rivals by my father or by none other than Freddie Fox, who had ridden Bahram to win the Triple Crown in 1935. Little did I dream then that the next jockey to ride a Triple Crown winner would be myself.

Crepello, Petite Etoile, Sir Ivor, Nijinsky, Alleged and all those other great horses came later. Brandy came first.

It's often said that jockeys are born and not made. If that's so, then I was always going to ride in races.

My father Keith, born in Stockbridge in Hampshire in 1904, had enjoyed a riding career which lasted nearly thirty years and brought around 500 winners under both codes – the first at Newbury on his fifteenth birthday. His most notable victory came in the 1939 Champion Hurdle at Cheltenham on African Sister, trained by his uncle, Charlie Piggott, a successful handler of jumpers between the wars.

Large-framed and 5 feet 7 inches tall, my father was hardly the ideal shape for a jockey, and once fully grown found it difficult to do under 10 stone. He had been apprenticed on the Flat to Newmarket trainer Bert Lines during the First World War before moving to Frank Barling, and although he won a few races between 1916 and 1920 he soon became too heavy to continue riding on the Flat, and returned to his father Ernie Piggott's stable. Among the famous trainers he rode for was Tom Coulthwaite, for whom he would have ridden 1931 Grand National winner Grakle but for being laid up with a broken thigh. (Compensation for that disappointment came thirty-two years later in 1963 when Ayala, trained by my father, won the National.)

My father was riding at a time when racing was free from many of the rules and regulations which govern it now – especially as regards the welfare of jockeys – and used to regale me with stories about his time in the saddle. A particular favourite was the occasion when he won a race by ten lengths, and as he was pulling up the jockey on the second came upsides and asked where he had finished: it was only then that my father realized the other jockey was drunk!

Another tale he loved to tell concerned his first ride in the Grand National. He fell at the fence after Becher's first time round, got to his feet and walked back to the stands, changed and went home. When he awoke the following day he thought it was Grand National day, and started getting himself ready to go to Aintree before it was pointed out to him that the race had already been run. He had suffered concussion in the fall and remembered nothing about the race; he had to go to the local cinema and watch the newsreel film to find out what had happened.

One of my father's great passions outside racing was motor racing at Brooklands, and it was doubtless from him that I inherited the love of speed – be it on a tearaway pony or galloping racehorse or in a fast car – which has been with me from my earliest years.

My father's younger brother Victor was also a jockey, a successful National Hunt rider who had to retire from the saddle after a bad fall in his early twenties. He then became a bookmaker in Malvern.

My grandfather Ernie Piggott rode mostly in Belgium and France early this century, and collected the first of his three champion National Hunt jockey titles in 1910. He won three Grand Nationals – on Jerry M in 1912 and on Poethlyn in 1918 (when the race was run at Gatwick) and again at Liverpool in 1919, before starting training at Letcombe Regis, near Wantage. His wife Margaret – my father's mother – was a sister of the jockeys Morny and Kempton Cannon, and her side of the family traced back in the eighteenth century to 'Old John' Day of Mere, in Somerset. Among Old John's sons were Sam Day, who rode the Derby winner three times (Gustavus in 1821, Priam in 1830 and Pyrrhus The First in 1846), John Day II, who trained Pyrrhus The First, and John Day III, who continued the family tradition of training near Stockbridge at Danebury. His daughter Kate married the stable jockey Tom Cannon – a famous contemporary of Fred Archer and George Fordham – and they produced four children: Tom junior, Mornington ('Morny' – six times champion jockey), Kempton (who won the Derby on St Amant in 1904) and my grandmother Margaret, who married one Ernest Piggott.

My mother Iris came from the great racing family of Rickaby. Her great-grandfather Fred trained the 1855 Derby winner Wild Dayrell, and her father – also Fred Rickaby – was a top jockey: he won the One Thousand Guineas and Oaks in 1891 on Mimi, and the Oaks again five years later on Canterbury Pilgrim. Her brother, a further Fred, won the One Thousand Guineas four times between 1913 and 1917 and five Classics in all (including the 1917 One Thousand Guineas on the great Diadem), but was tragically killed at the age of 24 in the First World War, to be survived by two sons, Bill and yet another Fred. My cousin Bill Rickaby was a top jockey for many years before his retirement in 1968, and Fred rode over the jumps for a while before emigrating in the late 1940s, after serving in the RAF, to start a training career in South Africa: he was champion trainer there.

My mother was an exceptionally good horsewoman, despite a weakness left over from a bout of polio during her teens, and she twice won the Newmarket Town Plate, a four-and-a-half-mile event for amateur jockeys which in her day was the only race open to lady riders, and is still held every October with its traditional prize of a bottle of champagne and a pound of Newmarket sausages. (My wife Susan maintained the family tradition by herself winning the Town Plate twice – on Fulminate in 1961 and Bingo two years later.) My mother often rode with me when I was very young, teaching me the essential basics of riding, but her influence on me stretched far beyond my equestrian education. Throughout my childhood she was a tower of strength, and even though I had a nanny my mother was always there: I found her easy to talk to, very down-to-earth and always ready to listen and then dispense the very best advice going.

My grandfather Ernie Piggott had retired from training but still lived in Letcombe Regis, in a wonderful old house dating from 1670, surrounded by a superb garden in which stood a huge old dovecote along with an even older granary sitting on stilts which looked like gigantic mushrooms. The garden ran down to the river, which flowed into a large lake in the grounds of the manor house next door, and I would sit on the bank for hours fishing for trout, while Brandy – the regular means of conveyance from home to my grandfather's – grazed on the lawn. One day she clearly became a little weary of this routine, strode up behind me, nudged me and pushed me into the river to remind me that she was still there!

After the war my grandparents moved up to Oxford, and although the family used to visit them regularly, I could not recapture the peace I had felt at their old house.

It is hardly surprising, given such a background, that I never seriously considered any walk of life other than racing.

My parents' only child, I was born in the town hospital at Wantage, not far from Newbury, on the morning of Guy Fawkes Day, 5 November 1935, and was named Lester Keith: Lester after my mother's brother Frederick Lester Rickaby, himself named after the American jockey Lester Reiff, and Keith after my father. For the next ten years the family lived near Wantage in the small village of Letcombe Regis in a modern brick house which my father built just before the outbreak of war. On the edge of the village, it was set in a large garden with a tennis court – tennis being one of the few hobbies I can remember my parents enjoying – and my father sunk a well in the garden: one of my earliest memories is of how good water from that well tasted compared with piped water! The landing at the top of the wide staircase housed my parents' extensive collection of racing books, in which I buried my nose at every chance I had, and from which I doubtless learned more effectively than from the more orthodox schooling to which I was subjected.

Throughout the war years food was scarce, bought only with ration coupons, and as fish and meat were a rarity we used to complement our diet by catching rabbits, pigeons and fish. If we helped a local farmer with the harvest, we were sometimes rewarded with a chicken. Many foods simply did not exist until after the end of the war in 1945, and the only ice-cream I ever tasted at this period – though in later life it has been one of my favourite foods – was made by a lady who cooked for the famous trainer Ivor Anthony in Letcombe Bassett. And it wasn't just food that was affected by rationing; most of our travel during my early childhood, if not by bicycle, was by motorbike and sidecar, usually with two persons crammed into the sidecar to economize on fuel coupons!

I was rising six when in 1941 I was sent to the King Alfred School in Wantage, a couple of miles from home, and almost from the start of my school days made the trip by bicycle, taking a short cut across the fields. Many of the other children there were evacuees from London rather than brought up in the locality, which made us country children feel somewhat different from them. For me at least, academic pursuits were far less important than sport: we played cricket, soccer and hockey, but the school sport which I really enjoyed was running (an enjoyment mirrored later by my daughter Maureen, who was school champion for three successive years and was almost up to County standard). School was in effect something that just had to be got through, a distraction from the centre of my life: horses.

I was first put up on a pony at the age of two, and learned the basics of riding from Brandy. When I was eight my father first allowed me to ride the yard's racehorses. The string would come back from daily exercise down a long hill, and I would walk up to meet them coming back, being legged up onto some reliable mount – first with one of the lads, then by myself – to ride the last bit home. The transition from ponies to Thoroughbreds was exciting to begin with, but after a while I began to find just walking the horses back to the yard somewhat boring compared with the fun I could have tearing around on Brandy, so I used to dawdle around the foot of the hill, with the result that my parents began to think I wasn't too keen to ride the racehorses. In any event, they never pushed me into race-riding, and allowed my interest to develop in its own time.

At around the age of eight my great passion – outside horses – was the *Dick Barton* programme on the radio, and one evening my parents noticed that I was listening with my ear pressed right up against the radio set, although it was at normal volume. Clearly I had a hearing problem. I was taken to the local doctor, who performed a series of tests using different tones before pronouncing that there was nothing to be done: I was not completely deaf, but my hearing would never be normal. I was fitted with a hearing aid, which I hated and left off. We simply went home and carried on as before, with me pressing my ear up against the radio to listen to *Dick Barton*.

Over the years plenty of people have tried to make out that my hearing disability caused me all sorts of psychological problems – it turned me in on myself, they said, and made me feel isolated – but for me it was much more straightforward: simply something that had to be overcome. When you're hard of hearing you have to find ways to get round it, and like many people with hearing difficulties I compensated by rapidly learning to lip-read. On the whole, talking one-to-one was fine, but in a crowded room it has been impossible to hear properly. Doubtless I've missed a great deal over the years, but most of it would not have been worth hearing anyway.

All the best riders have a natural talent, but they none the less need a good teacher to point them in the right direction at the outset, and in my father I had the perfect tutor. I've always thought that it is better for a young jockey to learn from an experienced rider not at the very top of the tree, as that way you get better all-round advice than from a champion who has established his own way of doing things. Eventually you find your own style, but you need to be taught the fundamentals, and in this my father – as patient and tolerant an instructor as I could

17

have wished for – was the ideal mentor. As he only had a few horses in the yard, he had that most precious commodity for a teacher, time, and painstakingly pointed out the mistakes I made and recommended how to rectify my faults. When I started race-riding, his continued teaching was invaluable, and when after a race he made no comment on my performance I knew I had done something right! And as I started going to the races more often I was able to watch the top jockeys at close quarters and learn from them: naturally I admired the phenomenally effective and successful Gordon Richards, though I cannot recall having particular riding heroes. To me they were all there to learn from, and I was in a hurry to acquire knowledge.

During the war my father served in the Royal Observer Corps, then in 1944 took out a licence to train a small string at the other end of Letcombe Regis, with just six or seven horses in a yard rented from the local landlord, Grimey Whitelaw. With very little racing taking place during the war years, low prize money in such races as were run and a very inactive market in buying and selling horses, it was difficult for small trainers to make much of a living, and the only other source of income was betting. Like many trainers, my father would bet on his horses and must have been reasonably successful at it, as we lived a comfortable enough existence – although the only holidays we ever took were in the West Country when we had runners at the summer meetings at Newton Abbot and Devon and Exeter: after the business was done, we'd stay on for a few extra days at Minehead.

Those forays to the West Country jumping tracks became an established part of my childhood years, though the first race meeting I ever attended was at Windsor in 1944 – one of the first National Hunt fixtures following a period of two years without any jump racing. My abiding memory of that first visit to a racecourse is not of horses or jockeys, but of the flying bomb which came over the track, sending the crowd running for cover as its engine stopped. The bomb came down about a mile away, and the explosion reverberated around the racecourse – but the programme carried on.

In the summer of 1945 we moved from Letcombe Regis to a training yard named South Bank, near the centre of Lambourn. This was to become one of the most famous yards in the area after Barry Hills had taken it over and sent out from there the 1973 Prix de l'Arc de Triomphe winner Rheingold – my first Arc success. Barry returned to South Bank for the 1991 season after his stint at Manton, and in 1994 had some 100 horses in training there – a far cry from the fourteen-box yard we took over fifty years earlier.

When we moved in the house and stables needed a fair amount of work, so we set to making it fit for my father's training operation, refurbishing the boxes and putting down a straw bed in the back paddock to use during the winter when we couldn't take the horses out onto the roads. My father decided to install a swimming pool on the front lawn of the house, and we built this mostly by ourselves, taking advantage of the fact that the lawn was on a steep slope, so one end needed excavating less than the other!

Riding was by now the entire focus of my life, but schooling had to continue. The distance between Lambourn and Wantage was too great for the journey to be made easily every day, and I started to board at King Alfred School – an arrangement I hated, as it meant being cut off from home and the life I loved there, and spending only weekends with the horses. Since there was little time for me to tear around the countryside on Brandy, she was put in foal and produced a lovely-looking youngster.

Despite the practical difficulties of keeping up my riding education while boarding during the week at King Alfred's, it was already obvious to me – and to my parents – that there was only one possible future for me: indeed, I can never remember even contemplating being anything other than a jockey. Eventually it was decided that my prospective career would stand a much better chance if I pursued formal education closer to home, so in 1947 I moved to a small school in Upper Lambourn which housed only a few pupils – a dozen at most – and was run by just two teachers: Miss Amy Westlake and her sister Mrs Paul. This change of school had another huge advantage for me over King Alfred's, as the much smaller class size there meant that I could hear everything that was said, whereas in the larger class at the Wantage school it was difficult for me to take everything in. Once I had moved to the school in Upper Lambourn I found my education a good deal easier.

By then, at the age of twelve, I was regularly riding out for my father and playing a part in running the stable, and my routine became a compromise between the demands of the yard and the necessity of still going to school. I would work in the yard first thing in the morning, then go to school, returning in time for evening stables. Although I had not yet ridden in public, I was starting to go to the races a good deal, and when necessary Miss Westlake would allow me to fill in the lost hours in the classroom on my return from the track, well after the other pupils had gone home. I learned a great deal more during those few years with Miss Westlake and Mrs Paul than in all the rest of my schooling, but at the beginning of the 1948 Flat season, academic education began to take even more of a back seat. That season I was officially apprenticed to my father, and at Salisbury on Wednesday 7 April 1948 the great day – the day I had been waiting for all my life – finally came: my first ride in public.

A one-mile apprentice handicap worth just £138 to the winner was the opening event on the Salisbury card, and my mount was a three-year-old filly named The Chase.

I had ridden The Chase in all her work at home, though not in her one previous race that year, and I knew her well. In the Salisbury race she carried 6 stone 5 pounds, but much of that was made up of lead weights, as at the time I weighed only about 5 stone. The race itself seemed to be over in a flash – The Chase finished in the middle of the field – but it so thrilled me to be race-riding at last that as soon as I dismounted I was asking my father when I could have my next ride. He was not one to be pestered, and, despite my impatience that the rides seemed rather slow in materializing, refused to rush me back into action.

I rode The Chase in her next three races – at Bath the following week in my first outing against senior jockeys (who included Gordon Richards), and then at Kempton Park and Worcester – and had two rides on a horse named Secret Code, finishing second on one occasion, before taking the mount on The Chase again for my seventh race in public, the Wigan Lane Selling Handicap at Haydock Park on 18 August 1948, during the summer holidays.

Among the other entries was a horse called Prompt Corner, which had been trained by my father but was then in the charge of Ginger Dennistoun. Ginger and my father decided to work the two horses together at home off the weights of the Haydock race so they could decide which to take, and Prompt Corner, ridden by Sam Wragg, narrowly won the gallop from me on the filly. Ginger suggested to the old man that we needn't bother to run ours, at which my father replied: 'I didn't take into consideration Lester's seven-pound allowance!' – the seven-pound weight concession The Chase would enjoy as I was then an inexperienced jockey.

We went up to Haydock and were staying near the course, when Ginger paid us a visit before racing to tell us that Prompt Corner was 'not off' – that is, would not be trying to win. Bill Rickaby – my cousin – had been booked to ride Prompt Corner but bad weather prevented his flying up to Haydock, so Davy Jones (who had won the 1945 Cheltenham Gold Cup on Red Rower) was put up instead. Apparently Ginger Dennistoun decided late on that Prompt Corner should try his best after all, then changed his mind again when he was unable to get his money on, so the last instruction to Davy Jones was to go easy. As The Chase and I took up the running close home Jones, just behind me, was screaming 'Go on! Go on!' – which is just what we did, winning by a length and a half.

That was my only win that year, from twenty-four rides, and the thrill of that first ever victory remains vivid. Not that I was allowed time to let it go to my head: my parents, though understandably delighted by my first win, made as little of it at the time as they could, and after the race I just got changed and went home with my father in the horse box.

I was twelve, and as there had been few winning jockeys as young as that the press wanted to make a story of it, and later came to South Bank to take photographs of the prodigy in various poses around the yard.

Most of my early mounts were for my father, but gradually other yards began to use me. My father had arranged for me to ride work for various other local trainers, and these connections resulted in rides, which boosted my confidence. The following year – when my racing schedule still had to be fitted around school holidays – my six winners (from 120 rides) included four for outside trainers: two for Fred Templeman and one each for Frank Hartigan and Atty Persse. However, my rise was hardly meteoric, as over a year passed between my first victory, on The Chase, and my second, on Forest Glade at Newbury on 20 August 1949.

By 1950 rides were coming thick and fast, and on 20 September that year I reached another milestone when winning the Brighton Autumn Cup on a filly named Zina and thus losing my claim: that is, I had ridden too many winners to be given a weight allowance to balance my inexperience, and from then on would be riding against senior jockeys on equal terms. The next day I rode my first ever winner at Ascot – Tancred in the Buckingham Palace Stakes – and followed up with two other winners at the same meeting. Then the following week I won my first big race, the Jockey Club

Stakes at Newmarket on Holm Bush, trained by Arthur Budgett. So the quality of my winners was improving, and the quantity was sufficient to make me leading apprentice for the first time with fifty-two winners, and eleventh overall in the jockeys' table.

Having left school at the age of fourteen in 1950, I was now free to concentrate on race-riding, though life still had other distractions. Public interest in my career was increasing along with the number and quality of my winners, and late in 1950 I was invited to appear on a radio programme hosted by the comedian Ted Ray, where my fellow guests were two promising teenage singers named Shirley Bassey and Petula Clark: Petula's memory is obviously not as good as mine, for when years later I reminded her of our meeting on that show, she had no recollection of it!

I found myself enjoying that early exposure to media interest, despite being understandably nervous, and since then have always tried to maintain a cordial and helpful relationship with the media – just as long as the questions they ask are of a sensible nature. Media exposure of racing personalities must be good for racing, though tabloid intrusion is a quite different issue.

A less pleasant aspect of the 1950 season was the succession of brushes with the racing authorities, usually occasioned by my being judged to have tried too hard to win – not a charge I would deny, though I'd put this down to a natural by-product of ambition coupled with inexperience, rather than reckless hot-headedness.

At the Lincoln Spring Meeting I was severely cautioned for crossing, and at Hurst Park later that spring was cautioned and suspended for the rest of the meeting. (Unlike today, when a suspension commences several days after the offence, giving you time to book a quick break in the sun, bans in those days took immediate effect – even to the extent, in some cases, of a jockey being taken off rides later the same afternoon.) Later that summer I was again cautioned at Kempton Park and at Worcester, with a £20 fine for boring being added to the punishment at the latter track.

But worse was to come in an incident in a two-mile handicap at Newbury in October, when my mount Barnacle beat Royal Oak IV, ridden by Scobie Breasley, by three-quarters of a length, but was then disqualified as I had been judged guilty of 'boring and crossing' Scobie's mount three furlongs out. The Jockey Club was starting to take a closer look at my riding, and I was summoned to appear before the Stewards at Newmarket a few days later, on Cambridgeshire Day.

My interview with the Stewards of the Jockey Club went very badly – so badly that they suspended me for the rest of the season (though they did allow me to keep my ride in the Cambridgeshire that afternoon). For the first time I felt that I was being victimized, singled out for harsh treatment which was not warranted by the nature of the infringements I was judged to have made. Maybe my enthusiasm to win had got the better of my judgement on occasions, but no-one had been hurt in any of the incidents which had incurred the authorities' displeasure, and I felt very hard done by.

I was fuming, and the outcome of the Cambridgeshire did not improve my mood. My mount Zina raced down the far side of the track, with Kelling and Valdesco, her main rivals in the closing stages, spread out across the course. I had a good lead inside the final furlong and at the line was sure that I had won narrowly, so I steered Zina into the winner's enclosure, only to learn that the judge had placed Kelling first and Zina second. I was shattered, and although I did manage to get second again in the Cambridgeshire forty-two years later on Montpelier Boy in 1992, it remains one of the big races I have never managed to win.

With no more riding that season, my parents took me off for my first overseas holiday, skiing at Arosa in Switzerland, where for ten wonderful days I felt relaxed and pampered. We all tried to ski and I found myself getting along quite well – though I had to leave my parents behind a good deal as they found skiing rather difficult to come to terms with! Since those days I've always enjoyed skiing, though given a choice would opt for sun rather than snow.

When we returned home I started to ride gallops at Baydon, near Lambourn, for Major Bay Powell, who had a few Flat horses although he was better known as a trainer of jumpers, and three of my first four winners of 1951 were for his stable. But just as things were looking very promising for the year, my luck ran out. At Lincoln I was riding a filly named Pandite, who broke her leg and fell just before the winning post: I snapped my collarbone and was out of action for a couple of weeks.

Once this reverse had been put behind me I soon got back into the swing of things, and at the end of the 1951 season was champion apprentice for the second successive year with fifty-one winners – one fewer than the year before – and had landed my first win in what nowadays would be classed a Group One race, when riding the French-trained three-year-old colt Mystery IX to a half-length victory over Mossborough in the Eclipse Stakes at Sandown Park.

But above all 1951 is memorable for the first really top-class horse I partnered, one who on his day was one of the best I ever rode: Zucchero.

Trained as a two-year-old at Whatcombe by Michael Blackmore, Zucchero had shown a great deal of promise but an even larger measure of temperament – a trait attributed by some to his sire Nasrullah. By the end of his two-year-old career, in which he had won just one small race at Worcester from seven outings, he had been moved from Whatcombe, via Ryan Jarvis, to Ken Cundell, for whom I was by then riding regularly.

Ken put one of his best lads in charge of Zucchero in an attempt to sweeten him up and gradually the horse improved. The persistent trouble, however, was Zucchero's behaviour at the starting gate – this was of course long before the days of starting stalls – and he would often get left when the tapes went up, which, given that we knew he was a horse of considerable ability, was deeply frustrating.

I first rode him in the Henry VIII Stakes at Hurst Park, when he played up at the start and got well behind in the race, eventually finishing fourth. He then returned to his best behaviour when landing the Blue Riband Trial at the Epsom April meeting easily by three lengths, and looked to have a good chance in the Derby.

At the age of fifteen, this was my first ride in the race and my excitement was tempered with a hope that Zucchero's behaviour would match the occasion. I was instructed not to carry a whip on the horse until I got to the start – not that he would respond to the whip anyway – and Ken Cundell, not wanting to leave anything to chance, came across to the Derby start to lead him in. At the crucial moment, as the starter called us forward, Ken ran with the horse to try to get him off on terms, but Zucchero's old habit got the better of him. He dug his toes in and simply would not set off, and although he eventually deigned to canter away, it was far too late to get him into the race. When he was in that mood there was simply nothing you could do about it, and although it was deeply disappointing for my first Derby to end in such a manner, that was that.

Zucchero's mulishness at the Derby start became even more aggravating after his next three races had proved what a top-class horse he could be when in the mood. Ridden by Gordon Richards, he won the Chepstow Stakes the week after the Derby, then I was back in the saddle when he won at Windsor and Sandown Park. In July we lined up against a top-class international field – including Arctic Prince, who had won the Derby in which Zucchero had declined to put his best foot forward, both that year's Guineas winners in the shape of Belle Of All and Ki Ming, and the brilliant French horse Tantieme – for the King George VI and Queen Elizabeth Festival of Britain Stakes at Ascot: the inaugural 'King George'. On this occasion

Zucchero showed his true worth, having a great battle with Supreme Court inside the final furlong before just going down by three-quarters of a length. He had not won, but he proved that when in the mood he could be a brilliant horse.

A blot on an otherwise highly satisfactory season came with a nasty fall at Lingfield Park in August, when a horse named Persian Wood fell in front of my mount No Light when making the steep descent into the straight. My horse cannoned into him and I was fired into a concrete post, breaking my left leg and collarbone (again!) so badly that it ended my season. I spent three weeks in East Grinstead hospital and three months in plaster, and was unable to get around much until the following January.

It is always a hard grind to get back into trim after a lay-off, but although plenty of swimming and riding put me on the road to fitness, there was the problem of weight to deal with. By early 1952 I was sixteen and growing taller than was ideal for an aspiring jockey, and I began to realize that if I wanted to continue to ride on the Flat I would have to take rigid control of my weight and force it down to under 8 stone 7 pounds. So I made a conscious decision to cut out all fattening foods and concentrate my diet on lean protein, fruit and black coffee. Such a regime soon proved as boring as it sounds, and every now and then I would alleviate the diet with chocolate and ice-cream – and I was also developing a taste for champagne. In this way, and with the later assistance of cigars to suppress the appetite, I have been able to keep my weight throughout my riding career at about two stones below what would be normal for my height. This is a daunting – if inevitable – task that faces the majority of jockeys, but having been forced to think about my weight at such an early age I was able to make wasting a natural part of my life, something I simply didn't think too much about once I had conquered the hunger of the first few months.

It had to be done, so I did it.

2

The Derby and the doghouse

Towards the end of 1951 I was approached by J. V. Rank, one of the country's leading owners, about taking a retainer to ride his horses, which were trained at Druid's Lodge, on Salisbury Plain, by Noel Cannon. Druid's Lodge was one of the best-known training establishments in the country, famed for its gallops and for being the home of the famous Druid's Lodge Confederacy, the legendary group of gamblers who around the turn of the century pulled off some of the biggest betting coups in the history of racing.

Druid's Lodge had long since ceased to operate as a training yard when Rank bought it in 1934 from Percy Cunliffe, last survivor of the original members of the Confederacy; he installed Noel Cannon there the following year. The new regime had met with a good deal of success, albeit interrupted by the war, and I was looking forward to riding for one of the most powerful owners in the land. But sadly J.V. died early in 1952 before I had a chance to get to know him. The running of the stable was taken over by his wife Pat, whose main interest in life was betting, and we came to an arrangement that I would continue to ride the horses through the year until the whole string had been sold off. Most of the horses were backward and showed little form until well into May, but among them was a three-year-old who would give me one of my less pleasant memories of that year: Gay Time.

Unplaced in the Two Thousand Guineas Trial at Kempton Park and behind Thunderhead II in the Guineas itself, Gay Time came good when winning the ten-furlong Druid Stakes at Salisbury in late May, exactly a week before the Derby, and that sign of his rapid improvement encouraged us to have a go at Epsom: although he started at 25–1, I thought he would win.

On the day, nothing went right.

Gay Time wrenched a shoe off while he was being saddled, and by the time he was ready to join his rivals they had all finished the parade and were on their way across the Downs to the start, which meant that our colt had to walk all by himself in front of that huge, excited crowd (in those days Epsom was packed to the rafters on Derby Day), an experience which would have put a strain on the nerves of the calmest young horse.

In the race itself he did not get away too well, and with thirty-three runners it was difficult to make up ground to get into the position I wanted by Tattenham Corner. But once we straightened up for home he began to pick up, and with a furlong to go only Tulyar, ridden by Charlie Smirke, was ahead of us. We'd got to within about three-quarters of a length when Tulyar, on the inside, started to lean out towards Gay Time, and although we were just beaten I thought I'd have a good chance of getting the race on an objection.

That thought soon disappeared. Just after passing the winning post Gay Time stumbled as we crossed the road which in those days went across the track a short way beyond the line. I fell off, and he galloped away into the woods beyond where the new stables now stand. By the time he was recaptured and brought back, the Clerk of the Scales told me that I'd run out of time in which to lodge my objection, so the result stood. I was deeply disappointed at this turn of events as I thought I probably wouldn't get as good a chance again of beating Tulyar, and I was right.

Gay Time's next outing was in the King George VI and Queen Elizabeth Stakes at Ascot in July. The month before I had ridden my first Royal Ascot winner when Malka's Boy won the Wokingham Stakes, and now I was very hopeful of another big win on the Royal course, which has always been one of my favourite tracks. We took the lead a furlong out and for a moment looked like taking our revenge for the Derby, but Tulyar collared us and won cleverly by a neck.

I did not ride Gay Time again. By the time of his next race, the Gordon Stakes at Goodwood (which he won at 15–2 on), he had been sold to the National Stud and leased to the Queen and was subsequently trained by Noel Murless.

By this time I could drive a car. I had been patiently taught to drive by my mother on the Downs and along local dirt tracks, and passed my test – at the second attempt – in Newbury. This made me feel much more independent, as my parents no longer had to drive me to the races or across to other yards to ride gallops – particularly to Druid's Lodge, where I had to be two mornings a week.

My first car, an almost-new Rover, cost me £1,000, a great deal of money in those days – especially for a sixteen-year-old! Nearly every week I used to go to the cinema in Newbury, about twelve miles away from home along very twisting roads, and on one of these nights out I very nearly collided with another car, both of us finishing up on the bank by the side of the road. I had clearly been driving too fast and expected a mouthful from the other driver as we both emerged from our vehicles, but to my great relief he laughed off the whole episode, saying, 'I was young once, too!'

It would have been good to have had that man as a racecourse steward.

Zucchero was still in training, and after a couple of unsuccessful outings we managed to land the Princess of Wales's Stakes at the Newmarket July Meeting (by which time he was being trained at Lambourn by Bill Payne) at 20–1. Doug Smith rode him when unplaced in the King George, but I was back in the saddle when he took the Rose of York Stakes at York in August, and I was not pleased to be denied the opportunity of partnering this wayward but brilliant horse in the

Washington International at Laurel Park, Maryland, in October.

This was the first ever running of what was for many years the only big American race with invited overseas runners, and I was very miffed that Ken Cundell, Zucchero's former trainer who had second claim on me in 1952, wouldn't let me go. Charlie Smirke took the mount, and finished third behind Wilwyn, ridden by Joe Mercer's brother Manny. There was some consolation that autumn, however, in the form of a trip to Greece at the invitation of George Cambanis – owner in later years of several very good horses including Tolmi, Stilvi and the 1980 Irish Derby winner Tyrnavos – who arranged for three English jockeys to go and ride in Athens for a few weeks. It was my first race-riding trip overseas, and I thought I deserved a break after a season which had brought me seventy-nine winners – my highest total yet – from 620 rides. I was very well looked after in Greece in a good hotel right on the beach, the weather was glorious, and after riding work at the racetrack in the mornings I would sunbathe – then a novelty but a habit I soon got into!

The racehorses in Greece were a mixture of Thoroughbreds which had been brought over from northern Europe and Arabs from the Sahara, and the races were run on sand (which must have suited the Arabs): there were no grass tracks. I rode eleven winners during my stay, a highly satisfactory first foray into international racing.

I stayed in Greece until the end of January 1953, then returned to England to prepare for the new season. In February my apprenticeship formally ended; now I was up against the senior riders. This is always a difficult time for a young jockey, and many highly promising apprentices never really make the transition to the senior ranks: some grow heavier than they had anticipated, others cannot take the discipline and rigours of the riding life, and others are simply found not to be good enough once they're out on their own. I was determined to come through what was likely to be a difficult patch of my career, but had no illusions that it would be easy.

Nor was it. At the end of the 1953 season I had ridden just forty-one winners, my lowest total for three years, and the year had been unhappy in other ways. After the Rank connection had failed to get off the ground, I had a new retainer for Sir Malcolm McAlpine, whose horses were trained at Epsom by Victor Smyth. I won a good many races for them, including the Gold Vase at Royal Ascot on Absolve, but soon after that we parted company. I had never really got on with Victor Smyth and found the McAlpines and some of his other owners difficult to please, so we agreed to go our separate ways.

A more intractable problem now loomed on the horizon. Still only seventeen, I was growing rapidly, and towards the end of the 1953 season was finding it very difficult to ride at under 8 stone 5 pounds. There was only one thing to do: contemplate giving up the Flat for a career over jumps. I had always ridden the jumpers at home and schooled them over hurdles, so this was not as difficult a transition as it might sound – though I never rode in a steeplechase.

My first winner under National Hunt Rules came on my third ride, at Wincanton on Boxing Day 1953 on a horse named Eldoret, trained by Bill Payne, and in February 1954 I landed a double for my father at Ludlow. After I had won a hurdle for my father at Worcester on 1 March on Carola Pride, he revealed that he wanted me to ride another of his, Mull Sack, in the Birdlip Hurdle the following day at the National Hunt Meeting at Cheltenham – what nowadays we call the Festival. Mull Sack was a safe enough conveyance, but since this was such a big meeting my father decided that we should leave nothing to chance, and should walk the course on the way home from Worcester. This was my first visit to the Cheltenham track, and my father – who had ridden plenty of winners there – explained the problems set by its gradients and turns. My schooling session was completed when we made our way up that famous finishing hill in the dark, but it was certainly worth the effort, as the following day Mull Sack, starting a 10–1 chance, found enough finishing speed after jumping the last in third place to go on and win.

This was a special thrill for me as my father's family had been associated with Cheltenham for many years: my great-uncle Charlie had ridden winners there, as had my grandfather Ernie, my uncle Victor and my father. (Much more recently, another winner there was one Percy Piggott, but he was a horse!)

On the Saturday after winning at Cheltenham on Mull Sack I enjoyed my greatest success as a jump jockey when partnering Prince Charlemagne (whom I had ridden behind Pinza in the 1953 Derby) to win the top four-year-old hurdle race of the season, the Triumph Hurdle – in those days run at Hurst Park, the course near Hampton Court which closed in 1962. I continued to ride over hurdles sporadically during the next few years, my last jumping winner coming on Jive on 18 February 1959 at Sandown Park. In all I won twenty National Hunt races, fourteen of them for my father.

Jump jockeys are a different breed from Flat riders, and there's a real camaraderie in the changing room which is not always mirrored on the level. I rode with some of the all-time greats of the game – including Bryan Marshall, Fred Winter, Tim Molony and Dick Francis – and thoroughly enjoyed the experience.

In those days hurdle races seemed to be run at a much slower gallop than they are today, and at a noticeably more leisurely pace than a long-distance race on the Flat. Riding in a hurdle race is in some ways more difficult than racing on the Flat – the jumping naturally adds a whole extra dimension – but I've always felt that you need to be fitter to ride on the level, as a Flat race puts incessant strain on the leg muscles in a way that a jumps race, in which you're constantly changing position, does not.

Hurdle racing was fun, but I still felt that my future lay with the Flat, so long as I could control my weight. For a start, Flat jockeys can earn a significantly better living than their National Hunt counterparts, as Flat races are on the whole much more valuable than jumping, and with the number of falls the jumps lads take, their working life is usually curtailed that much sooner: most of the recent greats, such as John Francome and Peter Scudamore, have not ridden beyond their early thirties.

So, with a Cheltenham National Hunt Meeting winner and a Triumph Hurdle winner under my belt, I went into the 1954 flat season in a good frame of mind. In a year of great highs and great lows, that mood was not to last.

At that period I was riding a good number of horses for the Newmarket trainer Joe Lawson. By then he was in his seventies, but he had handled many useful performers in his day and, in the twilight of his career, had a very live prospect indeed in the shape of a handsome chestnut colt by Nasrullah named Never Say Die.

Nasrullah was also the sire of Zucchero and had been thought genetically responsible for some of that horse's quirks, but Never Say Die could not have been more different. A tough, easy-going type, he was simplicity itself to ride. He had won once from six outings as a juvenile – at Ascot in July 1953 – but on the whole had failed to live up to expectations. When I rode him for the first time in the Union Jack Stakes at Liverpool in late March he was less than fully fit and did well to be beaten only a length by Tudor Honey, ridden by my cousin Bill Rickaby. Never Say Die's next outing was the Free Handicap at Newmarket, where he started favourite but disappointed, finishing well down the field. It was thought that the seven furlongs of the Free Handicap may have been too sharp for him so he was brought back to the Rowley Mile in May for the Newmarket Stakes over one and a quarter miles. Ridden by Manny Mercer as I had gone to Bath that day, Never Say Die was caught close home and beaten half a length and a head into third.

On the form book his Derby prospects did not look glowing; then, the week before the big race, he turned in his best piece of work ever and Joe Lawson, who was well aware that the horse acted best around a left-handed course, gave him a good chance. But it was not surprising that in the Derby he went off a 33–1 chance: he had never run over one and a half miles, he was bred for speed rather than stamina, and his form was patchy.

It was a very open race that year, with Rowston Manor and the French-trained Ferriol going off 5–1 joint favourites and the Two Thousand Guineas winner Darius third choice at 7–1. I was able to ride the race I wanted, laying up handy in the early stages and never getting detached from the leading group. At Tattenham Corner there were four in front of us, but I knew that I had enough horse under me to beat them when I wanted, and two furlongs out sent Never Say Die to the front, travelling up the centre of the track and easily cutting back the front-runners. He just kept galloping, and powered home by two lengths from Arabian Night and Darius. As Derbys go, it was a pretty simple race!

It was a fantastic feeling to win the Derby so young – the previous year Gordon Richards had landed it for the first time at the age of 49 – and so soon after the disappointment of Gay Time, although I was sorry that Never Say Die's American owner Robert Sterling Clark could not be there to see his home-bred colt carry his colours to victory.

Much was made at the time – and has been made since – of my apparent calmness after the race. Inwardly I was ecstatic, but I have never been one to display my emotions too publicly, and I managed to keep my euphoria to myself. Quite simply, I never allowed myself to appear elated, then or since.

As an eighteen-year-old Derby winner, the youngest jockey to win the race this century, I was understandably subjected to a fairly intense inquisition from the press as soon as I had weighed in, but once that was over I was driven home by my parents, and went to bed.

That was the good moment of my season with Never Say Die. The bad came at Royal Ascot fifteen days later. There were eight runners in the one-and-a-half-mile King Edward VII Stakes, the race immediately following the Gold Cup on the Thursday of the Royal meeting. Arabian Night, second in the Derby but now receiving eight pounds from Never Say Die, started favourite at 13–8, marginally preferred to Never Say Die on 7–4. Rashleigh, ridden by Gordon Richards, was third choice in the betting market at 5–1.

Everything went normally until soon after we had made the turn into the short home straight. Gordon on Rashleigh was on the outside, with Garter (Bill Rickaby) and Dragon Fly (Doug Smith) on his inner. Never Say Die was just behind this trio, full of running. Then a gap opened up between Dragon Fly on the inside and Garter, one off the rail, which looked inviting, so I pushed Never Say Die up to go through it. At that moment Gordon started to bring Rashleigh in towards the inner, causing Garter to be sandwiched and bumped from each side by both Rashleigh and Never Say Die. For a few seconds there was a fair amount of scrimmaging, then we sorted ourselves out and ran straight for the post – where Rashleigh won by a length from Tarjoman and Blue Prince II (neither of whom had been involved in the incident), with Never Say Die fourth.

I was hauled before the course stewards, informed that I had caused the rumpus by trying to force my way through when there was no gap, and suspended for the rest of the day. Worse, I was told I had to see the Stewards of the Jockey Club at the course the following day, which did not augur well. And worse still, when I learned that I would be appearing before the Duke of Norfolk I knew I'd be for the high jump, even though my record that season had to date been reasonably good, with only one earlier suspension. The Duke ruled Ascot with a rod of iron and following my various scrapes with the racing powers that be was hardly my greatest fan. The interview with the Stewards of the Jockey Club that Friday dealt me a severe blow: I was not to be allowed to set foot on any racecourse for the next six months, and meanwhile I had to go and work for a trainer other than my father (whom they presumably considered a bad influence on me).

I was furious, but there was nothing I could do about the ban, and my season, which had seemed so marvellous when Never Say Die won the Derby, disintegrated.

After the dust settled I was able to reflect on the incident and my punishment, but no amount of calm recollection could remove the conviction that I had been extremely harshly treated.

It has to be remembered that all this happened not long after the end of the war, when race-riding on the Flat was dominated by a generation of older jockeys – Gordon, Charlie Smirke, Charlie Elliott, Doug and Eph Smith, Edgar Britt and Bill Rickaby among them – who had had their own way on the track for a good while and possibly resented the arrival of a new generation of young jockeys. Because of the war that young generation of riders was tiny in comparison with the established riders: the usual process of integrating a group of young performers, which happens in any sport, had been disrupted by the hostilities.

Compared with today, the technology for examining the Ascot incident was not just primitive, it was non-existent. There was no camera patrol in those days, so when it came to the enquiry it was simply a matter of my word against those of my rival jockeys, all set against the stewards' recollections of what they had seen.

My general approach to race-riding was that you had to look after yourself: it was every man for himself, and you couldn't be seen to be pushed around. This may have incurred the displeasure of my seniors, who lost no opportunity to complain to the authorities that my riding was out of order, but the fact of the matter was that I was just doing my best to win races. Maybe I had acquired a reputation for being reckless on occasions – admittedly I'd been suspended nine times since 1950, mostly for rough riding – but Gordon, as is typical of all great riders, himself hated to be beaten: this time his own forcefulness was overlooked and the blame dumped on me.

The sentence made no sense at all, but it had to be endured.

Up to that point I'd had a marvellous season, having already ridden more winners than in the whole of the previous year, and the suspension was a body blow: it felt like I was back at square one. To make matters worse, I was beginning to put on weight at a worrying rate, and I knew that it would be hard to combat this if I had to cease race-riding for a few months. In my blacker moments I wondered if I'd ever get going again.

As my sentence had to be served with a trainer other than my father, it was arranged that I should go to work for Jack Jarvis in Newmarket. I still couldn't see the point of this move, but at least I was allowed to return home to Lambourn at weekends.

My mother had arranged for me to stay in Newmarket with her sister Florence, whom I knew as Auntie Bo. She was married to Fred Lane, who had won the Derby on April The Fifth in 1932 and although by now retired was still riding out for Noel Murless. After staying with them for a few days I moved to stay with 'Aunt Squiff', Grace Rickaby – mother of Bill and Fred and widow of the Fred who had been killed in the First World War: she was an exceptionally good cook, which for someone who is eating only a small amount means a lot!

In those days Newmarket was about half the size it is today, with far fewer horses in training there, and I soon got to know the gallops like the back of my hand. At the beginning of the year horses were always worked on the gallop known as Waterhall, coming over to Racecourse Side about a week before the season started. Although there is now a wider selection of canters and gallops, the way trainers use them is fundamentally the same as forty years ago, though the surface tends to get more cut up these days with so many more horses in the town.

Jack Jarvis was one of the leading trainers in Newmarket, with a yard containing around seventy horses supported by some of the biggest owners in the sport, including Lord Rosebery. He too was from a famous racing family and had trained some top-class horses in his time (the best being Blue Peter, winner of the 1939 Derby), but during my spell with him was suffering from poor health and was rarely seen around the yard as he was laid up in bed most of the time: he would write down his orders regarding each horse and send them out to us. Jarvis worked his horses very hard, and on the racecourse they always looked the lightest of all the horses sent out by the top trainers of the day, but he had plenty of winners, so his owners weren't complaining.

My cousin Bill Rickaby was riding for him while I was there, and I would see a great deal of Bill and his wife Bridget, who was Jack Jarvis's niece. The Rickabys lived in a wonderful house named Falicon Lodge with their two daughters Amanda and Melanie (aged five and two during the time I was with Jack Jarvis); tragically, Amanda died of leukaemia at the age of sixteen.

The whole set-up at the Jarvis establishment was hugely different from my father's small yard. The other lads – most of whom were much older than I was and many of whom had been with Jack Jarvis all his career – tried their best to be helpful and instruct me in the ways of a large training operation, but I didn't feel I was learning much, and thought that being sent there was something of a waste of time.

Naturally I missed the race-riding during the suspension, and no mount was so galling to lose as Never Say Die in the St Leger. It was the ideal race for him as he was the only true stayer in the field and was running on a left-handed track – he could not handle himself so well going right-handed – and, ridden by Charlie Smirke, he won as he pleased by twelve lengths: a brilliant performance.

Time went by.

In July, Gordon Richards suffered a very nasty accident at Sandown Park when a filly named Abergeldie reared up and fell backwards on him, and soon after that he decided to retire. This left Noel Murless, probably the greatest trainer in the land at that time and Gordon's main retainer, looking for a replacement stable jockey. Rumours went around about who had been approached, and then in September my world suddenly brightened up with word on the grapevine that I had a good chance of getting the job. But before I could phone Noel Murless to pursue this possibility I had an approach from Gordon Richards himself. He was about to start training, and was putting together an impressive stable of horses for some very big owners. Would I join him as stable jockey?

This was a difficult decision. Gordon would no doubt be a force to be reckoned with, but as a brand new trainer it would surely take him a couple of years at least to get up to full speed, whereas the Noel Murless establishment at Warren Place was already one of the top yards in England. After a good deal of soul-searching I decided to avoid giving Gordon an answer until I had asked Murless if he wanted me – and to my great joy he responded that he did.

It was now over three months since my last ride, and I had let my weight rise to well over 9 stone as I had assumed that I would not be riding again that season. But then I heard that the Jockey Club was considering giving me my licence back before I had served my full sentence – doubtless because Noel Murless trained for several Jockey Club members, and it was appreciated both that he needed his newly appointed stable jockey riding rather than sitting around on the sidelines, and that his new jockey's weight problem was not alleviated by idleness.

Towards the end of September I was officially notified that I could ride at Newmarket the following week, which didn't leave me much time to lose that excess weight: I had some 10 pounds to shed even to get down to a reasonable weight. So I returned to Lambourn and went about in a sweat suit for three days, riding out and running three times a day, and somehow managed to lose the necessary pounds.

On 29 September 1954 I was back in the saddle, and the first ride of my return proved a winning one: Cardington King in the Isleham Stakes at Newmarket. The crowd gave me a rousing reception when I returned to unsaddle and momentarily my earlier resolution never to look elated was forgotten. After such a dreadful summer, suddenly everything was looking bright again, and the prospect of riding for one of the top stables in the country was more than I could have dared contemplate even a few weeks earlier.

One disappointment was that I was not to ride Never Say Die again, dearly as I would have loved to. He was due to run in the Jockey Club Stakes at Newmarket at the very end of September, but at the time his owner Robert Sterling Clark and Her Majesty the Queen were neck and neck in the owners' championship. Had Never Say Die run and won at Newmarket, Mr Clark would have become leading owner, so he magnanimously declined to run the horse, thereby giving the Queen the title. Never Say Die did not race again, but was presented by Mr Clark to the National Stud, where his offspring included the 1962 Derby winner Larkspur.

Between my return to the saddle and the end of the 1954 season I notched up three winners for Noel Murless: Evening Trial at York, Princely Gift at Newmarket, and – ironically! – Rashleigh at Sandown Park.

It had been a year of extraordinary ups and downs, with my first Derby and then the still bitterly rankling suspension. But I had to look to the future, and for me the immediate future – and what turned out to be a period of twelve years with the country's top trainer – lay at the top of Newmarket's Warren Hill.

3

Up the hill to Warren Place

Warren Place, at the top of Warren Hill on the road from Newmarket to Moulton, was then – and, occupied by Henry Cecil, is still now – one of the great training yards in the country, and Noel Murless was undoubtedly one of the great trainers.

A tall, slim man who was always elegantly dressed, Noel had an air of unarguable authority about him, and did not waste words in exerting it: in all the time I rode for him, he rarely gave me detailed instructions before a race.

When I joined Noel in the autumn of 1954 he had been at Warren Place for only two years, having moved there towards the end of 1952 from the equally famous training establishment of Beckhampton in Wiltshire, where he had succeeded the legendary Fred Darling. Noel had ridden for a time as an amateur and then briefly as a professional before going to Ireland to become assistant trainer to Hubert Hartigan and then setting up on his own at Hambleton, near Thirsk, in 1935, moving from there to Beckhampton in 1947. At the time of my arrival he had already clocked up his first champion trainer's title in 1948 and won two Classics – the 1948 One Thousand Guineas with Queenpot and the St Leger the following year with Ridge Wood – and there was no doubt that the position as his retained jockey was the plum job in British racing.

I may at the time have had the reputation of a somewhat brash teenager in a hurry to get to the top, and I'd enjoyed a fair amount of success during my six years' race-riding, but I knew perfectly well that I still had a great deal more to learn, and at that stage of my career could have had no better tutor than Noel Murless.

The greatest characteristic of Noel's approach to his horses was kindness, which in those days was something of a revolution (Fred Darling, great trainer as he was, could be a real tyrant to his string), and he pursued this both on and off the racetrack. In a race, he was adamant that the jockey should be sparing with the whip, and taught me a good deal about finesse in the saddle: he was well aware that many horses had been turned sour through being subjected needlessly to the stick, and would not tolerate it in his jockeys. Similarly, he appreciated that the Thoroughbred is a thin-skinned animal and can be driven demented by too hard a brushing in the stable, and would insist that the lads go easy when grooming. As a consequence he had a stable full of well-adjusted inmates, and his career results testify to the wisdom of his approach. This is not to say that he was always easy on his horses: they were trained as hard as any when they needed to be, but he was insistent that they be looked after in a race – especially those having their first run.

The general routine during my first year at Warren Place was that I would ride work for Noel every Wednesday and Saturday – thereby gradually getting to know the whole string – and would spend the rest of the week, racing commitments allowing, back in Lambourn, where I was still helping my father run his yard.

These regular trips between Newmarket and Lambourn meant that I could get in a great deal of driving practice, and although the road network then bore little resemblance to what we have now, I did not hang about on the journey home as I was then the proud owner of a 120 type Jaguar, a small, fast, dark grey car which frequently got me into trouble for speeding. Nor was I alone in this; there was a bunch of young jockeys of that time – including Brian Swift, Geoff Lewis, Joe Mercer and Jimmy Lindley, to name just a few – who were always tearing around the country in a manic hurry.

The art of fitting everything which needs to be done into not enough hours is one which has to be mastered by every jockey even today, but back then, before the advent of jockeys' agents, it was much more difficult. As well as riding work early in the mornings before setting off for the races, we used to have to call trainers for rides – and of course did not have the convenience of mobile phones to help us.

Light aeroplanes alleviated the strain of travelling to and from racecourses, and in the early 1950s we Newmarket-based jockeys usually flew in De Havilland Rapides owned by Marshalls, based at their airport in Cambridge. Rapides were biplanes primarily used as air taxis, and we'd spend much of the time *en route* to the races larking about in the air: more than once we took along bags filled with water to drop on some unsuspecting soul a thousand feet below!

One person who definitely would not have approved of such juvenile behaviour was my new boss, for whom my regard and respect rapidly grew.

Each Sunday he would give me the runners for the week, and my plans revolved around which horses he wanted me to ride and where they would be running, though my agreement with him allowed me to accept outside rides. This was just as well in 1955, as Warren Place was going through a quiet period. Few of the two-year-olds showed much early promise, and the three-year-olds were such a moderate bunch that none was good enough to run in the first Classics. By the end of June the stable's biggest winner was Little Cloud, in the Northumberland Plate at Newcastle.

It was through riding Little Cloud that I first met his owner Sir Victor Sassoon, one of the great racing figures of the period. Confined to a wheelchair on account of injuries incurred in a plane crash while serving with the RFC, he had won his first Derby with Pinza – trained by Norman Bertie – in 1953, and Noel, who at that time was his breeding adviser, became his principal trainer the following year. Sir Victor's family had originated in Baghdad before moving to Bombay in the nineteenth century, and from there Sir Victor had gone to live in Shanghai. His lifelong interest in racing had started when his friend the trainer J. H. Crawford had been looking for someone to take over the bloodstock interests of one of his owners who had run into financial difficulties. Sassoon acquired this individual's entire breeding interests, in both England and India, and followed up by buying Fitzroy House Stables in Newmarket and a stud at nearby Woodditton. In an effort to improve the quality of bloodstock in India he also founded the Eve Bloodstock Scheme to import European mares and fillies. He used to come to England every summer from the Bahamas, where he lived after leaving Shanghai when it was overrun by Communist China.

Noel did not have that many owners at the time and Sir Victor Sassoon was certainly the biggest. Although I cannot claim to have got to know him very well, I always found him a kind man, and deeply knowledgeable about his horses.

Given the comparative lack of talent at Warren Place in 1955, I was fortunate to be able to take a good many outside rides. It was on one of these that I landed my second Eclipse Stakes, for Harry Wragg on Darius, winner of the previous year's Two Thousand Guineas and third to Never Say Die in the Derby. But my best outside ride that year was a great big black horse named Nucleus, one of the last runners in the colours of Dorothy Paget.

Miss Paget was a large, rather intimidating woman, who belied her immense wealth by always coming to the races dressed in the same clothes – a long, shapeless coat of indeterminate age and an old beret. A retinue of staff moved around with her, always at her beck and call, and she followed a strange way of life, eating a huge meal at midnight and then not getting out of bed until noon. Her trainers didn't see much of her

– though she was given to phoning them up at her whim in the middle of the night! – and often had to keep her informed by sending her photographs of her horses. She was a gambler of prodigious proportions and had owned some great jumpers – notably Golden Miller, who won the Cheltenham Gold Cup five times and is the only horse ever to have won the Gold Cup and Grand National in the same year – as well as many good performers on the Flat, notably Straight Deal, winner of the 1943 Derby, run at Newmarket on account of the war. I had ridden for her several times before teaming up with Nucleus, but I only ever saw her at the races: she never said very much, just asked what I thought about the horse and the race and left it at that.

Certainly the best horse I ever rode for Dorothy Paget, Nucleus was trained by Helen Johnson Houghton, twin sister of the great jumping trainer Fulke Walwyn and mother of the present master of Blewbury, Fulke Johnson Houghton. Her late husband Gordon had trained successfully after the war but was killed in a hunting accident, and Helen wanted to continue with the yard. Hard as it may seem to us now, just forty years ago the Jockey Club did not allow a woman to hold a training licence, so her horses had to run in the name of her great friend Charles Jerdein.

Helen was a marvellous trainer, quite rightly showing far more patience with her horses than she ever showed with human beings, and making her opinions forcibly known. In the swearing stakes, however, she was outdone by the stable duck, which used to take up residence in the breakfast room whenever it felt like it and, clearly feeling quite at home, would become very annoyed when asked to move, only doing so with much palaver and flapping of its wings.

Nucleus did not race as a two-year-old, but as a three-year-old in April 1955 won first time out at Wolverhampton and followed up at Hurst Park at the end of May. He then came second in a good race at Birmingham, and in July went to Royal Ascot – that year rescheduled from the traditional June date on account of a prolonged rail strike – for the King Edward VII Stakes, a race which after the previous year's Royal meeting was not exactly my favourite event of the fixture! But the 1955 renewal worked out much more happily, with Nucleus adding to his laurels when taking the lead a furlong out and winning easily from Eph Smith on True Cavalier. Two weeks later he was beaten in the Gordon Stakes at Goodwood – a race which may have come a bit soon for him after the delayed Ascot meeting – but came good again when beaten just three-quarters of a length in the St Leger at Doncaster by the great filly Meld, who had already landed the One Thousand Guineas and Oaks. Nucleus went on to win the Jockey Club Stakes at Newmarket, and was then invited to Laurel Park in Maryland for the Washington International.

This was a great opportunity for me – my first ride in the USA. Charles Jerdein and I travelled over to New York by Stratocruiser, a plane with bunks in the first-class section in which we were able to get our heads down – which was handy, as the journey lasted about fifteen hours. The advantage of a journey that long was that there was no jet-lag to combat, and after flying down from New York to Washington we were fresh enough, after checking into the Mayflower Hotel, to go out sightseeing.

I had of course heard and read a great deal about American racetracks, so was prepared for the great contrast between the Laurel Park circuit and the familiar courses back home. In the USA almost all tracks are the same – left-handed ovals with circuits of dirt and of grass – and are privately owned and control their own betting. A jockey needs a licence for each state he rides in, which in later years could be a nuisance when I was making a flying visit. The home jockeys rode much shorter than was usual in Europe at that time, with their inside – that is, the left-hand – stirrup leather several holes longer than the outside, as they were virtually on a continual turn: this style of riding was nicknamed 'acey-deucey'.

It wasn't only the racing scene which was very different from England. In those days everything in America had a reputation for being bigger and better than in Europe, and the meals we were served certainly confirmed this: they were huge, with steaks about three times the size we were used to. This was too much of a temptation for the Russian jockeys who had come over to ride in the International, who were obviously not used to good food at home and gorged themselves. They were then confined by their minders to the sauna, from which they were not allowed to emerge until they had got down to their riding weight.

In the Washington International itself, the European horses were at a disadvantage in every respect. For a start, they'd had a very long journey (transatlantic horse travel in those days was much longer and more wearing than it is now); they were racing on very strange territory; and furthermore, the Americans had a completely different style of racing, going flat out from start to finish. Although most American races were started from stalls – which were not to be introduced in Britain until over a decade later – for these invitation races the old-style starting gate was used to give overseas challengers a helping hand. Not that this helped Nucleus much: he didn't take well to all the unfamiliar aspects of the race, and ran disappointingly to finish unplaced.

By the time I returned home, the 1955 Flat season had come to a close. I finished third in the jockeys' table behind Doug Smith and Scobie Breasley with 103 winners. Of these, thirty-three were for Noel Murless. My first season at Warren Place had gone well enough despite the lack of high-class horses, and I could look back on good victories in the Hardwicke Stakes at Royal Ascot on Elopement – he also finished third to Vimy in the King George (that year run as part of the delayed Royal meeting) four days later; on Sir Victor Sassoon's Princely Gift in the Hungerford Stakes at Newbury and the Portland Handicap at Doncaster; and on my first ever success in France when Patras won the Prix St

Roman at Longchamp. Furthermore, for once I had managed to keep myself out of the stewards' room, mostly due to Noel's calming influence.

I went into the close season pleasantly satisfied, and decided that for that winter, at least, I'd forgo my busman's holiday over hurdles.

Three-year-old talent was again thin on the ground in the 1956 season, but there were enough highly promising two-year-olds in Warren Place to offer the prospect of great days just around the corner, and at no stage did I find myself thinking that taking the Murless retainer had brought disappointment: it was simply a matter of time before the Classics were in our sights. In the event I did not have to wait long.

We had a filly of immense promise in the shape of Carrozza, by the 1945 Derby winner Dante, who was leased to the Queen by the National Stud for her racing career. She won the Rosemary Plate at Hurst Park in May, but shortly afterwards reared over backwards and hurt herself, which meant confinement to her box for several weeks. She ran twice at Newmarket in the autumn, finishing runner-up on each occasion, and went into winter quarters quietly fancied for her Classic year.

Another promising two-year-old was Arctic Explorer, third in the Royal Lodge Stakes at Ascot, but the star turn of our juveniles in 1956 was undoubtedly Sir Victor Sassoon's sturdy chestnut colt by the Italian sire Donatello, who had won the Ascot Gold Cup – Crepello.

From the time he arrived at Warren Place as a yearling, Crepello was a big favourite of Noel's, and with good reason. He was a beautifully made horse with a handsome white face, though he had rather straight front legs – not ideal for a potential Derby candidate. He was heavy-shouldered, too, and as a consequence wore bandages on his forelegs for support all the time he was in training.

Crepello was bred to get two miles, but once we started working him on the gallops we realized that he possessed unusual speed, and it was decided to run him first time out in the Windsor Castle Stakes at Royal Ascot over five furlongs. Unfortunately in that race we came up against a speedy two-year-old of Geoffrey Brooke's named Fulfer and were beaten a head, but – as so often on a Murless two-year-old making its debut – I'd had orders to give Crepello as easy an introduction as possible, and even in the circumstances of Royal Ascot did not put him under too much pressure. It was a highly encouraging debut, and after that he was kept quiet until the autumn, when he confirmed his promise in finishing fourth behind Pipe Of Peace in the Middle Park Stakes at Newmarket. Two weeks later he won the Dewhurst Stakes – then as now the most important two-year-old race of the year – by a deceptively easy three-quarters of a length from the Queen's Doutelle.

By the end of the 1956 season the stable seemed to be on a springboard to Classic success, but the year had its sad moments, notably the death of Nucleus. He was unbeaten in his first three races as a four-year-old, but not long after landing the Winston Churchill Stakes at Hurst Park was discovered dead in his box early one morning. A post-mortem revealed a brain tumour, the existence of which had never been suspected – though thinking back on his style of running I recalled that he often carried his head at an odd angle. At the time I thought nothing of it, but he may have been showing discomfort.

I was again third in the jockeys' table – with my best total yet, 129 winners – behind Doug Smith and Scobie Breasley, and returned to Lambourn to spend the winter helping my father. I also returned to riding over hurdles, winning on six of my nine rides in the 1956-7 season (five of those winners on horses trained by my father) and coming second on one of the remaining three. Not a bad strike rate, I thought!

After two seasons at Warren Place it was time to take stock. My time there had so far been less than spectacular, but I felt strongly that those two years had laid the foundations for major success which could only be just around the corner.

By now I was 21 and still growing, and it was becoming difficult to keep my weight down to 8 stone 6 pounds – though luckily the calibre of horse at Warren Place was such that I was unlikely to be required to ride light. But I had to find a way to control my weight for the rest of my riding career, and started to regularize my diet: dry toast and coffee for breakfast, plus something light such as chicken or fish for lunch or dinner. I've never been one for salad or vegetables and dislike rice and potatoes, and chocolate (good for energy) and ice-cream continued to be my downfall. The occasional gin and tonic went down well, too, especially as we held the belief that it could stop you growing!

If I was not having to ride too light that day I would stay on at Warren Place for breakfast after riding work. Noel's wife Gwen – who had ridden point-to-point winners in her native Scotland – was always there, and often we would be joined by their daughter Julie – now Julie Cecil, the successful Newmarket trainer: I rode her first ever winner, Golan Heights at Newmarket in April 1991. Back in my days with her father, Julie would come out on the gallops during the school holidays, and turned out to be an accomplished rider, winning the Newmarket Town Plate in 1958 – beating a girl named Susan Armstrong on Florizel, trained by my father Keith, by a neck. Less than two years later Susan Armstrong would become Susan Piggott.

The early weeks of the 1957 season augured well for Warren Place. Our first winner was Shearwater in the Craven Stakes, then Sir Victor Sassoon's Sujui won the Fred Darling Stakes at Newbury and the following week Carrozza took the Princess Elizabeth Stakes – then a traditional Oaks trial – at Epsom, and Sun Charger a Classic trial at Sandown Park. The trials were going our way, and Crepello was still to make his reappearance.

Crepello went to the Two Thousand Guineas without a preliminary race. Although he had been working exceptionally well he was showing an inclination to pull, and the plan for the Guineas was to ride him from well off the pace and make up ground at the Bushes, about two furlongs out before the downhill run. The race worked out beautifully, Crepello – second favourite at 7–2 behind Scobie Breasley's mount Pipe Of Peace, who had won the Greenham Stakes at Newbury on his reappearance – coming up to collar the leaders easily passing the Bushes and taking up the running. But, like so many good horses, once he got to the front he started to idle, and as the post approached I had to get after him to resist the late challenge of Quorum. It was my first Two Thousand Guineas, and my second Classic.

Crepello continued to work really well during the run-up to the Derby, but the expected hard ground at Epsom and the undulating nature of the track were a worry for a horse with suspect forelegs. None the less, his Two Thousand Guineas performance clearly made him the form horse of the race, and he started a hot favourite at 6–4, with the next in the betting the 10–1 chance Prince Taj.

During the preliminaries Crepello was very much on his toes, but that was quite normal for him. Once the race was under way he took a nice hold, and it was a simple enough matter to settle him and start to follow what was becoming my usual Derby strategy: keep a handy position five or six places off the leaders until the straight, and then start to pick off the front-runners and ride a finish. There was a big field – twenty-two runners – but we were able to keep an ideal position all the way, laying up in the first half-dozen and steering well clear of trouble as beaten and outclassed horses started to back-pedal on the downhill run to Tattenham Corner. As we turned for home I was becoming increasingly confident, but I didn't let him go until inside the two-furlong marker, at which point he took himself easily to the front past a then obscure 33–1 shot named Ballymoss. After the Guineas I was aware that Crepello tended to idle in front so I kept him up to his work, and he was not troubled to get home a length and a half clear of Ballymoss, with Pipe Of Peace another length back in third.

As a present for winning him the Derby, Sir Victor Sassoon gave me his Lincoln Continental, a car he used only when he was in London. At this time the Americans were making the biggest and longest cars, and few could have come bigger or longer than this. Unfortunately I wasn't in possession of it very long, as one wet day in London I was unable to stop at a set of traffic lights on the Great West Road and rammed into the rear of another car, shunting it into the middle of the road. The poor driver was shaken but unhurt, and although his car was slightly damaged he was able to drive off. But there seemed to be substantial damage to my Lincoln – especially to the radiator, as all the water ran out – and I had to abandon the car at the nearest garage. It transpired that the car would need a new grille and radiator and these would have to be sent from the USA, so rather than go through all the waiting I decided to part with the car: the Duke of Bedford bought it from me to add to his spectacular collection of vehicles at Woburn.

Another gift I received after winning the Derby on Crepello was from my father's owner and great friend, the flamboyant hairdresser Teasy Weasy Raymond. As I rode back towards the winner's enclosure to meet Sir Victor Sassoon, Raymond ran up and thrust into my hand a gold watch which a few seconds before had been on his wrist!

Two days after the Derby, I struck Epsom Classic gold again with Carrozza. She was a small and tough filly whom I liked enormously, but I'd thought she lacked the speed for the One Thousand Guineas and had ridden Sir Victor's Sujui in that race, while my cousin Bill Rickaby rode Carrozza. They were fourth, running on at the finish; Sujui and I came nowhere. I had chosen the wrong one that day, but got it right for the Oaks.

Carrozza was not the Queen's only runner in the race, and Mulberry Harbour, ridden by Harry Carr, carried her first colours: I wore the distinguishing white cap.

It was a pulsating contest. The Oaks is run over the Derby course, and I always tried to ride the race in much the same way as the Derby, but the key difference is that Oaks fields are almost invariably smaller, and therefore it is easier to hold the ideal position of fifth or sixth coming into the straight. That was exactly the place in which Carrozza found herself as we came round Tattenham Corner. I pushed her into the lead with about a quarter of a mile to run and had to ride her hard as we were challenged by Jimmy Eddery – father of jockeys Pat and Paul – on Silken Glider. It was a great battle to the line and a desperately close decision, but Carrozza got there by a short head, and being led in by Her Majesty after the race remains one of the proudest moments of my riding career: I still treasure the cuff-links she sent me to mark what turned out to be my sole Classic success in the royal colours.

Carrozza ran only once more – fourth, finishing very lame, in the Nassau Stakes at Goodwood – and Crepello never ran after the Derby.

He seemed in such good form in the days after Epsom that the plan was to go for the King George VI and Queen Elizabeth Stakes at Ascot, which in its short life since the inaugural running in 1951 had soon established itself as the top all-aged middle-distance race in Britain. The announcement that Crepello would run scared off most of the likely opposition, but the night before the race Ascot was deluged with thunderstorms, and the ground became heavy. In the circumstances Noel felt that he couldn't risk the horse, and on the morning of the race – much to the chagrin of ante-post backers – Crepello was withdrawn.

He was then trained for the St Leger – and thus the Triple Crown – but during one of his gallops broke down on his forelegs: a terrific shame but, to those of us who knew the horse well, not a complete surprise. He never ran again, and was retired to Sir Victor Sassoon's Beech House Stud in Newmarket.

Crepello did not race against an older generation, and thus it has proved difficult to place him in the ranks of the great horses. I am constantly being asked to rank my nine Derby winners, and when doing so Crepello presents a problem. In terms of pure form over his whole career he cannot perhaps be rated alongside Nijinsky or Sir Ivor (though Ballymoss, runner-up in Crepello's Derby, developed into one of the great post-war middle-distance horses), but on Derby day he was probably as good as any of those more acclaimed horses, and was in many ways the ideal Derby runner – a horse who could be kept on the bit throughout the race and could then accelerate when his rivals were toiling. Had his legs stood the strain of training, I have no doubt that Crepello would have matured into a great racehorse.

Racing is constantly a matter of swings and round-abouts, ups and downs, and a few weeks after Crepello's untimely retirement was announced there arrived at Warren Place an iron-grey yearling filly with a mind of her own, a youngster who within a couple of years would have laid her claim to be considered one of the all-time greats.

4

Champion jockey

After the close of the domestic racing season in 1957 I accepted an invitation to join an international jockeys' tour of Australia. This was my first visit down under, and although Australia has since come to be one of my favourite countries – mainly because the weather suits me so well – I was surprised to find how far the country then lacked European sophistication. After a short stop in Sydney I arrived in Melbourne at the beginning of December for the first meeting at Flemington, home of the Melbourne Cup, where I met up with the other overseas jockeys: Leo Milani from Italy, Charlie Barends from South Africa, Pundu Khade from India, Peter Alafi from Hungary, Hein Bollow from Germany and Maxime Garcia from France.

The tour was peppered with press conferences and parties – one of which, at a Sydney restaurant named Romanos and built over the water in which sharks swam, ended with the famous Australian trainer Tommy Smith rolling around the floor in a fight with his jockey Athol Mulley; the barney was brought to a halt only when Tommy got a good whack around the head from Mrs Mulley's shoe!

At Doomben in Brisbane I rode the winner of the last of the invitation races, just beating Rae Johnstone, who was riding for the last time. I knew Rae – who had come to Europe before the war via India – very well, as in my first year at Warren Place he was riding the horses belonging to Lady Ursula Vernon, whose best horse was the very good colt Hugh Lupus. Although Rae was best known for a race he controversially did not win – the 1934 Derby on Colombo – he was in the mid-1950s closely connected with the great French owner Marcel Boussac, whose horses at the time seemed to be winning everything. Rae was a great connoisseur, invariably smart and polite, and after retiring from riding took up training in France, with a fair amount of success. He sadly died of a heart attack at the races – not a bad way to go – in 1972.

From Australia I moved on to Penang, where I found quite a community of English jockeys riding there for the winter, among them Jimmy Lindley, Joe Mercer, Eddie Larkin, Davy Jones and Sam Millbanks. I rode two winners over the weekend I was there but found that the excessively hot and humid weather made me heavy – presumably on account of water retention – and before long I was on the move again, this time to Calcutta.

India was a traditional wintering ground for English jockeys – particularly before the war – and the sweeping European-style grass tracks were almost like home ground for us. In the 1950s Indian Maharajahs – notably those of Baroda, Rajpipla, Morvi and Gwalior – were among the biggest owners in England, and often took their best colts and fillies back to India for breeding, so on my first visit there some of the bloodlines of the horses were familiar.

Less familiar were the attention and service I received. Labour was very cheap, and during my stay in Calcutta I had one man who looked after me all the time – even sleeping on the floor outside my hotel door! – and another man, who drove me everywhere I needed to go, was also available twenty-four hours a day and slept in the car.

I loved the racing in India, but not the food. Curry has never been among my favourite meals, so out there I tended to exist on a diet of ice-cream and fruit: mangoes, which I first ate in India, I now eat regularly.

In early January it was back to England to get myself in trim for the 1958 Flat season, the year that would see me ride my first runner for Vincent O'Brien, and – to illustrate how in racing terms this period was ancient history – the year the BBC first allowed their racing commentators to make any reference to the betting market; it was a further three years before any betting news other than starting prices could be broadcast.

I rode a couple of winners over hurdles before settling down to get to know the fresh batch of two-year-olds at Warren Place. The new crop contained one of the greatest horses ever to have been trained there, but at the time more attention was lavished on an older newcomer, the four-year-old Primera.

Originally trained in Ireland by Kevin Kerr and owned by his brother the bloodstock agent Bert Kerr, Primera had been bought during the winter by Constantine Dracoulis and his partner Charles St George, who with his brother Edward had recently started to get involved in racehorse ownership. They had acquired a couple of cheap yearlings to run in selling races, and initially their horses had been trained by Peter Thrale or Harold Wallington. The move to Noel Murless, and the purchase of Primera, represented a move into the big league. Both Edward and Charles worked in the City, where by 1958 Charles was a Lloyd's underwriter. His detailed study of racing and breeding made him one of the most successful British owners of the post-war period, and he soon became a close friend, whose Mayfair flat would usually be my base when I was in London.

Primera, the first horse Charles had in training at Warren Place, had shown only ordinary form before arriving there – his best performance was as runner-up in the Irish St Leger, which in those days had little status – so we were pleasantly surprised to discover once we started working him with the older horses that he was as good as any of them. On his first outing for the yard he won a small conditions race at the Newmarket Craven meeting in good style, and then took the Eaton Handicap at Chester. On his next appearance he disappointed when running unplaced in a handicap at Manchester, but with hindsight that day was more memorable for the racecourse debut of one of his juvenile stable-mates. She was that iron-grey filly I mentioned, and her name was Petite Etoile.

When you look back over the achievements of this wonderful mare – undoubtedly the greatest of her sex that I rode – it is curious that she showed so little of her potential as a juvenile. Certainly her career got off to an unfortunate start. On the way from the racecourse stables to the track she got loose and spent some time galloping around before finally being caught: whether this experience rattled her or not, she never threatened to upset the odds bet on her solitary opponent in the race, Chris, subsequently a top sprinter, and was beaten eight lengths.

Her antics that day did not come as a complete surprise, as Petite Etoile had always been – and would remain – a bit of a monkey, ready to lark about if her rider was not wary: we always had to be very careful with her at home and let her have her own way now and again. Perhaps she caught the inclination to play around a bit from her owner Prince Aly Khan, who had bred her at one of his Irish studs: Prince Aly was a dashing man who lived life to the hilt, including riding in races as an amateur, inheriting his father the old Aga Khan's racing and bloodstock interests in the early 1950s.

By the end of the 1958 season Petite Etoile had won two of her four races, but struck us as nothing particularly out of the ordinary: we had three or four young fillies as good in the stable, and our main hope for the One Thousand Guineas was Collyria, who had shaped promisingly on her solitary outing as a two-year-old, finishing runner-up to a very good horse named Saint Crespin III. Petite Etoile, we thought, was not in the same league.

I first met Vincent O'Brien at the Cheltenham National Hunt Meeting in 1954, the year I won the meeting's opener on Mull Sack, trained by my father. By then Vincent was already a training legend over the jumps, having won the Champion Hurdle three times with Hatton's Grace and the Gold Cup on four occasions – three with Cottage Rake and once with Knock Hard; he had won the previous year's Grand National with Early Mist and in 1954 and 1955 would run up a three-timer in the Liverpool race with Royal Tan and Quare Times. At our first encounter at Cheltenham, Vincent made me an unusual offer: 'Let me know if you ever want to ride in the Grand National.'

Vincent's formative years as a trainer had been spent with his father Dan O'Brien, a permit holder in County Cork, and he had for a while trained greyhounds before setting up on his own after his father's death in 1943; in 1951 he moved to Ballydoyle, near Cashel in County Tipperary, and set about transforming it into one of the finest training establishments in the world. By the late 1950s he was beginning to transfer his attentions to the Flat. His good colt Ballymoss had been runner-up to Crepello in the 1957 Derby and had gone on to win the Irish Derby and the St Leger, and it was in 1958 that I rode for him for the first time, on his Ascot Gold Cup contender Gladness.

A great big five-year-old mare who was a very late developer – she had not run until the back end of her three-year-old year – Gladness was by anybody's standards a great stayer, but Michael Vincent O'Brien has never been one to leave anything to chance, and before the Gold Cup the thoroughness of his preparation of the jockey – let alone the horse! – was remarkable. As I had never partnered the mare before he wanted to show me films of her previous races (an idea I think he'd borrowed from preparation for the Grand National), and set up a makeshift cinema in his hotel room at Ascot for that purpose. This was an inspired idea, and although I had never even sat on Gladness until getting the leg up in the paddock before the Gold Cup, I had a pretty good idea of the way to ride her: I kicked her into the lead at the home turn and she galloped on with great courage to resist anything her opponents – notably the very good stayer Hornbeam – could throw at her.

Gladness went on to win the Goodwood Cup easily before turning in one of the all-time great weight-carrying performances in the Ebor Handicap at York when coming off the pace in a race run at a strong gallop – her ideal conditions – and running clean away to win with the greatest of ease under 9 stone 7 pounds.

The other great horse with whom I was associated in 1958 was the four-year-old grey sprinter Right Boy, trained by Bill Dutton, on whom I won five races, including the Cork and Orrery Stakes at Royal Ascot, the July Cup at Newmarket, the King George Stakes at Goodwood and the Nunthorpe Stakes at York, for which he started at 100–8 on and was all out to win by half a length. The best sprinter I ever saw was probably the great Pappa Fourway – who won twelve races in all, including eight out of eight as a three-year-old in 1955 – but I have to rate Right Boy as the best I rode: he had explosive speed and was tremendously consistent.

In November I was off across the ocean again, this time to ride Orsini in the Washington International. I had won the German Derby on the horse the year before, and during the 1958 World's Fair in Belgium had won twice on him, at Brussels and Ostend: his owner Baron Thyssen had owned shell-making factories during the war, which understandably made him less than a hundred per cent popular with the Belgians, and after both races we were roundly booed on returning to the winner's enclosure.

In the Washington International, Orsini came up against Vincent O'Brien's top-notch colt Ballymoss, who earlier in the year had proclaimed himself one of the best middle-distance colts of recent memory by winning the Coronation Cup, Eclipse, King George and Prix de l'Arc de Triomphe. Ridden by his usual partner Scobie Breasley, he was expected to go well in the Washington International and was unlucky to be beaten in a rough race. Going round the Clubhouse turn before setting out on the final circuit, Scobie was tucked in behind me when my foot brushed against the hedge which bordered the track in place of rails. The dust flew up and as Orsini bounced back off the hedge Ballymoss ducked away, thereby losing his position – and any winning chance he may still have had was squashed by further scrimmaging down the back stretch. Ballymoss came third, Orsini fifth.

Sixth in the jockeys' table with eighty-three winners, one behind Joe Mercer in fifth (Doug Smith, with 165, was champion for the fourth time), I turned my attention towards my by now regular winter trip overseas, this time to South Africa and Rhodesia.

South Africa has beautiful scenery and is a good destination for European jockeys as the racetracks bear a great resemblance to ours and races there tend to be run in the European manner, not – as in the USA – flat out from the start. Most of the big trainers had yards at large training centres and worked their horses on the tracks – in which they are similar to the Americans.

I rode during December in Salisbury (now Harare), capital of Rhodesia, and in Johannesburg and Port Elizabeth, then became too heavy to continue, so escaped to Nice for a brief holiday – which made me even heavier: by the time I got back to England I was tipping the scales at 10 stone, nearly 2 stone in excess of what I should have been. At that time I was still inclined to put on weight if I was not very careful, and on my overseas jaunt the heat had not helped.

And yet I found the lure of international travel very difficult to resist. Over the past couple of years I had won a few races on a horse named Illinois, who at the end of 1958 was sold to the USA. His new owner invited me over to stay in his house in Florida, and I travelled on the plane with the horse to New York – a long, cold trip including a stopover in Iceland to refuel. I felt very sympathetic towards the horse! But my limbs started to thaw out once we hit the heat of Miami, and I spent a marvellous few days with the new owner of Illinois in his house on one of the islands in Biscayne Bay.

Back home, I had two rides over hurdles in February for my father – both favourites, and both winners. The second of these, Jive at Sandown Park on 18 February 1959, turned out to be my last ride under National Hunt Rules, and my twentieth winner.

I never did get round to taking up Vincent O'Brien on his Grand National offer!

With the Flat about to start, I had some serious wasting to do.

The simplest way to lose weight is to eat less. Beyond that you can remove the excess poundage primarily by emetics (such as Fred Archer's famous mixture, which reputedly had the effect of dynamite) or sweating. Back then we didn't have saunas so had to make our own arrangements: hot baths were always very effective, but you can't do much else while sitting in the bath, and I needed to find a way of losing weight while engaged in other activities – specifically, the long stretches of driving to the races. My solution was to wear a plastic running suit, which covered me from foot to neck, and turn the heater in the car on full blast for the duration of the journey. I got my weight down, but my passengers didn't always enjoy their lifts.

The race which was exciting Warren Place in the early phase of the 1959 season was the One Thousand Guineas, for which we had three serious candidates. Petite Etoile had thrived through the winter and on her reappearance turned in a good enough performance when winning the Free Handicap at Newmarket under top weight to earn her place in the Classic line-up, but other Murless fillies were vying for my attention, notably Rose Of Medina and Collyria. Rose Of Medina had narrowly won the Princess Elizabeth Stakes at Epsom on her first outing but Collyria did not have a prep race before the One Thousand Guineas, and after a great deal of deliberation and discussion with Noel Murless I finally decided that Collyria, who had been working very well at home and was, on the strength of her solitary outing as a two-year-old, a filly of great promise, was the one to be on.

In the event I was wrong. Doug Smith was offered the ride on Petite Etoile and rode her to a cosy victory. Rose Of Medina (ridden by Doug's brother Eph) was fourth, and Collyria and I trailed in down the field; a fourth Murless filly, Parrotia, ridden by Bill Rickaby, was also unplaced. Disappointing as it was to have chosen the wrong one and missed out on what would have been my first winner of the One Thousand Guineas, this situation often happens to stable jockeys and you just shrug it off. (Interestingly, the fact that I had decided against Petite Etoile did not put off the punters: the winner started at 8–1, Collyria at 9–1.)

I also had a choice of Warren Place fillies in the Oaks at Epsom five weeks later. Few who had witnessed Petite Etoile's victory in the One Thousand Guineas considered that a filly with such exceptional speed – it is always speed which wins the Guineas races – would have the stamina to win the Oaks over one and a half miles, but I wasn't so sure. Admittedly she was not bred to stay, coming from the famously fast Mumtaz Mahal family, but the mile and a half at Epsom takes less getting than the same trip on more demanding courses where stamina is at a greater premium, and a gut feeling that she would get home swayed me in her favour.

Not that the market agreed with me. Petite Etoile was only third favourite for the Oaks at 11–2 – the betting was dominated by Cantelo at 7–4 and Mirnaya at 2–1 – but she proved the doubters wrong. I tracked the favourite Cantelo up the home straight, and even I was surprised by how well Petite Etoile was going two furlongs out. From then on it was simply a matter of whether her stamina would last, but she never gave me the slightest worry on that score, and about a furlong from the post I eased her out. She accelerated past Cantelo easily and won in a canter.

Petite Etoile was clearly a filly of exceptional talent, and she went through the rest of the season unbeaten to give her six out of six for the year. After the Oaks she went to Goodwood for the Sussex Stakes, then up to York for the Yorkshire Oaks, and rounded off her triumphant year in the Champion Stakes at Newmarket – much to the relief of her owner Prince Aly Khan. Aly used to bet on his horses with a fierce loyalty, and plunged on his great filly in that Champion Stakes despite her odds being a rather off-putting 11–2 on. There were only three runners – fellow three-year-olds Barclay and Javelot were the other two – and the early pace was very sedate, so that when we started going down into the Dip, all three still had plenty left in the tank. As I tried to come between the other two, Garnie Bougoure on Barclay closed the gap, so rather than make for the outside I found a way between Javelot and the inside rail and squeezed through to win by half a length. No wonder Prince Aly looked decidedly pale as I brought his filly back to unsaddle! He had plenty to celebrate, however: the exploits of Petite Etoile that year made him the first owner to win more than £100,000 in a season.

My 1959 season was dominated by Petite Etoile, but there were other great moments: Right Boy repeating his 1958 victories in the Cork and Orrery, July Cup, King George Stakes and Nunthorpe; Primera winning several big races – including the Ebor Handicap – before finishing fourth in the Prix de l'Arc de Triomphe; Tin Whistle, trained by Pat Rohan (who by then also had Right Boy), winning several good sprints; and a potential star among the Warren Place two-year-olds in the shape of St Paddy, who won the important Royal Lodge Stakes at Ascot by five lengths in the manner of a very good horse.

I had first met Susan Armstrong, daughter of trainer Fred Armstrong (universally known as 'Sam' because, he said, at birth he had a mop of jet-black hair which caused his family to bestow the nickname Little Black Sambo), in 1950. I was fifteen, she was eleven, and our first encounter was at a small hotel outside Doncaster, where I was staying for the races with my family: the Armstrongs joined the Piggotts for a snack lunch before setting off for the course.

Our paths did not cross again for several years after that, but gradually I began to see more of Susan at the racecourses, as she always accompanied her father's apprentices, in whose riding education she played a key role: at one time there would be as many as six lads under her tuition, all race-riding regularly. Like me, she had been born into a racing family and had grown up with racehorses. As a small child she rode a pony with her father's string on the Heath at Newmarket, to where Sam had moved from Middleham in Yorkshire after the war, and like me she graduated to riding racehorses when she was eight.

There were other connections between our families. Susan's mother, Maureen Greenwood, lived at Court Hill, a large house opposite my parents' house in Letcombe Regis, and when she and Sam were courting they often joined my mother and father to make a four at tennis. When Sam trained up at Middleham his neighbour had been Noel Murless, and he then trained at Warren Place, which had been bought by his principal owner the Maharajah of Baroda. From there he moved to train from St Gatien, close to the centre of Newmarket, where his son Robert – Susan's brother – now holds the licence. Warren Place, which had been sold when the Maharajah was stripped of his wealth after Indian independence in 1947, stood empty for a while before Noel Murless moved in.

Susan and I gradually got to know each other, and started going out together. During our courtship I still had to be very careful about my weight, so rather than go out for slap-up dinners we used to have a light meal and then perhaps take in a film.

On 22 February 1960 we were married in London at St Mark's, North Audley Street, with a modest gathering of some eighty family and close friends. My best man was John Sutcliffe, whom I had known since he was a schoolboy as our parents were great friends, and I used to stay with his family in Bognor Regis whenever I was riding at Goodwood. John's father had had horses in training with my father before taking out a licence of his own, and over the years John and I had become close friends. The wedding reception was held at Brown's Hotel, where Susan's parents had held their own reception after their wedding in December 1935, when I was six weeks old.

Susan and I honeymooned in Nice for ten days, staying at the Westminster Hotel on the Promenade des Anglais and driving out from there to Villefranche, Cannes and Monte Carlo to eat in the excellent restaurants: a particular favourite was Chez Bidou, at the far end of the quay in Villefranche, where we continued to eat regularly during our frequent summer trips to the South of France. One day the restaurant's proprietor – Bidou himself – sold up and moved to Singapore, but since we've frequently spent parts of the winter out there, we've been able to keep in touch. While we were in Nice we took the opportunity to watch the local racing at Cagnes-sur-Mer, eating lunch on a terrace which commanded an excellent view of the track.

On returning to Newmarket we moved into a spacious house I had bought near the Tattersalls Sales complex, which we christened Florizel after the horse trained by my father on whom Susan had been narrowly beaten by Julie Murless – now Julie Cecil – in the 1958 Newmarket Town Plate. Over the years we added to the house, and put in a small swimming pool enclosed in a sort of greenhouse.

Warren Place was never a stable to hurry its big guns, and in 1960 it was the beginning of May before the undisputed queen of the establishment, the four-year-old Petite Etoile, saw a racecourse. She reappeared in the

Victor Wild Stakes at Kempton Park and started at 7–1 on to beat two opponents – which she duly did. Next stop was Epsom for the Coronation Cup, but meanwhile we had a three-year-old of whom big things were expected.

We had always thought a great deal of St Paddy, a well-made colt by the Queen's horse Aureole and owned by Sir Victor Sassoon, though he had a tendency to pull very hard. The first time he raced as a two-year-old, at York, he had bolted on the way to the start, which had not exactly been planned as part of his education! He failed to give his true running that day – a horse which bolts can never be expected to have enough energy left to race properly – and thereafter was fitted with a gag, a special type of bit which restrains a hard-pulling horse. St Paddy's five-length victory in the Royal Lodge Stakes – only the second race of his life – had been extremely impressive, and we were hopeful of a nibble at the 1960 Classics.

Noel and I did not really expect St Paddy to have the speed for the Two Thousand Guineas, but he ran well enough to finish sixth behind Martial: once it became clear that he did not have the toe to be involved in the finish I was not hard on him, and he rewarded this tender handling when scoring an impressive victory in the Dante Stakes at York, then as now one of the most significant trial races for the Derby.

St Paddy did not start favourite for the Derby, that honour going to the French-trained colt Angers, with Irish challenger Die Hard, trained by Vincent O'Brien, second choice. Tragically Angers broke a fetlock on the run down Tattenham Hill, but as far as St Paddy was concerned the race was run to suit him – a nice strong gallop from the start which meant that he didn't have to waste energy fighting for his head – and everything went according to plan. He was always going sweetly under me, and held a good position in about fifth, just behind the leaders, as we came into the straight. Taking up the running two furlongs out, he accelerated and ran on without my having to ask him a serious question. The winning distance over runner-up Alcaeus was three lengths. My third Derby, just six years after my first.

This win gave a particular joy to Sir Victor Sassoon. Not only was he winning his fourth Derby in eight runnings – following on from Pinza, Crepello and Hard Ridden – but he had bred St Paddy himself. Despite usually being confined to his wheelchair, he managed to walk on crutches into the winner's enclosure, and that evening gave a wonderful celebration party at the Savoy. I managed to get there for a while but could not stay long, as the following day I had another Epsom date – with Petite Etoile in the Coronation Cup.

Even by the standards of the Warren Place string, who were all flying at that time, Petite Etoile had been working exceptionally well at home, and in the Coronation Cup she absolutely hacked up, sauntering home in a half-speed canter from the previous year's Derby winner Parthia. Tragically her owner Prince Aly Khan was not there to see her triumph: he had been killed in a car crash at Saint-Cloud on the outskirts of Paris not long before.

All in all that was quite a day at Epsom, as Indigenous, my mount in the opener, the Tadworth Handicap, broke the British speed record for five furlongs (which had stood since 1933), scorching down the hill to win in 53.6 seconds, despite carrying 9 stone 5 pounds. While it was good to have played a part in setting such a record, I felt that the time might well have been exaggerated, as even at Epsom it is very difficult for a horse to run five furlongs in under 55 seconds, and timing in those days was of course done by hand, with a consequent sacrifice in accuracy.

With an excellent Royal Ascot – four winners, including Tin Whistle in the Cork and Orrery Stakes – and the prospect of big-race rides on Petite Etoile and St Paddy, the midsummer period was going well. I was then brought down to earth with a bump – literally – in a small race at Brighton in August on a horse named Barbary Pirate. This colt, trained by Richmond Sturdy, had given me my first victory of the season back at Lincoln in March, and at Brighton was looking like the winner when about a hundred yards out his saddle slipped and I ended up on the deck. The skull caps which we wore at that time had no chin straps, but luck seemed to be on my side, as my cap stayed put, and I was able to walk away feeling just a little shaken. I rode in the following race, but gave up the rest of my mounts that afternoon.

Those skull caps – the first which were mandatory under the Rules of Racing – were a far cry from what jockeys wear today. They were made of leather, which afforded little protection, but were arguably better than nothing. Their one major drawback was that they were very heavy, and had to be included in the weight the horse was allotted to carry (unlike now, when the jockey leaves off his helmet when weighing out and weighing in). Naturally if I had to do light I needed to find a way round this problem, so used to substitute for the leather cap one made up of one layer of a bowler hat – minus the rim, of course!

That year one major technological advance in British racing came with the introduction of the camera patrol, whereby each race was filmed from various different positions around the course – most significantly, head-on up the finishing straight – so that the stewards could have a proper opportunity to consider incidents in running, cases of apparent non-trying, and so on. On the very first day the system was used at Epsom, Scobie Breasley and I had a minor skirmish in the selling race, which Scobie won. The stewards hauled me in and had a good look at the patrol film before deciding to let me off with just a slapped wrist – doubtless taking into account the difficulty of maintaining a straight course at Epsom, plus the fact that I did not win. Once the film patrol had become accepted and established it made stewarding much fairer, and there were moments when I found myself regretting that this sophisticated technology had not been available at Royal Ascot in June 1954!

One particularly pleasing victory in the summer of 1960 which you won't find in the form book was my win in the celebrity donkey derby at the Finmere Show, held in aid of Stoke Mandeville Hospital, in which my mount prevailed after a rough race. A less pleasant memory is the ride on Petite Etoile in the King George VI and Queen Elizabeth Stakes at Ascot, after which I came in for a great deal of stick – not, in my view, justified.

Petite Etoile had done well since Epsom and at Ascot started 5–2 on favourite to beat seven opponents, none of whom, on form, was remotely in her class. But if on paper it seemed a simple enough task, I had my doubts. The ground was a little soft that day, and the Ascot mile and a half can prove a good deal more searching than that distance at Epsom: I had reservations about whether Petite Etoile really got twelve furlongs. Furthermore, the filly had been coughing, and as a consequence had had to forgo her planned appearance in the Princess of Wales's Stakes at the Newmarket July Meeting.

Planning to ride Petite Etoile in the usual way in the King George, I kept her well back until the turn into the straight, where I made my move up the inside. But the way was blocked, and in switching to challenge on the outer the filly was bumped by Kythnos. Once she'd righted herself we set off in pursuit of the leader Aggressor, ridden by Jimmy Lindley, and perhaps for the first time in her racing life she really had to dig deep. She responded gamely, but my fears about her lack of stamina proved right, and she just couldn't peg back Aggressor, being beaten half a length.

She did not race again that season, but Warren Place still had its three-year-old star up its sleeve. St Paddy was let down a little after the Derby, and was probably not fully fit when beaten half a length by Kipling in the Gordon Stakes at Goodwood: he blew up inside the final furlong, and there was no point in being hard on him. From there he went to York to win the Great Voltigeur

Stakes in August, then rounded off an excellent season by winning the St Leger very easily, striding to the front still on the bit three furlongs out and easing down near the post to win by three lengths from Die Hard.

Maybe St Paddy lacked the sheer brilliance of some of my other Derby winners, but he was a horse I'd always liked, and I felt he never quite got the credit he deserved.

The 1960 season brought me my first jockeys' championship: with 170 winners I was seventeen clear of Scobie, with Doug Smith and Joe Sime also in the frame. I felt a great sense of achievement at having reached the top of the tree after all the hard work on what felt like a very long road from Brandy to Petite Etoile.

5

The end of the Murless years

They always say that pride comes before a fall, and while still feeling very pleased with myself for having become champion jockey I was stopped by the police near Newmarket for speeding, as I had been several times over the past few years. The case went to court in Bury St Edmunds, where despite being defended by Michael Havers – father of actor Nigel and later to become Attorney-General – I was landed with a hefty fine of £50 (then the maximum), plus 25 guineas costs, and banned from driving for six months. The ban was a major inconvenience, but deep down I realized I had been lucky that this was my first, considering that I had always had a great fondness for speedy cars, and for driving them as fast as I could!

That winter Susan and I had been invited by St Paddy's owner Sir Victor Sassoon to stay at 'Eves', his home in Nassau – a favourite spot of many racing people, including E. P. Taylor, who was to become famous as owner–breeder of Northern Dancer, James Cox Brady, head of the New York Jockey Club, and Josephine Bryce, who had many good horses in training with Susan's father. Sadly, our hosts Sir Victor and his Texan wife Evelyn Barnes (known as 'Barnsie'), his former nurse whom he had recently married, were away as they had already made plans to go to India, so we shared the guest house, two flats on the opposite side of the pool from the main house, with Susan's parents, who had come out by ship. Apart from one incident when a stray ball from the adjacent golf course shattered the windscreen of our car as we were driving past, we spent several weeks relaxing in the sun, swimming and playing tennis – the ideal tonic after the rigours of a long season.

I had received an invitation to return to India to take part in a series of special cup races in honour of the Queen, who was making a state visit in February 1961, and flew there from Nassau via Miami and New York, for the first time travelling on the new generation of large passenger jets, the Boeing 707. Susan had decided not to accompany me to India for the best of reasons – she was pregnant – and after we had said our goodbyes in New York I jetted off to Bombay, where I was installed in the famous Taj Mahal Hotel, right on the waterfront. Needing to shed a few pounds before getting back into the saddle I decided to take a hot bath, but my anticipated relaxation turned into a nightmare when a swarm of ants, which I had apparently disturbed, started to run around the rim of the bath, trapping me for what felt like ages: I had to keep topping up the water until they decided to go back to their nest, but at least the weight was lost!

With both the five-year-old Petite Etoile and the four-year-old St Paddy still in training, there was a great deal to look forward to as the 1961 Flat season got under way. The first winner from Warren Place that term was Aurelius, who landed the Craven Stakes at the first Newmarket meeting in the manner of a promising horse. Aurelius would go on to bring yet another Classic to the yard, but early that season the three-year-old colt we all confidently predicted would be our star turn was Pinturischio, owned and bred by Sir Victor Sassoon.

A fine big son of Sir Victor's first Derby winner Pinza, Pinturischio was not blessed with the best of forelegs but had been working extremely well at home – so well that he was favourite for the 1961 Derby before he ever set foot on a racecourse. He had not run as a two-year-old and made his debut in the Wood Ditton Stakes at Newmarket in April, winning so easily that we were convinced he should take in the Two Thousand

Guineas on his way to Epsom. He started 5–2 favourite for the Guineas but could finish only fourth behind the shock 66–1 outsider Rockavon. Although disappointed, I was convinced that the race had brought him on a great deal, and was still certain that over a mile and a half at Epsom he would prove very hard to beat.

Tragically, he never got as far as Epsom. Three weeks before the race he became ill, and it transpired that he had been 'got at': the nobblers had struck. Pinturischio made a rapid recovery and Noel resumed his Derby preparation, but he was then got at again. Not only was he withdrawn from the big race, he was unable to run ever again.

There's simply no knowing how good Pinturischio could have been, as he never had the chance to prove himself. My opinion at the time was that he certainly would have won the Derby, as there was simply nothing around to beat him. His late withdrawal left me for once without a mount in the race, but the result had a sting in its tail. After riding a horse named Psidium for trainer Harry Wragg in his prep race in France I was offered the mount for the Derby, but at the time had no reason to doubt the participation of Pinturischio, so declined. It was therefore somewhat galling to sit at home in Newmarket and watch on television as Psidium, ridden by the French jockey Roger Poincelet and starting at 66–1, came from last to first to land the race. These things happen. I could not feel too miffed, especially as I considered that result something of a fluke: Psidium had never shown that sort of form before the race, and never ran again.

Although the Derby had passed me by I enjoyed a memorable Royal Ascot with seven winners, including St Paddy in the Hardwicke Stakes, Aurelius in the King Edward VII Stakes, and the very good stayer Pandofell in the Gold Cup.

Petite Etoile won the Rous Memorial Stakes at the Royal meeting starting at 15–2 on, but by then I was getting the distinct feeling that she was not quite as good as she had been. Noel had found her increasingly difficult to train at five, and she never really showed her old sparkle during 1961. Her season had begun with a rather scrambling victory in the Coronation Stakes at Sandown Park in April, from where she went for a repeat in the Coronation Cup at Epsom, which she won cleverly by a neck from Sir Winston Churchill's Vienna. After her Royal Ascot victory she started at 11–4 on for the Aly Khan International Memorial Gold Cup at Kempton Park – named in honour of her late owner – but was galloped into the ground by another of Sir Winston's good horses in the shape of High Hat, given an inspired ride by Duncan Keith. She then picked up the winning thread again in the Scarborough Stakes at the Doncaster St Leger meeting, but in the final race of her career, the Queen Elizabeth II Stakes at Ascot, was beaten half a length by Le Levanstell.

She had been a great servant to the yard, and it was sad to see her depart in the autumn for a stud career which proved a disappointment, never producing any offspring remotely as good as herself.

St Paddy, on the other hand, had a highly satisfactory year, winning four of his six races. He was beaten into second place in the King George VI and Queen Elizabeth Stakes at Ascot on soft ground which did not suit him by the champion French three-year-old Right Royal V; and in the last race of his career, the Champion Stakes at Newmarket, the distance of ten furlongs and the completely straight course were not really to his liking either: he was turned over by the French raider Bobar II. But his four victories included the Jockey Club Stakes and the Eclipse Stakes – in which he made all the running and broke the track record. If ever St Paddy was a great racehorse it was that day, but sadly Sir Victor was unable to be at Sandown Park as he was too ill to travel from his home in Nassau following a heart attack. A month later he died. His presence was very greatly missed at Warren Place, and his racehorses ran in the colours of his wife until they were found new homes. At the time of his death two of my three Derby winners had been in his colours and I knew that he had been a great influence on my career. A hitching post in the shape of a jockey wearing Sir Victor's colours still stands by the front door of our Newmarket home.

With Pinturischio out of the reckoning our Classic hopes hinged on Aurelius, a temperamental horse who was turning out to be the pick of the Warren Place three-year-olds. He bypassed the Derby on account of the firm ground, and after his Royal Ascot victory went to York for the Great Voltigeur Stakes, with the St Leger by then very much on the agenda. Just Great narrowly beat him at York, but we were hopeful of reversing that form at Doncaster, and when Just Great whipped round as the tapes were going up before the St Leger he virtually handed the race to Aurelius, who took full advantage of his main rival's behaviour and lasted home from Bounteous and Dicta Drake to give me my second St Leger.

Aurelius stayed in training as a four-year-old, winning four races and finishing a close-up second to Match III in the King George at Ascot (while I, as we shall see, was otherwise occupied), and then went to stud – where he proved a complete flop: completely incapable of performing in the required way, he was gelded and sent jumping. He blossomed in his new career to such an extent that he won over both hurdles and fences, actually finishing second to Saucy Kit in the 1967 Champion Hurdle at Cheltenham, only to be disqualified for interference on the run-in. I had always found him a horse of great ability but suspect temperament – he never seemed to be trying very hard – and despite his Classic victory I cannot claim he was one of my favourites.

As the end of the 1961 season approached I seemed to be in with a good chance of retaining my jockeys' championship title, but Scobie Breasley caught up with me and finally beat me by seven – 171 to 164.

* * *

Yet for all the racing activity, the high point of 1961 was the birth on 3 May of our first child, Maureen. I had been riding that day at Chester, and after flying back from there to Cambridge tore over to the Evelyn Hospital to see the new arrival. She was such a pretty little thing, and it was very strange to hold in my arms such a small person. Although she weighed in at 7 pounds 13 ounces, she remained on the small side for the first few weeks of her life – no doubt in sympathy with her father's constant regime of wasting! – but soon started thriving and putting on the pounds.

It is not easy for a professional jockey, constantly on the move and having to tear around the country in search of winners, suddenly to change his lifestyle, but to make Susan's life easier during the period following Maureen's arrival we employed a nanny: she was a real old-fashioned woman in her fifties, super-efficient but rather domineering, who made it quite clear that she considered young parents totally unsuited to the task of looking after a baby. She refused to take any time off, which in our comparatively small house made for a rather crowded and occasionally unharmonious existence.

Maureen was nine months old the following winter when I was due to take part in another international jockeys' tour of Australia, and Susan and I felt that to subject our daughter to the heat – there was little air conditioning in those days – would have been unfair. So we left Maureen with her nanny and set off to Singapore, where I was riding at the Christmas meeting, and stayed at what became our regular base there, the Goodwood Park Hotel. On the racing front, the track at Singapore turned out to be excellent: flat, and with going that managed to absorb all the rain the monsoons had chucked at it. I rode a double there on Boxing Day, then we were off to Australia, where we joined up with the other visiting jockeys – Roger Poincelet, Enrico Camici, Eddie Arcaro and the Japanese champion Hideo Takahashi – in Melbourne, before moving on to

Adelaide and Brisbane. Although I could manage no better placing than a third, I hugely enjoyed the trip, especially as the Australians made us so very welcome. At the airport in Adelaide hundreds of people turned out to greet the visiting jockeys, and the Australian press were always professional, asking well-researched and sensible questions. They've remained so throughout the years.

After Australia we managed a brief holiday in Honolulu *en route* to California, where in Los Angeles we were the guests of film producer Raoul Walsh, a great friend of Charles St George. Raoul was an excellent host and gave a fascinating insight into the world of the movies, taking us round the studio where he was making a film with Peter Fonda. We went racing at Santa Anita – a track with probably the best scenery in the world as a backdrop, just fifteen miles north of Los Angeles – and then spent a few days in Las Vegas. Susan decided to fly home from there but I went down to Arizona to stay with friends of Noel Murless, Keifer and Lucy Mayer: every day for two weeks we spent all the daylight hours in the saddle, herding cattle for mile upon mile on fast, nimble-footed ponies, a very far cry from the Classic racehorses I'd left behind in Newmarket. We returned each evening to the wooden ranch for a long bath, dinner and a good sleep. It was as well that American saddles were so comfortable!

In 1962, for the first time for eleven years, I rode a winner on the first day of the season, scoring a treble – two of them for my father – on the opening day at Lincoln.

But at Warren Place things were uncharacteristically quiet. Pinturischio had been retired to stud, his career destroyed by the nobblers; Aurelius had serious question marks hanging over his temperament; and among the three-year-olds the only Derby possibility was Young Lochinvar. In the event the prospects of Young Lochinvar or any other potential Derby mount became completely academic, as just before the Epsom meeting

I again found myself in trouble with the Stewards of the Jockey Club.

In a selling race at the Lincoln evening meeting on 30 May I was riding a filly named Ione for the small Staffordshire trainer Bob Ward, who had another runner – Polly Macaw – in the same race. Polly Macaw, backed down to even-money favouritism and ridden by Peter Robinson, won, and my mount Ione – who started at 11–8 despite being forecast favourite in the morning papers – ran on to finish second. The racecourse stewards, suspecting a stitch-up which had allowed the originally less fancied stable companion to win following hefty support in the betting ring, accused me of not letting Ione run on her merits. This came as a big shock to me as the winner had landed the race so easily and always proved the better horse, but my protestations of innocence fell on deaf ears, and the case was referred to the Jockey Club Stewards in London.

After a hearing lasting two and a half hours Bob Ward's licence to train was withdrawn and I found myself suspended for two months. I thought this an excessive punishment, but then again any penalty would have been unjustified as I knew perfectly well that I had done nothing wrong. In those days the Stewards had no guidelines to follow with regard to punishment by fine or suspension and looked at each case differently. For whatever reason, I was hammered.

I emerged from my meeting with the Jockey Club Stewards at their London headquarters, then in Cavendish Square, to find a gaggle of reporters and photographers milling around waiting for me. But luckily Peter O'Sullevan – long established as the finest racing journalist and commentator of his time, and a close friend of many years' standing – was waiting outside in his car. He signalled me in and whisked me away to find my own car – only for me to reach home and find another gathering of journalists outside the house. This was the first time I had experienced the tenacity of the press in full pursuit of a story – and it was certainly not the last.

That suspension ruled me out of the big midsummer race meetings, including Epsom, Royal Ascot, the Newmarket July Meeting and Ascot's late July fixture in which I would have ridden Aurelius in the King George, and it was in a highly disgruntled frame of mind that I watched the Derby at home on television: Larkspur, a Vincent O'Brien colt I had ridden in the Irish Free Handicap in April, won, but the race was marred by the fall of seven horses on the run down Tattenham Hill. Young Lochinvar, the representative of Warren Place, finished well down the field.

Susan and I then took up an offer from Teasy Weasy Raymond to make use of his house in the South of France, where for a couple of weeks we swam, waterskied and tried to forget about racing. Teasy Weasy – christened Pierre Raymond Bessone – had been born in Nice, and although he moved to England at an early age he always spoke with a hint of a French accent. His main home in Britain was near Windsor, and we would stay with him for Royal Ascot – to which he would turn up flamboyantly dressed in a brightly coloured morning suit (a different colour for each day) set off by his characteristic blue carnation. He revelled in upsetting the Ascot establishment with his garish attire and pranks such as arriving at the entrance to the Royal Enclosure riding a white horse!

I returned to the saddle at Windsor on 30 July 1962, by which time my total of winners for the year was an abysmal thirty-six. By the end of the season this had risen to ninety-six, which put me fourth in the table. All in all, the 1962 season was best forgotten.

In the New Year I decided to try my luck in Florida, and flew out to Hialeah, only to fall foul of the local stewards and receive a ten-day suspension on account of my whip action, which they described as 'unconventional' and even 'intimidating'. Charles St George, who had just flown in from a holiday in Jamaica, suggested I go down there and ride the following weekend as the Florida suspension would not apply on the island. I leapt at the idea and spent a few weeks lapping up the Jamaican warmth – while England was in the grips of one of its worst ever winters – and riding a few winners before returning to Newmarket to see what Warren Place had in store.

My first winner of the 1963 season came at the end of March at the Liverpool meeting – then a mixture of Flat and National Hunt – but my win on a horse named Forgotten Dreams in a minor race was as nothing compared with one of the greatest triumphs the Piggott family had ever achieved.

My father was still training a few jumpers, and at Liverpool I helped him saddle Ayala, co-owned by himself and Teasy Weasy Raymond, for the Grand National. Teasy Weasy had paid just £250 for this strapping chestnut, and although Ayala was a bit slow (which doubtless accounted for his National starting price of 66–1) he was a very safe jumper for whom the Liverpool fences would hold no terrors. I had schooled the horse myself at home and knew that he had just come to himself – though my confidence did not extend to contemplating a return to riding over jumps! In Pat Buckley my father had booked a very good lightweight jockey, and we thought we might just have a squeak.

Ayala jumped well throughout the race, though on the run back towards the stands he seemed to be a little outpaced, and at the last fence was behind Carrickbeg, ridden by John Lawrence – now Lord Oaksey – who looked all over the winner going to the 'elbow' halfway up the Aintree run-in. But Carrickbeg started to tire and Pat Buckley never gave up pushing away: with the winning post rapidly approaching, Ayala kept on closing the gap and got his head in front in the shadow of the post to win by three-quarters of a length.

The National triumph realized a lifetime's ambition for my father, but Teasy Weasy had commitments elsewhere and could not be at Liverpool for his greatest triumph as an owner – one he was to repeat thirteen years later with Rag Trade. I made my way back to Newmarket while my parents headed off home, stopping for a celebration dinner at Burford: they had plenty to celebrate, as the Grand National victory had catapulted my father to the top of the National Hunt trainers' table, where he was to remain right to the end of the term.

But the beginning of the 1963 flat season was not all roses, and that spring I found myself in trouble with the law again over a motoring offence. Driving into the racecourse car park at York the previous October I had found myself in the wrong lane, and in trying to extricate myself cut in front of two cars and almost ran over a policewoman. She flagged me down, and during questioning I stupidly gave my name as Edmund Brown (in fact the name of one of the biggest owners in the north), as I assumed she knew who I was. Since I heard nothing for a while after, I assumed that the incident was closed, but six months later received a visit from the police, and the case ended up in court at Reading, where I was fined £50. Riding commitments at Birmingham kept me away from the court that day, but I was amused to learn that the judge had given the opinion that since this was my ninth offence since 1955, perhaps I should consider taking my test again!

We had no particularly strong Classic hopes at Warren Place in 1963, and in the Derby I rode the French-trained second favourite Corpora, who finished only fifth behind the favourite Relko. But a poor Epsom – no winners – was balanced by a wonderful Royal Ascot, with six successes including Lady Sassoon's gigantic chestnut Twilight Alley in the Gold Cup. Twilight Alley next raced in the King George VI and Queen Elizabeth Stakes, but split a pastern that day and could never run again.

Quite apart from the thrill of riding six winners at the Royal meeting, that tally helped a great deal in my season-long struggle to pin back Scobie Breasley in the jockeys' championship. Scobie had got off to a flying start but I managed gradually to close the gap, and for most of the season we had a real ding-dong battle. Some newspapers commented on how thin and tired I was looking, and questioned whether the frantic travelling in search of winners was taking its toll, but the intense competition must have been doing me some good, as on 19 and 20 July I rode nine winners from eleven rides, and three days later at Leicester landed the first four races.

But one winner which landed me in trouble was Casabianca in the Royal Lodge Stakes in September, run that year at Newbury as the new Royal Enclosure was under construction at Ascot. Casabianca was a big, fat, lazy grey colt who really needed rousting along to show his best, and my use of the whip on him at Newbury did not meet with universal approval – particularly from one racegoer, who complained to the RSPCA. They instigated an investigation but no action was taken against me, and Noel Murless, who always insisted that his charges were treated fairly both on the racecourse and at home, staunchly defended me by explaining that Casabianca needed strong handling, and that the Newbury race had done him no harm whatsoever.

With just two weeks to go to the end of the season, the jockeys' championship was bubbling to the boil. I was trailing Scobie by one, then drew level (167 each), and the bookies were quoting 5–4 on the two of us. I pulled ahead by two but Scobie fought back level on 171 each. By the start of the final day at Manchester on 9 November the score stood at Breasley 176, Piggott 174. I managed to win the very last race – ironically named the Goodbye Consolation Plate – but it was not enough, and the final scoreboard read Breasley 176, Piggott 175 – a major let-down after I'd put in so much work to win the title. I was disappointed, but it was impossible not to give credit to Scobie, who was winning what turned out to be the last of his four championships.

Scobie was a great deal older than me – 49 on the day he won the 1963 championship, while I had just passed my 28th birthday – and in so many ways was typical of the Australian jockeys who at that period were making such an impact on European race-riding. Sitting very tight into his horse, he would never leave the rails unless he had to and liked to come as late as possible, yet in his quiet way he knew how to get to the bottom of a horse, and often the impression that he had given his ride an easy race was mistaken. The rivalry between us in the mid-1960s added a cutting edge to the Flat at the time, and I always knew that if he was riding the danger in the race I'd have to think just that little bit more, and constantly be keeping an eye open for the Breasley move up the inside rail.

The 1963 season had been exhausting, and soon we were off on our travels again, first for a spell in Majorca with the Queen's jockey Harry Carr and his wife Joan, and then after Christmas for a winter holiday in Nassau, where we took Maureen and her new nanny Ann Mather along with us. Ann was a bright and cheerful sixteen-year-old from Derbyshire, and Maureen loved her – as did our second daughter Tracy when she came along in April 1965: they christened her 'Annann'.

At the start of the 1964 season I reached an arrangement with Chantilly trainer Mick Bartholomew that I would ride for him on Sundays, and we got off to a dream start when his Rajput Princess gave me my first French Classic winner in the Poule d'Essai des Pouliches – the French One Thousand Guineas – in May.

At Warren Place we thought we had a live Derby candidate in the shape of Lady Sassoon's Sweet Moss after he had won the Dante Stakes at York, but in the big race he disappointed, finishing in the middle of the field. The rest of the season was providing a satisfying mix of quantity and quality until towards the end of September, just after winning the important Queen Elizabeth II Stakes at Ascot on Linacre, I flew across to Paris to partner Persian Garden in the Prix Henry Delamarre at Longchamp.

He was running on the rail when suddenly, seven furlongs from home, we found ourselves in the middle of a very nasty three-horse pile-up. Persian Garden had two horses fall on top of him – fracturing his skull – and I ended up with concussion. To this day I cannot remember what happened, but I later discovered that Yves Saint-Martin was held responsible for squeezing us onto the rail, and received a month's suspension from the French stewards. (Persian Garden, happily, recovered from his injuries, and later went to stud.)

I had regained consciousness by the time I reached hospital – the Clinic Juvenet in nearby Saint-Cloud – but the first three days were a blur. Not being able to speak French was something of a problem, and my companion in the room – French jockey Marcel Depalmas, who had also been hurt in the pile-up – was rambling deliriously. So it was not until the next day, when Susan arrived with Charles St George, that anyone could explain to me that the medication I had swallowed was actually a suppository!

I had sustained a hairline fracture of the skull, though this was not diagnosed until a good deal later following blinding headaches which affected me sporadically for some years. But while lying in that Paris hospital my main concern was not so much my head as the jockeys' championship. Having won the title just the once, in 1960, I was desperate for a repeat, and at the time of the accident had a lead of thirteen over my nearest pursuer, the Australian jockey Ron Hutchinson. I was well aware that if I didn't get back in the saddle quickly Ron would stroll away with the title, so on the Saturday – just six days after the fall – I persuaded the doctors that I was fit enough to leave hospital.

I donned a pair of black wraparound sunglasses, and despite a great deal of press interest no-one on the flight back to London seemed to recognize me. But when I emerged at Heathrow I was horrified to see a huge throng of photographers. Surely they couldn't all be there for me? Feeling dreadful and steeling myself for the worst – with my head in the state it was, I certainly did not feel up to popping flashbulbs or interviews – I made towards the pack, only to discover to my very great relief that all the attention was for the Beatles, then in the first manic flush of their popularity, who were about to leave on an overseas tour.

On my arrival back in Newmarket I was greeted by a huge pile of get-well cards, telegrams and flowers, which were much appreciated, and after ten days' quiet recuperating I thought it was time to climb into the saddle again. I got up on a quiet pony, but soon decided that I had been somewhat optimistic about my rate of recovery, and resigned myself to a slower convalescence.

Welcome relief from the aggravation and disappointment that day came in the jovial form of Tommy Steele and his wife Ann. I had met them in Jamaica the previous winter, and Tommy had kindly phoned after my accident to ask how I was – and also whether, when I was fit enough, I could give him some riding tuition, as he was about to make a film that required him on horseback, and he'd never ridden before. So we gave him a leg up on the long-suffering pony, and after a crash course in the riding skills Tommy proved a natural.

Just under three weeks after the accident I was back in the saddle – and the winner's enclosure – at Newmarket. Ron Hutchinson, despite being able to ride at under 8 stone (my lowest riding weight at the time was 8 stone 5 pounds), had not been able to take much advantage of my enforced rest, and although in the final few days of the season he narrowed the gap to three, I held on to take the title with 140 winners.

I was thrilled to have won my second championship, but had found the road back to full fitness very tough, and on reflection considered that perhaps I should have called it a day for the season after the Paris fall.

My mount in the Washington International that year was Belle Sicambre, trained by Mick Bartholomew for Mme Suzy Volterra, but the ground was too firm for the filly and she finished fifth. Then after a short holiday in Nassau I headed again for Jamaica, where I rode five winners over three weekends.

In 1965 the Flat season did not begin at its customary location: the track at Lincoln had been closed down. Along with most of the jockeys I was not heartbroken by this, as Lincoln was a pig of a place to get to, and the new opening meeting, at very accessible Doncaster, proved much more congenial. Among my early successes that year was on Fighting Charlie in a race at Lanark – my one and only visit to that track, until then the only Flat course in Britain at which I had not won.

Tracy, our second daughter, was born on 6 April 1965, like Maureen in the Evelyn Hospital. Tracy was a little bigger than her sister, weighing in at 8 pounds 4 ounces.

I was beginning to ride more frequently for the great trainer Paddy Prendergast, along with Vincent O'Brien the acknowledged master of his art in Ireland. My family had known Paddy for some time, and it was from him that my father had bought Anselmo, who in 1964 had been his one and only runner in the Derby. My father had met the pop singer Billy Fury through his manager Larry Parnes, for whom he trained, and when Billy wanted a Derby runner he asked my father to find him a suitable candidate: starting at 100–1 and ridden by Paul Cook, Anselmo ran a blinder to finish fourth to Santa Claus.

Paddy Prendergast asked me to ride Meadow Court in the 1965 Derby, and the colt, who had good form in both England and Ireland, started second favourite at 10–1. The identity of the favourite, though, was enough to explain why neither my mount nor anything else in the field that year had a prayer, for hotly fancied at 7–4 was the French colt Sea Bird II, who in the 1965 Derby put up one of the great performances of all time.

I rode this Derby in my customary way, and made my move halfway up the straight at about the same time as Pat Glennon on Sea Bird, but it was no contest. Sea

Bird had a tendency to hang to the left and Pat may have been worried that this quirk would repeat itself, so he never let the horse go at all, simply cruising into the lead, and that was that: he beat me by two lengths. It was quite extraordinary.

That day Meadow Court came up against a freak of a horse, but with Sea Bird out of the way showed himself a pretty good performer. At the end of June he gave me my first Irish Classic when he won the Irish Derby from Convamore, after which Bing Crosby, who had bought a share in the horse, entertained a huge and appreciative crowd of racegoers at The Curragh with his impromptu rendition of 'When Irish Eyes are Smiling'.

Things were going well, and they went even better in Royal Ascot week, when I beat the previous record for a jockey at the meeting by riding eight winners there, including Casabianca (still fat and lazy) in the Royal Hunt Cup, Sweet Moss in the Rous Memorial Stakes and Fighting Charlie in the Gold Cup.

Back at Ascot for the King George VI and Queen Elizabeth Stakes at the end of July, Meadow Court again took advantage of the absence of Sea Bird by winning cosily from Soderini and Oncidium, and Mick Bartholomew's highly promising two-year-old Kashmir II won the valuable Prix Robert Papin at Maisons-Laffitte.

In England a huge change in the running of races was introduced on 8 July, with the Chesterfield Stakes at Newmarket becoming the first race in this country started from stalls rather than the starting gate. This race – which I won on Track Spare – was a one-off, but before long starting stalls became a regular sight on British courses, a change very much for the better.

Of course, the arrival of stalls meant that horses had to be got used to the new technology and taught to go through them, but most adapted very well. Older horses seemed to take to the stalls without too much trouble, and the youngsters were introduced to them at home at a very early age. I was very much in favour of their introduction as so many horses got kicked in the mêlée when a field – especially a large one – was lining up at the old-style gate. One example which comes to mind happened a couple of years before stalls were brought in. At Wolverhampton I was riding a horse named Fauvist for my father-in-law Sam Armstrong in a 27-runner field. While we were lining up Fauvist got squeezed up, so went down on his knees and tried to savage the horse next to him who, in self-defence, lashed out and kicked his attacker on the jaw! Fauvist had to be withdrawn and I, covered in blood, hitched a lift back to the weighing room in the starter's car.

One horse who most definitely would have benefited from the more widespread use of starting stalls in 1965 was Young Emperor, a brilliant but wayward two-year-old trained by Paddy Prendergast on whom I won the Coventry Stakes at Royal Ascot and the Gimcrack Stakes at York. I would also have won the Richmond Stakes at Goodwood on him, had he not refused to start, and then turned round and bolted in the opposite direction!

On a rather humbler level, that year I won on a horse named Freda's Legacy the Wigan Lane Selling Handicap at Haydock Park – the race in which I had ridden my first winner seventeen years (though it felt like a lifetime) earlier.

The closing phase of the season was disappointing, with Meadow Court, who started at 11–4 on, failing to cope with very soft ground in the St Leger and going down by ten lengths to the outsider Provoke. He was even more disappointing in the Arc. Admittedly the 1965 race was one of the strongest ever contested, with Sea Bird winning from the French Derby winner Reliance, but none the less I expected Meadow Court to do better than ninth. He was a very good horse, but he just couldn't go in soft ground.

Despite the inevitable disappointments I'd had a good year, finishing up champion jockey again with

160 winners and well ahead of my closest rival Ron Hutchinson.

It was about this time that I was approached by Brian Epstein, manager of the Beatles, about his becoming my manager for promotional purposes – as opposed to racing matters, about which Brian knew nothing. After several meetings in London we decided that such an arrangement would not work, partly because I simply did not have the time to devote to the promotional ideas he had in mind, and partly because when it came to the crunch I did not really want to be managed.

I was off on my travels again, this time to Venezuela, where I had been invited to ride in Caracas. This was my first visit to South America, and I loved it. The majority of the horses there were American-bred, often by owners wealthy enough to have horses in training in England (for some of whom I had ridden), and generally the Venezuelan racing business was thriving. I stayed there for five days and thoroughly enjoyed myself, before getting ready for our usual winter holiday – sunbathing in Nassau (where Susan stayed with the two children) and riding weekends in Jamaica.

Five winners during the first week of the new season back home seemed like a flying start, but although I little knew it at the time, 1966 was to be a watershed year in my career.

With all the travelling and the increased number of rides I was getting, my weight was more or less looking after itself. The days of wearing a sweatsuit in the car while the heater blasted away flat out all the way to the races were long gone. For a while I was able to indulge my sweet tooth more often, particularly with favourites: prior to the Paris accident in 1964 my preference was for Mars Bars, but after that, for no apparent reason, it switched to Fudge Fingers. Even more curiously, before that fall I loved grapes, yet for several years after it I just could not face them.

Paddy Prendergast had decided he needed a stable jockey, and took on the young Australian prodigy Des

Lake. But when one door closes another one opens, and I was able to add another string to my bow in France following an offer from Countess Batthyany, one of the biggest owners over there, to ride for her whenever I could.

Warren Place housed nothing for the Two Thousand Guineas but Paddy Prendergast had two live contenders with Young Emperor and Celtic Song, and I was asked to stand by for whichever the new stable jockey decided against. This turned out to be Young Emperor. Then Mick Bartholomew asked me to ride Kashmir II, but as I thought Young Emperor had the better chance I declined Mick's offer – rather unfortunately, as Kashmir II, ridden by Jimmy Lindley, won, with Great Nephew (sire of Grundy and Shergar) second and Celtic Song just pipping Young Emperor for third place.

All in all, Guineas week 1966 was not a happy one for me. I had declined the ride on the Two Thousand winner, and in the One Thousand Lady Sassoon's Soft Angels, to whom we at Warren Place gave a good chance, behaved disgracefully at the start – this was before stalls were used in the Classics – delaying matters for a considerable time and then finishing only fifth. This was sad, as she had been a lovely two-year-old, winning the Royal Lodge Stakes by five lengths, but she succumbed to her temperament and never showed comparable form at three.

The importance of a good temperament in a racehorse should never be underestimated: it is good for a horse to be high-spirited, but any fractiousness or irritability uses up too much energy before and during a race, and although temperament is not always passed down the bloodlines, it's one factor which breeders must constantly bear in mind when planning matings.

Vincent O'Brien asked me to ride his Right Noble, owned by the American industrialist Charles Engelhard, in the White Rose Stakes at Ascot, and after the horse had won very impressively there Vincent offered me the mount in the Derby, for which Right Noble was now favourite. Noel Murless had no obvious Derby candidate, so I agreed.

The trouble started when Vincent subsequently asked me if I would also ride his Irish One Thousand Guineas winner Valoris in the Oaks. Again I agreed, but this time there was a hitch – and a very serious one. Noel intended to run Varinia in the fillies' Classic, and was far from amused by the prospect of his stable jockey riding against his horse. When I told him of my preference for the Irish filly, he issued his ultimatum: ride Varinia, or else.

For me the issue was simple. I wanted to ride the winner of the Oaks. On her Irish One Thousand Guineas form – her only previous race that season – Valoris looked a stone-cold certainty, and I was going to ride her. Noel, naturally enough, took a different line, pointing out that I had been with him all that time and owed it to him to ride his filly. There was, however, one aspect of this whole sorry affair which did not get properly aired at the time. There existed, for the 1966 season, no formal agreement between Noel Murless and myself. Prior to then there had been a formal and binding contract between us, but over recent years I had been offered an increasing number of top-class rides from other stables – both in England and in France – and for that season had asked for (and been given) only a verbal agreement that I would ride for Warren Place when I could, and in return would have more freedom to choose outside rides.

Despite this, the Valoris–Varinia choice proved a flashpoint, and once news of the split got out all hell broke loose. There was even an investigation by the Jockey Club, but since in this case no formal contract existed between trainer and jockey, no breach had occurred, and no further action was taken.

And so there I was, after twelve years as stable jockey to the most powerful yard in the land, suddenly turned freelance – a position almost unheard-of in those days for any rider with pretensions to the jockeys' championship. To add to my woes, Paddy Prendergast had taken it into his head that I had something against his new stable jockey Des Lake – one day at Chester Paddy accused me of deliberately chopping Des off – and announced in banner headlines in the press that he 'would not put Piggott up again, even for the Crown Jewels'. He forbade his owners to request that I ride their horses.

Two important doors were shutting as the one at Ballydoyle was opening, and before the dust from the furore had fully settled, the Epsom Classics were upon us.

The night before the Derby I found myself doubled up in excruciating pain which continued through the small hours. On seeing a doctor in the morning I found that I'd had tiny crystal-like particles in my digestive system, the grating of which was causing the intense discomfort. I've never suffered from this condition since, but learned that its cause was insufficient liquid intake, and that it is not uncommon among jockeys.

I recovered well enough to ride Right Noble in the Derby, but this big horse – joint favourite on the day with Pretendre – was unsuited to the contours of Epsom, failed to act on the track and finished unplaced behind Scobie Breasley on Charlottown.

But Valoris, focus of all the controversy, did the business beautifully (just as well, in the circumstances!) and won from Berkeley Springs, with the rejected Varinia, ridden by Stan Clayton, third. (Valoris, incidentally, proved the truth of the old racing adage that a change of colours can bring a change of luck: her owner Charles Clore had had horses without success for twenty years before changing his silks brought him his first Classics.)

That summer my father, by then 62 years of age, announced his retirement from training. He'd had enough. He told us that he'd set off on a world tour but never got round to it: my mother enjoyed travelling but shared her life with a man who enjoyed his home comforts and always managed to talk her out of her more exotic travel plans, so instead they spent their time enjoying the garden and playing golf. A couple of years after my father's retirement they sold South Bank to Barry Hills and moved to a house in Kintbury, between Newbury and Hungerford, which was set back from the road and had a couple of paddocks behind, unused while my father lived there.

At the beginning of July, six weeks after the split with Warren Place (during which time I had had no contact with Noel Murless), Noel phoned and asked me to ride for him again as he wanted the relationship to continue. Naturally enough I was delighted, not only by the prospect of riding high-class horses for the yard, but also by the evidence that he was not harbouring any lasting bad feelings. I resumed riding work for him, and we had the first winner of our 'new' relationship when Jim Joel's Pink Gem won the Princess Maiden Stakes at the Newmarket July Meeting.

The same day I rode the winner of the Bunbury Cup, Showoff, who wore blinkers for the first time. The decision to fit them was taken only on the morning of the race, so punters studying the form in the morning papers would not have known about the blinkers, and there was a furore in the press – led by Tim Fitzgeorge-Parker in the *Daily Mail* calling for the overnight declaration of the use of any such equipment. This was a reasonable suggestion, but it was some years before it came about.

For a while that summer the dual link with Ballydoyle and with Warren Place seemed to work well enough, and between them they gave me the winners of both the great midsummer middle-distance races. For Vincent O'Brien I rode Pieces Of Eight to win the Eclipse Stakes at Sandown Park, and then the following week landed the King George VI and Queen Elizabeth Stakes at Ascot on Aunt Edith. This grand four-year-old filly had run unaccountably badly in the Hardwicke Stakes at Royal Ascot when partnered by Scobie Breasley during my estrangement from Noel Murless, and a dope test had been taken: the result had not been made public by the time the King George was run, and in the event nothing untoward was revealed. She became the first filly ever to win the King George when getting home by half a length from Sodium, and her Royal Ascot flop was never properly explained. Perhaps she was just missing me!

Thereafter the winners just kept on flowing, including a five-timer at Leicester on 19 July – three years to the day since I had pulled off the same feat at Pontefract. On 6 August I hit my century for the tenth time when scoring on Florescence for my father-in-law Sam Armstrong, and all in all August proved a quite phenomenal month, with forty-one winners in Britain and several trips across to Deauville adding to the tally. The possibility loomed of being able to ride 200 winners in the domestic season, which no jockey had achieved since Gordon Richards in 1952, and with another five-timer at Warwick on 5 September the prospect looked rosy.

Towards the end of August, Noel Murless asked Susan and me to pop up to Warren Place one Sunday evening for a drink. He wanted to tell us that, after a great deal of thought and consultation with his main owners, the decision had been taken that a fully retained jockey for 1967 was essential. The existing arrangement would carry on for the remainder of the 1966 season, but after that it would be over.

I was very sad indeed at the prospect of not riding regularly again for this great man, but could see his point of view, and we parted that evening on the best of terms.

There were, however, still several weeks of the current season to go, and Warren Place winners to be ridden before the door was finally shut on my time there. They were good winners: Royal Palace won the Royal Lodge Stakes at Ascot; Hill Rise, who two years previously had been runner-up to Northern Dancer in the Kentucky Derby, won the Queen Elizabeth II Stakes at the same meeting; and Fleet won the Cheveley Park Stakes at Newmarket.

Looking back on it, that was not the best of times to depart: Royal Palace the following year won the Two Thousand Guineas and Derby, and in 1968 developed into one of the best middle-distance four-year-olds of the post-war period; and Fleet won the One Thousand Guineas, which at that time was the one Classic I had never won. Yet the Murless horse which it was hardest not to be riding in 1967 turned out to be neither of those, but Busted, who as a four-year-old in 1967 was just brilliant, unbeaten in four races including the Eclipse and the King George.

I knew that I could have stayed at Warren Place, but it was time to move on, and the thought has never left me that had I not made the move then I would not have ridden such horses as Sir Ivor, Nijinsky and Alleged.

Those great horses lay in the future as the traumatic 1966 season came to a close. I had not hit the magic mark of 200 winners, but settling for 191 as I became champion jockey for the fourth time did not hurt too much. Shortly after the end of the season it was announced that George Moore had been asked to come over from Australia to ride as stable jockey at Warren Place in 1967, and that he would give his answer before Christmas. Few doubted what that answer would be.

For me, the Murless years had come to an end.

6

Freelance – and still champion

Before embarking – with no little trepidation – on a
new life as a freelance in the 1967 season, another
International Jockeys Series took me to Australia, and
en route we stopped off at Hong Kong. Racing was
still run in the colony for amateur riders only, but
even in those days the betting turnover was huge. We
found Hong Kong a fascinating place and would have
been happy to stay longer – especially as we found
that fellow jockeys Yves Saint-Martin and Bill Pyers
and their wives were also breaking their journey there.
Both were great friends. Yves, the finest French jockey
of his generation, had won the Derby on Relko in
1963 and was a familiar rider in the big British races,
while Bill Pyers, based in France, was one of that
great team of Australian jockeys who had made such
a name for themselves in Europe.

They too were on the Australian tour, so we all
moved on, and on Christmas Day 1966 gathered at the
Southern Cross Hotel in Melbourne for a welcoming
party. In the New Year the circus moved on to Adelaide,
from where we visited the famous trainer Colin Hayes at
his Lindsay Park Stud: Colin claimed that moving to the
high altitude of Lindsay Park had doubled his output
of winners, his theory being that training at altitude
and then bringing the horses down to sea level to race
significantly increases their lung power.

My mount in the International was to be Yangtze,
but he was found to be lame on the morning of the
race and was withdrawn, so I was switched to a horse
named Agrifo – who did me proud in the race itself,

holding on by a head in near record time. We returned to the winner's enclosure to a terrific reception.

Next stop was Brisbane, where I got into trouble with the local stewards over my whip. In Australia they had strict rules regarding the length and use of the whip, and while in both Melbourne and Adelaide we had been allowed to ride with our own whips, the Brisbane stewards refused to allow this: they said that mine looked like a golf club! The replacement sticks we had to carry were like fly-swats, but in my case it made no difference, as I needed no more than hands and heels to win the big race on Prunda, a great big seven-year-old gelding who carried 9 stone 8 pounds and started at 10–1. This old horse had won twenty-four races in his career and become a very great favourite with Brisbane racegoers, so the result was extremely popular: the papers described the reception we were given as worthy of a Melbourne Cup winner.

With the series completed, Susan and I headed off for New Zealand and then Tahiti, where our visit turned out to be not quite the idyllic experience traditionally associated with that island. The taxi taking us from one foul hotel to more congenial accommodation was driven by a woman smoking a particularly noxious cigarette, and in an attempt to counter its smell I had lit up a cigar. Suddenly a chicken ran across the road, the taxi swerved, and my cigar ash landed on my bare chest, giving me a nasty burn. Worse was to follow: while swimming in the shallow lagoon by our new hotel I felt a sharp pain in my big toe. Though I could see nothing in the water, the sting hurt intensely and started to turn red, so Susan sought the assistance of the hotel manager, a large French lady. 'Ah, the Nohu fish,' she pronounced knowingly, and bathed my toe in neat ammonia, which hurt more than the sting. Not my day.

We had planned to spend our time in Tahiti swimming and lazing about, but our peace was suddenly shattered one afternoon by the sound of a familiar raucous laugh – and there were Bill and Becky Pyers, just flown in from

Sydney. It was wonderful to see them, but our Tahitian lifestyles were somewhat at odds – we wanted to lounge around, they liked staying up half the night partying – so we didn't spend much time together.

From Tahiti we moved to Acapulco, where for the first time I tried my hand at windsurfing, a sport which had just started to gain popularity. I can't pretend I took to it, perhaps because after returning to dry land I was informed that the bay in which I had been trying to learn the necessary skills was apparently infested with sharks!

Then on to Mexico City, where the local Jockey Club fêted us at the racetrack, and home to Newmarket before taking Maureen off to Switzerland for a brief holiday.

It had been a hectic winter of travel, but one also marked by a particular personal sadness. My grandfather Ernie Piggott died early in 1967 at the age of 88. I hadn't seen too much of him during the last years of his life, but could never forget the part he played in my childhood and the pleasure I'd always had from visiting him in the old house.

I was back in the saddle almost as soon as I got home, first in France and then at the traditional St Patrick's Day meeting at Baldoyle, the now defunct racecourse near the sea just north of Dublin. It seemed that Irish trainers would be a prime source of rides in 1967, since as well as the Vincent O'Brien connection it appeared I could look forward to a renewed association with Paddy Prendergast, who had forgiven me for whatever I had done to upset him.

There was much speculation and comment regarding how I would fare as a freelance, but the domestic season started well enough with my first six winners being for six different trainers. Then a long losing spell in April – no winners for over two weeks – had the Prophets of Doom turning up the volume before the tide turned, ironically enough, on the Noel

Murless-trained Royal Saint in the Fred Darling Stakes at Newbury.

I was still riding abroad regularly, and one ride in Italy sticks in the memory. The race was at Milan and the horse, named Dragon Blond, duly won – which was just as well, since his starting price was 10,000–1 *on*! I have no doubt that the Italian racegoers would have lynched me had that one not got in, as they're not known for their tolerance of beaten favourites.

Back home, rides were undeniably harder to come by as a freelance, and by 21 May, well into the new season, I'd ridden only sixteen winners – exactly half my total at the same date the previous year.

Royal Palace had won the Two Thousand Guineas for Warren Place under the new stable jockey George Moore and was a hot favourite for the Derby, but it is an indication that Noel Murless and I remained on the best of terms that he offered me the Derby mount on the stable's second string, Sun Rock. When that colt was scratched I switched to Ribocco, trained by Fulke Johnson Houghton and owned by Charles Engelhard: I had won the Observer Gold Cup at Doncaster on the colt the previous autumn but he had not yet shown much as a three-year-old and started at 22–1 at Epsom. Ribocco was a small horse, standing barely 15 hands high, but like so many of the offspring of his sire Ribot could be temperamental and difficult, both to ride and in his box. On the track, he always took his time coming out of the stalls – 1967 was the first year in which starting stalls were used in the Derby – and he had to be left alone in the early stages of a race. I never really felt that Ribocco was putting his best foot forward, as it was just not on even to touch him with the whip: he hated being bustled up, and resented the stick. So the trick was simply to set him alight as late as possible and just hope for the best, and in the Derby I brought him with a late run on the very wide outside to challenge George Moore on Royal Palace. It might have looked for a moment as if he was a serious danger to Royal Palace, but that horse was always holding us and drew away to win by two and a half lengths.

At The Curragh in the Irish Derby I got my revenge on George when Ribocco beat his mount Sucaryl, following which Ribocco was third to another Warren Place star, Busted, in the King George. He was beaten at Goodwood when less than completely fit, then came good in the St Leger, coming with a strong run in the closing stages to beat the Queen's Hopeful Venture (another Murless horse) by a length and a half. Ribocco next ran a marvellous race to come a fast-finishing third behind Topyo and Salvo in the Arc, beaten a neck and a short head, but disappointed in the Washington International at Laurel Park, finishing well down the field in seventh place. He had had a long year and rewarded his connections with over £200,000 in prize money; and his two-year-old full brother named Ribero looked like providing me with yet another string to my bow in 1968.

A more obvious Classic hope for 1968 was Petingo, one of the first horses owned by Greek shipping tycoon Captain Marcos Lemos and trained by Susan's father Sam Armstrong. I won a maiden race on him at Newmarket in June, and then teamed up with him in the Gimcrack Stakes at the great York August Meeting, where he absolutely slaughtered his rivals, winning by six lengths. He rounded off his unbeaten juvenile term with a facile victory in the Middle Park Stakes, and clearly had Classic pretensions of the highest order.

Other landmarks that summer included winning the German Derby in Hamburg on Luciano, the Ulster Harp Derby on Dan Kano, the Gran Premio de Madrid – my first visit to Spain – on a locally trained horse named Toté, and my 2,000th domestic winner: Coonbeam at Leicester on 25 July. I ended the season as champion jockey again, but with just 117 winners, the lowest total of my eleven championships.

But above all 1967 meant the start of my partnership with the best horse I ever rode: Sir Ivor.

Throughout the spring and summer I had been gradually familiarizing myself with the set-up at Ballydoyle and getting to know Vincent O'Brien. Much has been written over the years about this great trainer and his achievements both on the Flat and over jumps, but for me his outstanding characteristic was his special insight into each and every one of the horses in his charge: he just seemed to know what each horse was capable of, and how to release that potential. He is surely the best trainer there has ever been at keeping the value of a horse – a fairly essential quality in the late 1970s and early 1980s when so many of the horses which passed through his hands were literally worth millions – and he knew instinctively that when running a horse in a race everything had to be one hundred per cent in its favour: nothing was to be left to chance. When I came to ride for him regularly this sometimes caused problems, as often he would have several horses in a big race and would not decide until the last possible minute which one he would actually run, waiting to see what the conditions would be like on the day. As a freelance I was often having to keep my riding options open until quite close to a race, and if Vincent was not yet ready to decide that could be awkward!

His famed attention to detail could be seen all around Ballydoyle, where, significantly, he never housed a vast number of horses, preferring to keep his string to a size where he could get to know each individual animal. Although the basic set-up was pretty much the same in the mid-1960s as it was when Vincent retired from training in 1994, he was constantly making improvements to the place, and everything was geared towards keeping the horses happy and relaxed – including playing music in the covered ride.

My agreement with Vincent excluded riding his horses in Irish races, so I had never sat on Sir Ivor before getting the leg-up on him in the parade ring before the Grand Criterium at Longchamp in October 1967. In physique he impressed me enormously – a fine big bay colt by Sir Gaylord with superb conformation. He had won two of his three races in Ireland, including the important National Stakes at The Curragh, and was very highly thought of. In the Criterium I could see why. Despite the bottomless going he won very easily by three lengths, and the way he quickened was really exceptional.

Now I found myself in a quandary, as I had a choice of Two Thousand Guineas mounts between Sir Ivor and Petingo – both very high-class colts and both giving every indication that they would train on into top-notch three-year-olds. Understandably both Sam Armstrong and Vincent O'Brien needed to know before the winter which colt I would ride at Newmarket, and after due deliberation I chose Sir Ivor, taking the long view that my Two Thousand Guineas ride would very probably become my Derby ride, and sensing that although on breeding Sir Ivor was not guaranteed to get one and a half miles, even at Epsom, his relaxed style of racing made it more likely that he would get home than was the case with Petingo, whom I always considered would get no further than a mile.

Sir Ivor's owner Raymond Guest was a great racing man who had already won the Derby with Larkspur (Vincent's first Derby winner) in 1962 and in the 1970s was to achieve notable success under National Hunt Rules with the great L'Escargot, dual winner of the Cheltenham Gold Cup and apart from Golden Miller the only horse ever to win the Gold Cup and the Grand National. He had always adored Sir Ivor, and in 1966 had backed the colt – then an unnamed yearling – to win the 1968 Derby, getting odds of 100–1 from the famous bookmaker William Hill.

Early in 1968 Vincent O'Brien took his major Classic contenders to Pisa in Italy to put a bit of sun on their backs and escape the raw Irish winter. Sir Ivor obviously found the change of climate particularly stimulating, as one day he dropped his lad and galloped loose into the centre of Pisa, chased by a pregnant Jacqueline O'Brien,

Vincent's wife: thankfully the horse was caught, and neither he nor Jacqueline came to any harm.

I saw Sir Ivor for the first time in 1968 when I flew over to Ireland to ride in the opening meeting of the season there at Baldoyle, and went down to Tipperary to give the colt a gallop. He looked absolutely terrific – clearly the trip abroad had done him good – and in the gallop gave me a feel as good as his looks.

His first outing as a three-year-old came in the Two Thousand Guineas Trial at Ascot, which he won handily by half a length from Dalry. Naturally enough, with so many big races to aim for, I had no intention of being hard on him that day, which was just as well as he had hit his head on the stalls and finished with blood dripping from his mouth.

Then Petingo won the Craven Stakes at Newmarket in the manner of a really good horse and became Two Thousand Guineas favourite over Sir Ivor. I began to wonder whether I had made the right decision. Spring in Ireland was, as it so often is, cold and wet, and Sir Ivor did not really thrive once he had returned home after the Ascot trip. His gallops were proving very disappointing, so Vincent decided to send him over to Newmarket two weeks before the Two Thousand Guineas and take advantage of the much drier ground there. He was billeted in the racecourse stables, where Sir Ivor responded well to his trainer's thoughtfulness, seeming to like it at Newmarket. Generally a tremendously relaxed horse who took changes in his stride, he allowed nothing to put him off his main interest in life: eating. He had a massive appetite, and between the Two Thousand Guineas Trial and the Guineas itself put on so much weight that Vincent had to step up his work. Once he'd arrived at Newmarket I rode him nearly every day, and in his one serious gallop before the big race he absolutely flew. I knew then that he was completely on song, and sure to win.

The same day as that gallop Petingo turned in an equally impressive piece of work, and the build-up to the race generated great excitement as people took sides. Petingo, unlike Sir Ivor, was unbeaten, but Sir Ivor might have the greater turn of foot. The rest of the field didn't count in the public imagination: this was a two-horse race.

And so it proved. There were two or three very speedy horses in the Guineas and we went fast in the early stages, with Sir Ivor near the rear of the ten-runner field. Then I had to ride him a bit to take a closer position. He came to collar Petingo coming out of the Dip and accelerated smoothly to go clear in a matter of strides, winning by one and a half lengths. Considering that there had been a great deal of rain in the preceding two days, the time for the one mile – 1 minute 39.26 seconds – was very fast.

Sir Ivor immediately became favourite for the Derby, and although some of the breeding pundits thought he couldn't possibly get a mile and a half, I was convinced that he would win. My reading of his pedigree gave him a reasonable chance of getting the trip, as I was sure that he'd get ten furlongs, and most years that is enough for Epsom.

Sir Ivor arrived at the course two days before the race, and I went down to work him on the track. I had not seen him since Guineas day, and he looked in tremendous shape – mature and trained to the minute. If he failed, it would not be for lack of condition.

The going was good and the weather fine as the thirteen-strong Derby field made its way across the Downs to the start after the formal parade. Nowadays the Derby field canters the whole way to the start, but until quite recently the runners would gather near the racecourse stables after the parade and walk across the road and then across the Downs. This could be an unnerving experience for a young horse, and although Sir Ivor tended to take everything calmly Vincent, with his typical attention to detail, was taking no chances. He arranged for his head lad Maurice O'Callaghan to be waiting after the parade to lead Sir Ivor down the long pathway to the start, having taken the colt over from travelling head lad Gerry Gallagher, who had looked after Sir Ivor during the parade itself.

In the event Sir Ivor behaved quite beautifully, staying completely relaxed and going into the stalls like a lamb. When the gates opened I jumped him out and kept him reasonably handy in the middle of the field, exactly where I wanted him to be. Benroy, ridden by Duncan Keith, set a good gallop, but halfway down the hill Sandy Barclay on Connaught – like the previous year's winner Royal Palace, owned by Jim Joel and trained by Noel Murless – took it up and went four lengths clear. I had to keep him in my sights but, being well aware of the doubts about Sir Ivor's stamina, could not make my move too soon, and at Tattenham Corner we were back in about fifth.

Halfway up the straight Connaught still had the lead, with Sir Ivor tucked in behind him, and for an instant or two I thought that he might get away from me. With two furlongs to go I still had a fair bit of ground to make up and thought it was time to move, so pulled Sir Ivor out and asked him to quicken. He didn't respond instantly as, characteristically, he had got so relaxed that he wasn't really thinking about stretching out. But when he woke up the response was amazing. He just took off, flying past Connaught a hundred yards out and winning easing up. I had always expected him to win, but the sheer brilliance of his performance impressed even me. There's no doubt about it: of all my nine Derbys, Sir Ivor's was the most exciting.

Unfortunately Raymond Guest could not be at Epsom that day since his duties as US Ambassador in Ireland required his presence at the opening of a memorial to the late President Kennedy, but he was able to watch the race on television. That evening he hosted a wonderful celebration party at the Savoy: at the end of the room a large screen was set up on which the race was shown, so I was able to give him a full run-down of how it had gone. That was one race I certainly didn't mind seeing over and over!

Following that display of sheer brilliance, Sir Ivor then proceeded to be beaten in his next four races.

His immediate target after Epsom was the Irish Derby at The Curragh. Vincent's contract with stable jockey Liam Ward dictated that Liam should ride the Ballydoyle horses when they raced in Ireland – an arrangement with which I was perfectly comfortable – so for the big race I had to look elsewhere, and teamed up with the big, temperamental Ribero, like my 1967 Irish Derby winner Ribocco a son of Ribot and also like him trained by Fulke Johnson Houghton.

Ribero had missed the Derby and then been beaten twelve lengths by Connaught at Ascot, so on the form book had no chance against Sir Ivor, who started at 3–1 on, with Ribero joint third favourite at 100–6. But I knew that, despite his Epsom victory, Sir Ivor did not truly get a mile and a half, and in the race set out to test his stamina to the limit, sending on Ribero as soon as we straightened for home and making the best of my way for the line. Inevitably, Sir Ivor started to challenge us, but his effort – not helped by a strong head wind – petered out, and Ribero kept going stoutly to win by two lengths. I was probably one of the few people not shocked by Sir Ivor's defeat.

I was reunited with Raymond Guest's colt in the Eclipse Stakes at Sandown Park, where he came up against two absolutely top-class performers in the shape of Royal Palace and Taj Dewan. Royal Palace, winner of the Two Thousand Guineas and Derby in 1967 and ridden at Sandown by Sandy Barclay, had already vindicated the decision to keep him in training by landing the Coronation Stakes at Sandown Park, Coronation Cup at Epsom and Prince of Wales's Stakes at Royal Ascot, while Taj Dewan, ridden by Yves Saint-Martin, had won the valuable Prix Ganay at Longchamp earlier in the year and was one of the top four-year-olds in France. Despite the strength of the opposition, Sir Ivor started odds-on favourite, and over a mile and a quarter seemed to be running at his best distance.

It was a fantastic race. Yves took Taj Dewan into the lead about half a mile out and set sail for home, with Royal Palace challenging on his outer and Sir Ivor about three lengths adrift. For most of the way up the straight my fellow felt like he could pick off the two leaders whenever he wanted, but as Taj Dewan and Royal Palace knuckled down to a tremendous duel inside the final furlong he seemed not to be moving well: he was a heavy, big-shouldered horse and the firm ground at The Curragh may well have jarred him up. Although he rallied close home and started to make up the ground, he couldn't pin them back. Royal Palace beat Taj Dewan by an extremely short head – Yves was convinced he had won! – with Sir Ivor three-quarters of a length away in third.

Sir Ivor was sore after the race – which must have explained his less than typical effort – and was not fully wound up when beaten in his prep race for the Arc, the Prix Henry Delamarre at Longchamp just a week before the big race. But in the Arc itself he ran a blinder. We found a trouble-free passage up the inside rail and from a quarter of a mile out it was a two-horse race. Unfortunately for Sir Ivor, that other horse was one who on his day over a truly run mile and a half was even greater than he – Vaguely Noble – and try as he might, quickening gamely under pressure, he could not get on terms and went down by three lengths. Over the Arc distance Sir Ivor was never going to beat Vaguely Noble, who must have been one of the best horses I ever rode against.

In the Champion Stakes a couple of weeks after the Arc everything was in Sir Ivor's favour over the straight ten furlongs at Newmarket, and he won very easily from Locris.

That was his last race in Europe, but Raymond Guest was very keen to run him in the USA and on 11 November he lined up in a field of eight for the Washington International at Laurel Park. This was many years before the Breeders' Cup had been dreamt of and before the much greater ease of air travel for horses had made transatlantic raids a regular part of the programme of many a top-class racehorse, and for a European champion to travel to the USA to race was still fairly unusual: Sir Ivor was the first Epsom Derby winner to run in the USA since Papyrus in 1923.

At Laurel Park the weather was damp and gloomy and the going on the turf track so wet that my main problem was going to be getting Sir Ivor to last home in the conditions. The horse himself was in great form, almost bucking me off as Vincent legged me up into the saddle and carrying on the joke with the stalls handlers: it took three of them to get him loaded.

With a fast pace set from the start and my nagging worry about his stamina in the conditions, I was happy to keep Sir Ivor in the middle of the field for most of the race. Coming round the final bend into the home stretch I moved him up on the inside into third place, where he was poised to strike behind the leaders Czar Alexander and Fort Marcy. Then Carmarthen came up on the outside, and to riders in the stand I must have looked hopelessly boxed in. But I just waited a bit and then, well inside the final furlong, Carmarthen drifted towards the centre of the course, Fort Marcy ducked towards the rail, and there appeared a gap for Sir Ivor. I gave him a slap with the whip and he flew into it, showing that tremendous burst of speed which was his hallmark and going a length clear in a couple of seconds. With the race in the bag, I eased off a little so that at the wire we were three-quarters of a length to the good.

It had not been one of my worse efforts, so it was odd that our victory unleashed all sorts of crass criticism of my ride from the US press. They said that I had nearly lost the race – though I hadn't lost, had I? – and got the best horse beaten. I was given a very hard time, but then I've never thought that the American press understood the finer points of race-riding. And it may just be possible that I knew a little bit more about Sir Ivor than they did.

The fact is that the Americans look upon racing in a different way from Europeans. Over there they're used to dirt racing, where the horses give each other plenty of room and don't worry about being on the inside. Our horses, on the other hand, are taught to follow another one, so that when they're asked to race on the outside and a little behind their rivals they tend not to race as fluently. Sir Ivor needed to be ridden in a certain way and that was the ride I gave him.

The Washington International was Sir Ivor's last race; after that he was retired to stud, initially to Ireland and then to the Claiborne Farm near Paris, Kentucky.

Vincent O'Brien believed that Sir Ivor was the most intelligent horse he had ever come across, and always maintained – though he did not say whether or not this was anything to do with his intelligence! – that the horse had a special affection for me, as he invariably pricked his ears when I came along. Years after he had retired I visited the old horse in his stallion paddock at the Claiborne Farm, and from the greeting he gave me I think Vincent was probably right. Sir Ivor has lived to a grand old age, and as I write this in the summer of 1995 is still thriving at Claiborne at the age of thirty – the oldest living Derby winner.

Although others have strong claims to be called the best horse I ever rode, for me Sir Ivor stands above the rest. Maybe he did not have the imperious majesty of Nijinsky, but he was a beautiful individual to look at and as a racehorse was the complete professional: he knew what was required of him, and always did his best to deliver. He had phenomenal speed, but all the talent in the world is pointless without the will to use it, and Sir Ivor was a real trier. Put at its simplest, Sir Ivor knew how to race.

I was able to maintain my interest in the horse after he had retired by breeding from him. Raymond Guest had offered me the chance to send a mare of my own to

Sir Ivor, and I bought a lovely bay filly named Limuru, many of whose relatives I had ridden during the Murless years. I had had my eye on Limuru for some time, and when she was entered at a Doncaster evening meeting in July 1968 suggested to Susan, who was running a bloodstock agency at the time, that she should go and take a good look at the filly with a view to negotiating a deal with her owner before the race – in which I was riding a horse named Copsale for Susan's father Sam Armstrong. I flew up from Newmarket, leaving Susan to travel separately by car, but *en route* she drove into a fierce hailstorm which slowed the traffic to a crawl. Once clear of the hold-up she made an attempt on the land speed record and tore into the Doncaster car park – where she stepped out of the car to hear 'and it's Limuru from Copsale' coming over the commentary: Limuru would not be as cheap a purchase after the race as she would have been before! Susan rushed up to the weighing-room steps to find a very annoyed husband who – she says – gave her a sharp ticking off for arriving so late. But later in the season I did manage to buy Limuru and sent her to Sir Ivor – then standing in Ireland – for the 1969 covering season. The offspring, a bay colt who was sold to Petingo's owner Captain Marcos Lemos and named Cavo Doro, went into training with my father-in-law and after his two-year-old career was transferred to Vincent: I rode him to be a good second to Morston in the 1973 Derby, beaten only half a length.

Susan had established her bloodstock agency a couple of years before we bought Limuru. One of my father's owners asked me to select him a yearling, and as Susan was often popping over from our house to Tattersalls when the sales were on – usually taking Maureen and Tracy along to see the horses – I suggested to her that she might like to carry out this assignment, and she came up with a 970-guinea filly, later named Razia, who went into training with Fulke Johnson Houghton, winning first time out as a two-year-old and going on to breed winners herself.

After that highly satisfactory first foray into the bloodstock world Susan spent more time at the sales and began to build up a thriving business; in 1973 she joined forces with our Irish friend Cormac McCormack to form Susan Piggott Bloodstock Limited, which continued to flourish on a worldwide basis until I started training at the end of 1985, when, mindful of a possible conflict of interests, Susan wound up the business and Cormac formed a new one: he was instrumental in acquiring several owners for my stable, purchasing yearlings and handling the sale of horses from our yard when necessary.

My other English Classic winner in 1968 was Ribero, who emulated his older brother Ribocco by landing the St Leger.

The weather at Doncaster on Leger day was absolutely foul, with a downpour which had softened the ground well beyond the liking of the favourite Connaught – runner-up to Sir Ivor in the Derby – and Ribero himself. To make matters worse, Ribero had an abscess in his mouth which had burst the night before, so unsurprisingly he was somewhat mulish at the starting stalls. He was slowly into his stride and ten lengths adrift of the pace early on, but like all those Ribot horses he could not be hustled along, so I let him make up the deficit in his own time. Three furlongs out I was just behind the leaders, who were struggling in the mud and clearly going nowhere, when upsides loomed Bill Williamson on Canterbury. One by one the rest of the field – including Connaught – fell away, leaving just Ribero and Canterbury to fight out the finish. At the furlong pole I got first run but Bill started coming back at me, getting closer and closer, inch by inch. Ribero was flat out, giving his all, and I knew that there was no point in even picking up the whip. So I kept away at him with hands and heels and he plugged on through the desperate ground, with me praying that the post would arrive. At the line we were locked together, and most people – including the bookmakers – thought that Canterbury had won. They were wrong. We had held on by a short head and returned, covered in mud but victorious, to a great reception. That was one ride about which even I could allow myself a little satisfaction.

All in all 1968 had been a wonderful year, though it was marked by the first example of a phenomenon that was to live with me – as it has done with other jockeys – throughout my career. After riding a treble at Epsom in the summer I was informed by the police that the course had received a phone call from someone threatening to shoot me, and that I had had a discreet police escort all afternoon. Over the years this sort of thing happened again and again, and I soon decided that the simplest approach is to take no notice of these cranks.

Besides, I had much happier matters to look back on at the end of 1968.

My decision to go freelance had been fully vindicated by my position on top of the jockeys' championship at the end of the year: champion for the sixth time with 139 winners. I had ridden two very great horses: Sir Ivor, of course, and a big three-year-old on whom I was beaten a short head in the Earl of Sefton's Stakes (worth £437 to the winner) at Liverpool on Grand National Day 1968: Red Rum!

That autumn I was proud to be voted *Daily Express* Sportsman of the Year, celebrated at a wonderful lunch at the Savoy: 1968 must have been the Year of the Horse for *Express* readers, as the women's award went to show-jumper Marion Coakes – later, having married the jump jockey David, Marion Mould.

My travels that winter took me first to Calcutta, where I rode a treble on the first day, including the Calcutta Derby. Next stop was Hong Kong, where I spent a couple of days with my cousin Bill Rickaby, who had taken up a post with the Hong Kong Jockey Club, and then it was down to Australia for another International Jockeys series, in which the riders included

Masare Kurita from Japan, Jacky Taillard from France and Gianfranco Dettori (father of Frankie) from Italy. The way home again took in Honolulu, followed by our first visit to that glorious Californian city San Francisco, where we went through the full tourist menu – Fisherman's Wharf, Golden Gate Bridge, the lot – before returning to England to prepare for the 1969 season.

I got off to a flying start, the first day producing a winner in the shape of New Chapter, but my inability to win the first big race of the season, the Lincoln Handicap, continued – as it was to do right to the end of my riding career. In 1969 my mount was Kamundu, owned by the flamboyant bookmaker John Banks. I had known John for some time, and the previous winter, while I was in the Caribbean, had received a telegram from him asking me to fly back and ride his horse Hill House in the 1968 Schweppes Gold Trophy at Newbury – one of the big handicap hurdles of the jumping season! Hill House was notorious for manufacturing his own cortisone, which had landed his connections in trouble after the horse had won the Schweppes in 1967 for his previous owner. John Banks offered to pay all my expenses and throw in a hefty fee if I agreed to ride Hill House, but it had been nine years since I'd ridden over hurdles and after a due amount of reflection I decided to stay in the sun a while longer. Just as well: Hill House finished unplaced behind Persian War.

An offer to ride John's Kamundu in the Lincoln was somewhat more orthodox, but we could finish only third.

Ribofilio, another of the good Ribot colts trained by Fulke Johnson Houghton, who had done enough as a two-year-old to be installed winter favourite for the colts' Classics, made his seasonal reappearance in the Two Thousand Guineas Trial at Ascot, where he was ridden by Joe Mercer. (I was under suspension following a disqualification in Paris on Easter Monday.) He won very easily indeed and was then directed towards Newmarket for the Two Thousand Guineas itself.

Rumours of home setbacks abounded, but none of these was substantiated and he arrived at the Rowley Mile apparently in the peak of condition. In the parade ring before the race (for which he started hot favourite) he seemed a little quieter than he had been before his earlier races – though that is not uncommon with three-year-olds as they learn to settle down – and on the way to the start was definitely listless. In the race itself he ran like a dead horse: when the stalls opened he just could not get off on terms with his rivals, and two furlongs out I was so afraid that he would fall over that I had to pull him up. He was stringently tested after the race, but to this day the reason for Ribofilio's devastating failure in the Guineas has never been found.

Later in May I was back in trouble with the French stewards after finishing second on Fanghorn in the Poule d'Essai des Pouliches: they decided that I had not kept a straight line in the closing stages and demoted me to third, about which I was far from pleased: nor was I terribly impressed that the Jockey Club representative sent over to interpret when I subsequently lodged my appeal could speak little French. The appeal was thrown out.

In spite of his dismal run in the Guineas, Ribofilio was ante-post favourite for the Derby. It took him a good while to come right again after Newmarket, and rather than subject him to another race we took him to Sandown Park for a searching racecourse gallop over a mile and a quarter. I was left with a niggling feeling that all was not quite right, but the day before the big race he galloped six furlongs well enough at home, so we decided to run. He started 7–2 favourite for the Derby but pulled too hard in the early stages and in the end was beaten only just over three lengths when fifth to Blakeney. Who knows what might have happened had he elected to settle?

He returned to his best form when a gallant second to Prince Regent in the Irish Derby (for which he was again favourite), won a two-horse race for the March

Stakes at Goodwood, and then, having recovered from a brief bout of coughing, started favourite for the St Leger – the fourth time that year he had been market leader for a Classic. But the Leger trip was a little far for him and he could manage only second behind Intermezzo, ridden by Ron Hutchinson. I did not ride Ribofilio again that year, but always considered him the most genuine of those Ribot horses I rode.

Ribot, dual winner of the Arc in the 1950s and winner of the King George in 1956, and certainly one of the greatest racehorses ever seen in Europe, passed on some of his temperamental problems to all his offspring, and since I rode most of his best colts I had to learn the knack of getting the best out of them. Fulke Johnson Houghton, who trained the majority of the good ones, understood them well and used to brief me on their individual quirks. On the whole, you just had to sit and suffer, knowing that they had the necessary ability but had to do it in their own time, and that most of them would stop dead if touched with the whip. For 'riders in the stand' the way I sometimes rode those Ribots – just hands and heels – may have been hard to comprehend, but that was just the way it had to be done.

My most fruitful partnership of 1969 was undoubtedly with the Duke of Devonshire's great five-year-old mare Park Top. She was trained at Newmarket by Bernard van Cutsem, a tall, suave and urbane man liked by all, from the Jockey Club members with whom he mixed socially down to the youngest lad in his yard. He started out as a successful owner–breeder, and after taking out a licence himself trained mainly his own horses and those belonging to his friends – notably Lord Derby, at whose Stanley House yard he was based, and the Duke of Devonshire himself.

On Park Top that year I won the Prix de la Seine at Longchamp in May, the Coronation Cup at Epsom in June, and the King George VI and Queen Elizabeth Stakes at Ascot in July (in which race one of her rivals was Speed Symboli, the first Japanese-trained raider in a big European race). Park Top suffered from arthritis and when in her box wore a copper bracelet on one of her forelegs – and in her races she had to come very late to be at her most effective. At Ascot she was at her brilliant best, making rapid headway in the final quarter-mile to win comfortably from Crozier. However, she also gave me one of my more forgettable moments of 1969, when second to Levmoss in the Prix de l'Arc de Triomphe. I got a great deal of stick from local racegoers and the press for overdoing the waiting tactics on her, and for once the criticism hit home: I was very annoyed with myself that day, as I knew deep down that had I made my move sooner I would certainly have won.

That was one blot on the season. The other was the number of suspensions I had to endure, which brought me a total of nineteen days on the sidelines. Of these sentences, the one which really aggravated me was a seven-day break incurred in the St James's Palace Stakes at Royal Ascot. Geoff Lewis was on the Two Thousand Guineas winner Right Tack, I was on Habitat, and we were having a tremendous tussle when, as Right Tack got the upper hand, Habitat started to hang in towards him. It all happened so quickly that there was nothing I could do, but the stewards judged that I'd deliberately caused the interference – despite Geoff's insistence that the incident made no difference to his horse, which earned him a caution for giving false evidence! I thought the whole business was diabolical.

These enforced absences at one point looked like handing the championship to Geoff on a plate, and the occasional lean spell made matters more difficult, but at the end of the season I had notched up 163 winners to his 146, enough to give me my seventh championship.

In addition I rode forty-eight winners overseas in 1969: of these, thirty-one were in France, but perhaps the most memorable was in the USA: my second successive win in the Washington International, this time on the four-year-old Karabas, trained like Park Top by Bernard van Cutsem.

A tremendously tough horse, Karabas had been on the go since April, when he won the then prestigious City and Suburban Handicap at Epsom, and in all had won six good races in England and France before going to Laurel Park to take on an international field. He absolutely slammed them, and this time the American press were more polite about my riding. Not that I was too polite in return, and that year I was branded a 'rude bum', as opposed to simply a 'bum' on Sir Ivor in 1968. Karabas may have been no Sir Ivor, but he was consistent, resilient and genuine, and on his day was a horse of considerable class.

From Washington, Susan and I made our way to Japan for a series of races in Tokyo and Kyoto. We boarded the Pan Am flight in New York for the long trip across, pausing *en route* to refuel at Fairbanks, Alaska. This should have been only a brief stop, but the plane had developed a fault, which necessitated a three-hour stopover. The airport terminal was a large, barn-like building, only just visible above the snow, and although the sun was out the weather was so cold that any vehicle parked outside had to keep its engine running to avoid freezing up. Inside the terminal, however, the heat was almost unbearable – probably because this building appeared to be the meeting place for the entire population of Fairbanks. A variety of Eskimos and very large Americans, who had come in wearing fur hats and sheepskin jackets, were sitting in the restaurant eating huge plates of steak and chips. As usual I fancied an ice-cream, but it arrived as a massive portion in a container the size of an ice bucket, which even I could not empty!

Eventually we continued our journey to Japan, and our view of Tokyo as the plane came in to land was memorable: a vast sprawling city covered in haze, through which the snowy summit of Mount Fuji was just visible in the distance. The bright red sun was about to go down, and we learned later that the cause of its vivid colour was the ever-present Tokyo smog.

Japan in the late 1960s was an emerging racing nation, and a fascinating place in which to be ambassadors for the sport. Our visit had been arranged – on the initiative of the British Embassy – to coincide with a British Trade Week being held for the first time in Tokyo, and I was representing British jockeys along with Ernie Johnson (who had won that year's Derby on Blakeney) and Sandy Barclay. Others in the official party included Major Peter Smith, founder of the Jockeys Association of Great Britain, and Lord Derby, who was to present the cup for the big race.

Our time in Japan was hectic, full of receptions and sightseeing trips (though sadly we were denied the opportunity to go to the Wada Stud to see the stallion Speed Symboli, who had run in that year's King George at Ascot), and Japanese hospitality was wonderful – although conversation with our hosts was usually possible only through the army of interpreters assigned to us by the Japan Racing Association, and in all my subsequent trips to Japan the overriding problem has been that of language. We made many friends on that first trip, who later visited us in England and still keep in touch.

The main racecourse in Tokyo is Fuchu, established in 1933: it is dominated by a vast grandstand, six storeys high and extending over two furlongs. The surface of the track itself on that first visit left something to be desired, with rock-hard ground covered by very little grass – Japanese grass, we learned, is very sparse and has virtually no root system.

Among other memories of that first Japanese jaunt are the chaotic Tokyo traffic – the fifteen-mile journey from our hotel to the track took well over two hours – and the saddling arrangements once we reached the course. Japanese jockeys in those days rode with lead weights around their waists instead of (as in the West) in a cloth under the saddle, so we European jockeys, using weight cloths alien to the Japanese way of doing things, had to saddle our mounts ourselves, as the locals did not appreciate how to put on the weight-cloth.

The paddock was reached by a tunnel running from the weighing room, and the haul from one to the other was so long that Sandy Barclay wisely commandeered a bicycle for the round trip.

Nearly all home-bred, the horses we rode in Tokyo were noticeably lean, and all seemed to pull very hard. Their manes were plaited and decorated with pom-poms in the owners' colours, and some runners had a sprinkling of salt on their quarters or a medallion or ribbon around their necks – all symbols of good luck. Not that good luck was very apparent in the British jockeys' performances: I managed a third, but that was the nearest to a winner that any of the three of us came.

From Tokyo we moved to Kyoto, former capital of Japan and set in a beautiful situation below high mountains, travelling there on the famous Bullet Train: when we reached Kyoto we had to be ready to jump straight out with our bags as the doors would shut seconds after they had opened, and the train would zoom off on its way to Osaka.

The hotel in Kyoto was less glamorous than our billet in Tokyo, but we were amused to see a notice in the foyer greeting us:

WELCOME TO OUR GUESTS,
WONDERS OF THE ORIENT,
SIR AND LADY PIGGOTT

I love Japanese food, but Susan didn't like the raw fish and rice diet, and survived mainly on fruit and bread. Sandy Barclay shared Susan's lack of appetite for the local fare and at one function, where we had to sit shoeless on the floor while eating, I spotted the two of them discreetly depositing their rejected dinner under the low table.

We visited a huge training centre over the mountain from Kyoto, with its own full-sized racetrack used for both racing and training. Although at that time the Japanese did not have much idea about how to train racehorses, no expense was spared and they were very eager to learn.

All too soon an intriguing visit had to come to an end. Susan flew home for the Tattersalls December Sales, while I embarked on a whirlwind tour of Singapore, Perth and Calcutta, where I rode a few winners before arriving home a week before Christmas.

It had been a memorable year, and one in which I did my bit for all the jockeys in the weighing room by helping to set up the Jockeys Association of Great Britain, an amalgamation of the Flatrace Jockeys Association of Great Britain and the Professional National Hunt Jockeys Association. Lord Oaksey – father of John Oaksey, nowadays so familiar to Channel 4 Racing viewers – was elected President, and I became Vice-President, and since then the JAGB has gone from strength to strength.

But perhaps my greatest emotion at the end of 1969 was not reflection on past events so much as anticipation that 1970 would be even better, as it would mean a Classic partnership with the horse on whom in October I had won the Dewhurst Stakes at Newmarket. His name was Nijinsky.

7

The year of Nijinsky

You couldn't help falling in love with Nijinsky as soon
as you saw him. He was so big and imposing, with a
real presence about him: in looks as in performance, he
was simply outstanding.

Vincent bought Nijinsky in Canada as a yearling for
$84,000 for Charles Engelhard, and soon discovered he
could be a difficult horse to train. When he first arrived
at Ballydoyle he would not eat oats, and horse nuts had
to be sent over from Canada. By the time they arrived
the horse was eating oats! He had a constant problem
with his digestion and was subject to bouts of colic,
and was always a tense character. Consequently Vincent
decided to get as many races into him as a two-year-old
as he could, in the hope of settling him down, and by the
time he first came to England, for the Dewhurst Stakes
at Newmarket in October 1969, he had already raced –
and won – four times, and a huge reputation preceded
him. Liam Ward had ridden him in all his races in
Ireland, and Vincent's best lads were working him at
Ballydoyle, so the first time I teamed up with the colt
was in the parade ring at Newmarket.

Despite being so big, he proved a very easy horse to
ride – he just did what was required, and you could
do anything with him in a race. Maybe he was never
to show that instant burst of blinding speed which Sir
Ivor had possessed, but when he started to go, he just
went!

He won the Dewhurst easily, never coming off the
bridle and going clear in the final furlong to beat
Recalled by three lengths. The opposition wasn't up

to much that day, but Nijinsky was clearly a very good horse indeed, and he went into the winter hot favourite for the 1970 Two Thousand Guineas and Derby.

Yet however rosy Nijinsky's Classic prospects seemed, I had a more urgent priority as the 1970 Flat season opened – winning the Lincoln Handicap, at long last, on Prince de Galles.

Winner of the Cambridgeshire the previous autumn, Prince de Galles had a favourite's chance in the Lincoln, and I came by the ride in a somewhat unusual way, having found myself about three weeks before the race sitting next to his owner Arthur Swift while having my hair cut in the Grosvenor House Hotel in London. I was booked for the mount within a couple of minutes.

Trained by former jockey Peter Robinson, Prince de Galles was a top-class handicapper, and as the Lincoln approached our confidence grew – despite a hair-raising incident on Newmarket Heath a few days before the race. I was cantering Prince de Galles towards the start of the Waterhall gallop when a light aeroplane in trouble flew over us so low that the horse took fright and bolted. While the plane crash-landed on the Limekilns – mercifully without casualties – Prince de Galles was carting me round and round the Heath.

No harm was done, but a week before the Lincoln Prince de Galles put in such a disappointing gallop that Peter thought the horse was ill and considered withdrawing him from the race. He persevered, however, and a sparkling piece of work a few days later restored our confidence.

I had been trying to win the Lincoln for twenty years and had never gone into it with a better chance than in 1970. Whatever had been ailing him in the run-up to the race, Prince de Galles looked magnificent in the paddock, and started favourite at 9–4 – an extraordinarily short price for such a competitive event.

But in the race itself luck was not on our side. I tracked the leaders for the first six furlongs, then made a forward move and took up the running going into the final furlong, where we were challenged by Sandy Barclay on New Chapter, trained by my father-in-law Sam Armstrong. New Chapter, on the stands side, swerved towards us close home and landed me a hefty bump right on the line. Since we were beaten just half a length I felt there were strong grounds for an objection, but although the head-on film showed the bump clearly enough, the stewards couldn't tell if contact had occurred before or after the line, so allowed the result to stand.

All my four mounts that afternoon finished second. It just wasn't my day, but a few days later at Liverpool matters could have taken a much more serious turn. The Grand National meeting was still a mixture of jumping and Flat, and in a nine-runner handicap we were coming round the bend to the point where the National starts when suddenly the three horses in front faltered and ducked out, their jockeys shooting backwards in the saddle as if they had hit an invisible wall. It transpired that part of the Grand National starting gate was hanging down, and as we were on the turn at the time the impediment was not visible until it was too late to avoid it. I could see blood on the side of Tony Murray's head where he had taken the full force of the impact: he was lucky not to have been decapitated, and carried the scar of a badly cut left ear for the rest of his life. My horse was far enough back in the field for me to have time to see what was happening and duck down, and though I went on to win the race, it was a horrific moment.

But by the end of the first full week of racing I had notched up nine winners, five of them for David Robinson, and looked set for a good season.

I had ridden for David Robinson (no relation to trainer Peter) over the years, and at the beginning of 1970 he indicated that he wanted to use my services more frequently. As he had a large string of highly promising horses this was an arrangement I was keen to pursue.

David had made his considerable fortune in the television rental business and had earned a deserved reputation as an astute and highly successful businessman by the time he decided in the 1960s to build a racing empire and run it on strictly commercial lines. Though a somewhat remote figure to the racing public, David did enjoy being personally involved. He engaged the best judges to select his yearlings at the sales but liked to do the bidding himself, and devised a way of indicating his interest to the auctioneer without gesticulating. He and his wife would always sit in the same seats in the Tattersalls sale ring at Newmarket, from where David would be bidding so long as he was wearing his glasses. Once he removed them, the auctioneer knew that the Robinson limit had been reached, and he had withdrawn.

David installed Paul Davey and Michael Jarvis as his private trainers in separate yards in Newmarket, with a huge board in each yard office listing the horses graded by ability. Decisions about which horse would run where were made at a weekly meeting between owner, trainers, head lads and Robinson's own private handicappers, and the system worked extremely well.

David Robinson's main Classic hope that year was his 1969 Gimcrack Stakes winner Yellow God. I rode this colt on his seasonal debut in the Two Thousand Guineas Trial at Kempton Park, where he won easily from Gold Rod, but neither he nor any of the other horses on whom I won major Classic trials – Decies in the Blue Riband at Epsom, Roi Soleil in the Prix Djebel at Saint-Cloud and Breton in the Prix de Fontainebleau at Longchamp – seriously tempted me away from Nijinsky as my Two Thousand Guineas mount.

Nijinsky had wintered well, and made his reappearance in the Gladness Stakes at The Curragh on the first Saturday in April. Ridden as he was on all his outings in Ireland by Liam Ward (who in fact won more races on the colt than I did), he was never out of a canter to win by four lengths from the four-year-old Deep Run – later to become a legend as a National Hunt sire.

Nijinsky had grown into an even more magnificent individual as a three-year-old than he had been at two, and in the paddock before the Two Thousand Guineas he seemed to dwarf his rivals. His performance in the race matched both his looks and his starting price of 7–4 on. Keeping him on the bridle tucked in behind the front-runners during the early stages, I didn't ask him a serious question until a furlong and a half out, when he produced a wonderful surge of speed and swept through to win easily from Yellow God and Roi Soleil – on both of whom I'd won trials. It was a superb performance.

A few days after the Guineas I received a charming letter from Romola Nijinsky, widow of the great dancer:

> I was tremendously impressed with your magnificent winning of the Two Thousand Guineas race this afternoon on the beautiful horse, Nijinsky, and I send you my congratulations.
> I ask of you now only one thing – please win the Derby for us!

The day after the Two Thousand Guineas I won the One Thousand for the first time on Humble Duty, a lovely dark grey filly from the yard of the then up-and-coming young trainer Peter Walwyn. Peter had asked me to ride her in her prep race at Newbury as her regular partner Duncan Keith had been sidelined through ill health. Less than fully wound up, she was beaten by Highest Hopes. In the Guineas Humble Duty reversed the form in spectacular style: she had a terrific turn of foot and needed to come from behind, and once I unleashed her with over a furlong to go she just flew, shooting clear of her rivals and winning by seven lengths from the French challenger Gleam. That day she was quite brilliant – so brilliant that some even compared her with Nijinsky. But after that race

Duncan returned to the saddle and I never rode her again.

Having won both the English Guineas, I then picked up the Irish Two Thousand on Decies, trained by Bernard van Cutsem. But in contrast to Nijinsky's imperial performance at Newmarket, the race at The Curragh was a desperate affair. Decies was hampered when trying to make his run and had a good deal of ground to find in the last furlong. He managed it, but only just – a short head to spare over Great Heron, with Mon Plaisir, racing between us, a head further back in third.

Meanwhile Nijinsky, already being hailed in some quarters as a wonder horse, was enjoying a quiet preparation for the Derby – a good deal quieter than that of his jockey!

The week before the race was one of the most hectic I've ever had. I rode at Longchamp on the Sunday, Sandown Park on the Monday, then flew back to Paris that night to gallop Breton for Mick Bartholomew on the Tuesday morning. Tuesday afternoon it was back to Sandown to win the Temple Stakes on that great sprinter Raffingora, then into another plane, this time for the trip across to Ballydoyle. It was getting dark as we approached our destination, so Vincent had a bonfire lit to guide us in.

On the Wednesday morning I worked Nijinsky – the first time I'd sat on him since the Two Thousand Guineas – and was delighted by the way he went. Confidence for the Derby was high, but there were less glamorous races to be won, and after a snatched breakfast with Vincent it was back across to Brighton for two winners, then Paris again on Thursday, Newbury on Friday and Newmarket – where I had a full book of rides – on Saturday.

As I was being legged up for the fifth of my six rides that afternoon I felt dizzy and had to dismount. The dizziness soon passed and I was allowed to ride in the race, but the course doctor insisted I forgo my ride in the last. The weather had been very warm and the heat and all the travelling must have dehydrated me, but it was still a surprise when returning home that Saturday evening to get on the scales and discover that I weighed 7 stone 12!

Derby Day started well. My first ride of the afternoon was David Robinson's My Swallow, who won the Woodcote Stakes easily. My second was Nijinsky.

Nijinsky had so dominated his rivals in the Two Thousand Guineas that he had nothing to fear from those who reopposed him at Epsom. There was a slight doubt about his stamina – his sire Northern Dancer had failed to stay the mile and a half of the Belmont Stakes when going for the third leg of the US Triple Crown in 1964 – but I had no worries on that score. He had always settled well in his races and was a wonderfully amenable ride, so I had no doubt about his getting the trip.

Less easy to dispel was the notion that he might not act on the course. Epsom, with its ups and downs, is such an unusual track that you can never be sure whether a horse will adapt to it or not, and plenty of my Derby rides patently did not. Nijinsky was such a big horse that there had to be a niggling doubt as to whether he could show himself to best effect on Epsom's contours – but there was only one way to find out.

In any case, my view of the ideal Derby horse has always been that size is less important than manner of racing. You need a horse that can lay up handy, a few places behind the leaders: getting too far back at Epsom can be disastrous, as there is no part of the course where you can readily make up ground forfeited early on. You have to get up into a reasonable place and keep out of trouble as beaten horses fall back on the downhill run towards Tattenham Corner. Nijinsky you could put anywhere in a race, which made him the perfect Derby runner.

The major factor dictating how I rode that Derby was the nature of the opposition. Whichever way you looked at the form book, there was only one danger – the

French colt Gyr, who had been a leading two-year-old and whose Derby preparation had consisted of victories in the Prix Daru and the Prix Hocquart at Longchamp. A strong galloper with a huge stride, there was some doubt about his own ability to act on the course, but I knew him to be a top-class racehorse, so my strategy was simple. Ride to beat Gyr.

Apart from the bout of colic which affected Nijinsky on the eve of the race and from which he thankfully made a rapid recovery, the final question mark against him come Derby Day itself was whether his temperament might prove his undoing. But the extended preliminaries – the parade in front of the stands followed by the walk across to the mile-and-a-half start – did nothing to ruffle him.

With only eleven runners, it was a small field by Derby standards. Nijinsky started at 11–8 (the only time in his career he ever started at odds against), with Gyr 100–30. Approval (winner of the previous season's Observer Gold Cup for a first-season trainer named Henry Cecil) and Stintino were the only other two horses seriously considered in the betting, but for me this was a two-horse race.

It soon became obvious that it would be a one-horse race. Nijinsky adapted beautifully to Epsom. I kept him on the bridle in the middle of the field and at Tattenham Corner was about fifth, with Gyr on my outside. Once into the straight Gyr – who like Nijinsky had come down the hill without trouble – made his move, and two furlongs out had gone clear. For a moment it appeared to those in the stands that Nijinsky might be in trouble, but once I showed him the whip – without needing to use it at all – he quickened to pass Stintino and collar Gyr inside the final furlong, coming right away to win by two and a half lengths in a time only fractionally outside the then record for the race set by Mahmoud in 1936.

This was my fifth Derby victory, but the first time I'd ever been invited up to the Royal Box – to which, accompanied by Charles Engelhard and Vincent, I was summoned to meet the Royal party.

That night we had a more prolonged celebration at London's premier nightspot, Annabel's. The champagne was flowing, but Mr Engelhard was virtually addicted to Coca-Cola, and spent the evening working his way through a crate which he kept beside his chair. It had already taken its toll on his teeth and was beginning to affect his general health, and despite the hubbub all around him he fell asleep before dessert was served.

The following day it was back to work at Epsom, where Park Top was beaten in the Coronation Cup by Caliban, and on the Friday Raffingora set an electrically timed world record for five furlongs when getting up in the last stride to win the Cherkley Sprint by a short head under 10 stone – a fantastic performance. (The official fastest five furlongs ever – Indigenous at Epsom in 1960 – was hand-timed.)

Nijinsky's next race was to be the Irish Derby at The Curragh, and as Vincent's stable jockey Liam Ward would be continuing to ride him in Ireland I was free to look elsewhere for a mount in the race, which I found in the shape of David Robinson's Meadowville. Although he had not figured in the Epsom Derby he had won the Lingfield Derby Trial earlier in the season and was a progressive sort, and I was expecting a big effort from him in Ireland, even if that did not mean beating Nijinsky.

A fall at Newbury a few days before the race left me with snapped bones in my right foot, and David Robinson, always a cautious man, was beginning to have doubts about my fitness to ride his horse at The Curragh, but Susan managed to persuade him that I was up to the job and I kept the ride. The best I could hope for that day was second to Nijinsky – which is exactly where I finished, a respectful three lengths behind the easy winner.

Nijinsky's complete superiority to the rest of the three-year-old generation was by now in no doubt, and it was time to prepare him for his first encounter with older horses in the King George VI and Queen Elizabeth Stakes at Ascot at the end of July.

King George week began well for me, with victory in one of the best races of the 1970 season, the Prix Robert Papin at Maisons-Laffitte. By mid-July the two-year-old form is beginning to work itself out and the Robert Papin is one of the first opportunities for top juveniles from different countries to face each other. I had the ride on My Swallow, unbeaten in his previous three races, and our main rival was none other than Mill Reef, undefeated in two outings, the more recent of which was the Coventry Stakes at Royal Ascot, which he'd won by the huge margin of eight lengths.

This promised to be an epic race, and so it turned out. I made the most of my rail draw, getting My Swallow to break fast and make the running while Geoff Lewis kept Mill Reef covered up in third, but with a furlong to go Mill Reef had mounted a challenge. Halfway through the final furlong I still had the advantage, then Mill Reef drew level. Both horses ran on with the utmost gameness under strong pressure, and twenty yards out Mill Reef probably just headed me, but as the line came My Swallow stuck his long neck out and got there by a short head.

The pair would next meet in the famous 1971 Two Thousand Guineas won by Brigadier Gerard, but My Swallow was a quite brilliant two-year-old, as he demonstrated after the Prix Robert Papin in the Prix Morny at Deauville. With Mill Reef staying at home this time, My Swallow won hard held.

Another significant winner for me at the same Deauville meeting was Gold Rod, whom I had beaten on Yellow God in the Two Thousand Guineas Trial at Kempton early in the season. Gold Rod's owner–breeder Mrs 'Lottie' Dickson was one of my favourite owners: a great enthusiast for the sport, she had bottomless faith in her little horse, who made up in courage what he lacked in breeding and who in Reg Akehurst had a trainer who could be guaranteed to get the very best out of him.

I had ridden Gold Rod for the first time when he finished second to my One Thousand Guineas winner Humble Duty (by then reunited with Duncan Keith) in the Sussex Stakes at Goodwood, and after that there was just no stopping Lottie: her belief in her horse was unlimited. Gold Rod, to his credit, always did his best to live up to her opinion of him, and Lottie has been part of our extended family ever since.

But the week before Gold Rod took on Humble Duty in the Sussex Stakes, the eyes of the racing world had been firmly fixed on Nijinsky and his attempt to see off the older horses in the King George.

He faced a strong field at Ascot, including two other Derby winners – the 1969 Epsom winner Blakeney and Hogarth, who had won the Italian Derby in 1968. Then there was my old friend Karabas, on whom I'd won the Washington International the previous year, the 1969 French Oaks winner Crepellana and the Coronation Cup winner Caliban.

That day Nijinsky was at his absolute peak, and victory was never in doubt. He took up the running a furlong out while still on the bridle and was going so easily in the closing stages that I eased him down, which allowed Blakeney to close up a little. But it only took a gentle push at Nijinsky for a stride or two to put the issue beyond doubt. He was never better than he was that day.

All seemed set fair for a triumphant second half of the season – but then, early in August, Nijinsky contracted American ringworm, a skin condition which caused almost all his hair to fall out, sapping his energy and severely affecting his training programme. Vincent felt that in the circumstances the colt should be brought along slowly and bypass the St Leger – which in any case was a quarter of a mile further than Nijinsky had ever run before and would put additional strain on him – so that he could be spot on for his main end-of-season target, the Prix de l'Arc de Triomphe at the beginning of October. But Mr Engelhard was dying and knew it, and he was desperately keen to have Nijinsky set the seal on his greatness by becoming the first horse for thirty-five years to win the Triple Crown. A staunch traditionalist, Mr Engelhard had already won the St Leger with Indiana, Ribocco and Ribero, and another victory in the race with the greatest of all his horses would mean a huge amount to him. So once the ringworm had cleared up Vincent was prevailed upon to train Nijinsky for the Doncaster Classic in the middle of September.

In the race before the Leger I had a ride on another of Mr Engelhard's horses, Leander, trained by Jeremy Tree. As the stalls opened, Leander stumbled and I fell off – upon which half a dozen men suddenly emerged from the nearby trees asking where I had been shot! They were plain-clothes policemen who had been keeping an eye on me all day following a threat telephoned to the racecourse by an escaped inmate of Rampton, the nearby mental institution. At the track I had been shadowed by the police but not told of the threats, and now, with Leander careering loose around the course, imminent assassination was less of a worry than retrieving my saddle so that I could weigh out for Nijinsky. Eventually a mounted policeman recaptured Leander and my valet 'Son' Hales retrieved the elusive piece of equipment.

When I saw Nijinsky in the paddock before the St Leger – not having set eyes on him since Ascot – it was clear that some of the gleam had gone out of his eye, and in the parade before the race he seemed quieter and calmer than usual. At the time I put this down to the fact that by now he had raced several times and was more confident and relaxed, but with hindsight you have to wonder whether he wasn't still feeling the after-effects of his illness.

He walked sweetly into the stalls, jumped out well and settled. Looking to find out any limit to Nijinsky's stamina, the leaders set a good gallop, and with a mile to go there was only one horse behind us, but the pace was beginning to tell on the front-runners and one by one they fell back.

With its long, wide home straight, Doncaster is no place for the horse with suspect stamina and I did not want to get to the front too soon, but after the three-furlong marker I asked Nijinsky to move up, and he steadily sidled past his rivals until hitting the front 300 yards out to a tremendous roar from the crowd. At the post we were a length in front of Meadowville.

Nijinsky had won the Triple Crown, and the headlines screamed the ease of his victory. Certainly it had looked facile, but the few correspondents who questioned the ease of his win were quite right: however it may have appeared, Nijinsky was all out at the end of the Leger and could not have won by much further. The hard question to be faced now was whether he had left the Arc behind on the Doncaster Town Moor.

The Prix de l'Arc de Triomphe came just three weeks after the St Leger, and the revelation by Vincent that Nijinsky had lost an abnormally large amount of weight through his exertions – 29 pounds – was not encouraging, so it was in a spirit of hope rather than excessive confidence that Susan and I flew to Paris after racing at Newmarket on the eve of the Arc. We enjoyed a quiet dinner at the small hotel on the Champs Elysées where we always stayed for Longchamp meetings, and retired early.

The following day dawned warm and sunny. We left promptly for the track as I was riding in the first and there is always a huge crowd on Arc day, but I have never, before or since, seen such a crowd as there was at Longchamp that afternoon – nor some of the scenes that took place.

The paddock at Longchamp is an amphitheatre, with terraces commanding a view for thousands of people. By October 1970 Nijinsky was the most famous racehorse in the world, and it seemed as if racegoers had come from around the globe to see him. There were only fourteen runners in the Arc, but in addition to their connections the paddock was swarming with camera crews from several different countries, who were causing havoc. A Japanese film crew homed in on poor Nijinsky, and one of them even thrust a microphone under the horse's mouth. Even the best efforts of Vincent's travelling head man Gerry Gallagher could not deter these people, and by the time I entered the ring with the other jockeys Nijinsky – always a temperamental horse – had flipped. He was awash with sweat, snorting and dancing around, a look of terror in his eye: I had a job to get up into the saddle. In the parade and going to the start I was increasingly unhappy with his state of mind, and felt that he must have used up a great amount of nervous energy.

An additional problem was that I was drawn on the outside, and in France you have to keep your position for over a furlong before tacking over towards the inside rail. Once the race was under way, Nijinsky found it difficult to keep his place early on and stay up handy as he normally could. Half a mile from home he was still towards the rear of the field, but made a forward move when I asked him approaching the short final straight – where his finishing run was blocked by four horses in line ahead of us. I had to pull to the outside, thus losing a little ground, and by the time I straightened him up to go for the post Yves Saint-Martin and Sassafras were still in front on the rails. Nijinsky put his all into pulling back Sassafras and with a hundred yards to go just got his nose in front, but then he faltered and began to hang to the left. He could find no more, and we were beaten a head.

There was a shocked silence as we turned at the top end of the track to canter back towards the stands, and then the customary jeers which the French like to hurl at beaten favourites, before the crowd switched to cheering in the home-trained victor and Yves, always the darling of the Parisian tracks.

(I was to face another volley of abuse at Longchamp just a week later after the defeat of Park Top in the Prix Royallieu. She was long odds on but on ground much softer than she really liked could only dead-heat for third place. This failure earned us the full wrath of French racegoers, who went berserk, throwing all sorts of things at us and issuing threats which even my limited French could just about comprehend. The Duke of Devonshire, Park Top's owner, became thoroughly fed up with the racket in the unsaddling area and swung round to face the crowd, giving them a two-fingered salute in very un-ducal fashion. The mare never ran again, and at stud proved a shy breeder. Those foals she did produce were no good as racehorses.

The recriminations over Nijinsky's defeat were fierce, and I came in for a great deal of stick, mostly based on the accusation that I had lain too far out of my ground. Certainly Nijinsky would have won had he not swerved almost in the shadow of the post, and certainly he would have won had his initial finishing run not been blocked on the final bend. Yet according to the form book he ran up to his best – beating Gyr and Blakeney by further than when they had last met – and his sad experience at Longchamp that day is best put down to sheer bad luck.

What is particularly upsetting about the Arc defeat is that it led to Nijinsky putting in one final racecourse appearance in the hope of bowing out on a winning note. Had he won the French race he would then have been retired to stud, unbeaten and doubtless acclaimed as one of the greatest horses of all time. As it turned out, his last race in the Champion Stakes at Newmarket just thirteen days after the Arc simply compounded the downbeat end to his great career.

Bearing in mind what he had gone through in the parade ring at Longchamp, we had to be apprehensive about how he would react to being on the racecourse again at Newmarket, and as soon as I saw him in the paddock that day I could tell that the Arc experience had left its scar. He was a mental wreck, and although as usual he settled down once the race was under way, he never gave me the familiar feel. When I asked him to go on and win his race there was no response, and we were beaten one and a half lengths by Charles St George's Lorenzaccio, a good horse but one Nijinsky in his prime could have picked up and carried.

Immediately after the race David McCall, Charles Engelhard's racing manager, announced Nijinsky's retirement to stand at stud at Claiborne Farm in Kentucky. I visited him there on and off over the years before his death early in 1992, and even in old age he had that tremendous presence which had struck me the first time I saw him. A great racehorse, he went on to be a great sire, numbering Derby winners Shahrastani, Golden Fleece and Lammtarra among his offspring.

Nijinsky possessed more natural ability than any horse I ever rode, before or since. It all seemed so easy for him, but at the same time he always boiled up a little inside. He had a pathological hatred of vets, and Demi O'Byrne, who was virtually personal physician to the horse, had to come into his box as casually as possible, usually with a carrot in his hand: a stethoscope was out of the question!

Looking back, it's clear that the attack of ringworm affected Nijinsky mentally, which in turn diminished his ability on the racecourse. He was probably as good at two as he ever was – which is the case with many big horses – but during the summer of his three-year-old career, and especially in his Derby and King George, he was one of the greats.

8

Musical chairs

Life after Nijinsky soon provided a ride on his Champion
Stakes conqueror Lorenzaccio in the Washington International. He finished fifth, and from there we were
off on our winter travels again.

I had been invited to Puerto Rico, where the sunshine
was a wonderful contrast to wet and cold Washington,
and rode for one day at San Juan without adding
that exotic location to my list of winning venues. An
invitation to go on another tour of Australia and New
Zealand had been declined – giving rise to pointless
press speculation that I was about to retire – and
instead we set off for Barbados.

Nowadays half the Flat trainers in Britain seem to
make for Barbados in the winter, but back then it was
much more select! One trainer with a home there was
the amusing and charming Jeremy Tree, who handled
horses for such big owners as Jock Whitney and Charles
Engelhard and for whom I often rode. One day he
suggested that Susan and I should spend some time in
Barbados – and what better time than after that hectic
1970 season?

We stayed at the Coral Reef Club, next to Jeremy's
house, and there we found Gordon Richards and his
wife Marjorie, along with Sir Michael Sobell (for
whom Gordon, having retired from training, was now
racing manager) and Sir Michael's son-in-law Arnold
(now Lord) Weinstock. After dinner each evening the
Richardses, Sobells and Weinstocks took a walk around
the grounds discussing their hopes for the coming season,
and before long we found ourselves joining in this ritual.

We also spent a good deal of time with another old rival – Scobie Breasley, now retired from riding, who had a house down the coast. Susan even found a local stud that had as a stallion a horse named No Complaint which her father had trained! We travelled home via Miami – with one hiccough when Susan discovered that her US visa had run out – and arrived back rested and refreshed for the new season.

There was no Nijinsky on the horizon, but everything was looking good – and then came the bombshell: Nijinsky's owner Charles Engelhard, aged just 54, died. One of the great racehorse owners, he had believed in spreading his horses around a number of trainers – at the time of his death he had some 300 horses in various countries – and many people had cause to be grateful for his generosity. His passing put a real dampener on the start of the new season.

It was clear that I was going to have some difficulty retaining the jockeys' title I had now held for seven consecutive years, since Geoff Lewis was retained by Noel Murless and Frank Durr was riding for the David Robinson empire, and I would have my work cut out getting the necessary quantity of rides. Furthermore, my association with Vincent O'Brien meant that I would be riding more in Ireland – on, among others, a colt named Minsky.

Charles Engelhard's widow Jane had taken over his horses after his death, and Minsky – a full brother to Nijinsky, trained by Vincent – was the most promising of these. He won the Gladness Stakes and then the Tetrarch Stakes at The Curragh, and was considered good enough to take his place in the Two Thousand Guineas. But this of course was 1971, and Minsky understandably played little part in the famous race in which Brigadier Gerard swooped to beat Mill Reef and My Swallow. At least Minsky got into the money by finishing fourth, five lengths behind My Swallow.

By the middle of May I was still without a Derby ride, though not short of offers. Eventually I settled for The

Parson, trained by Noel Murless. Although Geoff Lewis was Noel's retained jockey, his agreement allowed him to be released to ride Mill Reef, so the mount on The Parson – a backward sort who had run well to finish second in the Dante Stakes at York – became available. I rode work on the colt at Newmarket a couple of times and decided that although he was still a maiden he was sure to get the Derby trip and had a good chance of being placed. I was wrong, though he ran respectably enough to finish sixth behind Mill Reef, one of the great Derby winners. Derby week was not too disappointing, all the same, as I rode eight winners at the meeting before being brought down to earth with a bump – a nasty fall off Noel Murless's filly Maina before the Oaks which necessitated a quick break in the South of France.

One blot on a season which up until that fall had been going well enough was a controversial incident in the Irish Two Thousand Guineas at The Curragh. Riding Sam Armstrong's Sparkler, I fought out a furious battle with Freddie Head on King's Company throughout the last quarter of a mile, but our chance was ruined when King's Company rolled towards us a furlong out, completely knocking Sparkler off his stride. I was confident of getting the race on an objection but the stewards chose to turn a blind eye, and I was so furious that in the heat of the moment I declared that I would never ride in Ireland again. Come Irish Derby time I was naturally reflecting on the wisdom of this outburst, and when I took the ride in the Classic on Paddy Prendergast's Lombardo, who had been fourth to Mill Reef at Epsom, that gave the press the opportunity for some snide headlines. Lombardo ran second to Irish Ball, who likewise had finished one place in front of him at Epsom.

That summer some changes took place in our family arrangements. Ann Mather had got married in 1967 (with Maureen and Tracy as her bridesmaids) and her successor had stayed for a couple of years, but as both girls were now at school we decided no longer to have a nanny living in. Just around the corner from our house lived Len and Nellie Hobden. Len had been a horsebox driver for Susan's father, and Nellie housekeeper for both Susan's grandmother and her mother, and now they started to help further generations of the Armstrong family by working for us – Len in the garden and Nellie around the house. Maureen and Tracy – to whom they rapidly became 'Uncle' and 'Auntie' – loved them, and when Susan was at the races with me or we were away overnight the girls would stay with the Hobdens: our phone could be switched through to their house, so that any trainers trying to contact me could leave messages there.

One particularly significant mount that summer came at Chester, when I won a fillies' race on a lovely two-year-old named Mrs Moss: the next time I sat on her was over twenty years later at Woburn Abbey, where a life-size statue of the Marchioness of Tavistock's now legendary brood mare (dam of Jupiter Island, Krayyan, Precocious, Pushy, and so on) was unveiled.

And I had a truly Glorious Goodwood at the end of July, winning no fewer than eight races at one of the hottest (in two senses) meetings of the year, including the Foxhall Maiden Stakes on Some Hand – owned by Muriel Haggas, whose grandson William was to marry our daughter Maureen in 1989.

The 1971 season also saw an addition to my Classic haul in the shape of the St Leger (my sixth victory in the Doncaster race) on Athens Wood for the Newmarket trainer Harry Thomson – 'Tom' – Jones. When I'd won the Great Voltigeur Stakes at York on this horse in August I'd been impressed by his tenacity, so when Tom – for whom I did not ride very often – offered me the Leger mount I snapped it up. In the Classic itself Athens Wood did not let me down, leading from the start and then battling on bravely up the straight as various rivals tried in vain to collar him. Inside the final furlong we had a rare old tussle with Homeric, ridden by Joe Mercer, and Falkland, whose jockey Greville

Starkey had ridden Athens Wood earlier in the horse's career. It was real hammer-and-tongs stuff, but Athens Wood held on bravely to win by a neck from Homeric with Falkland just a head away in third. Athens Wood may not have been the most glamorous or famous of my Classic winners, but few were braver.

That autumn I looked yet again like having to choose between two horses as my main ride in the following season's colts' Classics. On the one hand there was Vincent's star two-year-old Roberto, whom I first rode in the Grand Criterium at Longchamp after he had been ridden to victory in all his three races in Ireland by the new Ballydoyle stable jockey Johnny Roe: at Longchamp he lost his unbeaten tag, coming fourth, but this big, powerful colt by the American sire Hail To Reason was impressive, and he had to enter my Classic calculations for 1972. The other prime contender was Crowned Prince, trained at Newmarket by Bernard Van Cutsem. This colt, who ran in the name of Frank McMahon (co-owner, with Bing Crosby, of Meadow Court), had cost $510,000 as a yearling at the Keeneland July Sales in the USA – almost treble the previous record for that prestigious auction. On looks and on breeding alone he seemed worth that amount, and his efforts on the Newmarket gallops served only to increase the feeling that he was potentially a star. So when the time came for the acid test on the racecourse, in a two-year-old maiden race at Newmarket in August 1971, there was a great sense of expectation among his connections and the betting public alike. Frank McMahon and the colt's breeder Leslie Combs flew over from the USA to witness his first appearance, and in the ring he was backed as if defeat were simply out of the question: he started at 7–2 on, an absurd price for any two-year-old making its debut.

The race was a disaster. Crowned Prince broke well enough and in the early stages travelled smoothly, but when I shook him up and asked him to go on there was no response at all, and eventually I eased him and allowed him to come home a desperately disappointing sixth. Gloom and despondency all round, with Bernard van Cutsem's wife Mimi in tears and only Bernard himself managing – typically – to remain phlegmatic in defeat.

Both Bernard and I knew that Crowned Prince had considerable ability – he had shown us that often enough on the gallops – but we were beginning to suspect that the horse sometimes let his temperament get the better of him, and would sulk if upset.

Despite the disappointment of that debut, Bernard was convinced that Crowned Prince could bounce back, and immediately announced that the colt would be trained for the Champagne Stakes at Doncaster in September – which gave us just under three weeks to sort him out. We boxed him over to Yarmouth for a racecourse gallop, fitted blinkers to get him to concentrate a little more than he may have been inclined to, and were pleased with the result – and even more pleased when, with the blinkers on, he redeemed his reputation in the Champagne Stakes. A short-priced favourite despite that earlier reverse, he won on the bridle – despite breaking slowly and swerving left a little – by a length from a horse named Rheingold, of whom we shall be hearing more. It can be imagined that this result caused connections no little relief!

His next outing, and the one in which he was to lay his reputation as the country's top two-year-old on the line, was the Dewhurst Stakes at Newmarket. Thinking that Crowned Prince had probably learned to concentrate by now, we decided to leave off the blinkers. This time he broke smartly from the stalls, tucked in nicely behind the leaders, and when I asked him to go on and win his race quickened in the manner of a very good horse indeed to win going away by five lengths, with Rheingold again filling the runner-up berth.

Crowned Prince was immediately installed as winter favourite for the Two Thousand Guineas and Derby. Although he did not in the event get as far as either

With my father, 1948.

With my mother, 1948. *P.A. – Reuter*

A quiet wedding, 22 February 1960. *Sport & General*

Taking a break with the stable lads, 1948.

A typical all-action finish from Gordon Richards as Denizen gets the better of me on No Light at Lewes in August 1950.
Hulton-Deutsch

My first Derby.
Never Say Die wins
from Arabian Night
(Tommy Gosling,
quartered cap) and
Darius (Manny
Mercer). In fourth
place is Elopement,
whom I would later
ride for Noel
Murless. *Popperfoto*

The greatest filly I ever rode: the peerless Petite Etoile.
The Observer/*Jack Eaton*

A proud moment: The Queen leads in Carrozza after our victory in the 1957 Oaks at Epsom, her first Classic win.
Sport & General

Going out the side door: the fall from Barbary Pirate at Brighton in August 1960. The winner was Colin Moss (stripes) on Bob Barker. *Sport & General*

Catching up on the home news in the jockeys' changing room at Aqueduct, New York, where I was riding late in 1967 while British racing was suspended on account of the epidemic of foot-and-mouth disease.
Hulton-Deutsch

Winning the Gran Premio in Madrid on Toté in 1967.
Zarkhijo Madrid

The right choice. Sir Ivor slams Petingo, whom I could have ridden, in the 1968 Two Thousand Guineas at Newmarket.
Popperfoto

I really earned my riding fee here: Ribero (right) just beats Canterbury (Bill Williamson) in the 1968 St Leger...
Press Association

...and a few minutes later Charles and Jane Engelhard greet their weary winner.
Sport & General

Mountain Call stretching his legs in the paddock at Newmarket, 1968.

The Triple Crown is in the bag as Nijinsky wins the 1970 St Leger from Meadowville (Johnny Seagrave)... *Gerry Cranham*

...and is admired afterwards by trainer and jockey. *Gerry Cranham*

My 3,001st winner in Britain: Dahlia wins the 1974 King George VI and Queen Elizabeth Stakes. *Sport & General*

The great stayer Sarago in familiar surroundings – the winner's enclosure after the Ascot Gold Cup. *Gerry Cranham*

Minutes away from my eighth Derby, as Gerry Gallagher escorts The Minstrel in the parade before the 1977 race. *Gerry Cranham*

race, I had plenty to ponder as I set off in November on my winter travels.

This year I had been invited to ride in Argentina and Brazil, and then go on to South Africa – a long haul, and one which started energetically, for upon checking in at the hotel in Buenos Aires (after a flight which had taken us via Paris, Madrid and São Paulo) I was told to report back to the lobby in an hour in my riding gear, as I was required to gallop the horse I was partnering in the big race! After a whirlwind tour of the city we arrived at Palermo racetrack just as it was getting dark, but since racing there took place under floodlights, the idea was to accustom me to this new experience. I was baffled, though, when our guide asked me if I needed a saddle: apparently the horses there were usually ridden bareback in their work! Not wanting too many new experiences on my first evening in the country, I used my racing saddle, but could only just get the tips of my toes into the irons as I was wearing more substantial jodhpur boots rather than racing boots. Eventually I felt ready to venture out on to the racetrack – a vast circuit with a good sand surface – and after putting the horse through his paces was about ready to call it a day. No such luck. We were expected for dinner at the home of one of the Jockey Club members. In the event it turned out to be an extremely relaxed and enjoyable evening, setting the tone for the days which followed: everywhere we went, including a trip to a couple of stud farms standing ex-European stallions, everyone was extremely friendly.

The first day of the racing action, at the beautiful San Isidro course just outside Buenos Aires, brought me a winner and a second from four rides, but the main reason for our visit was for me to ride in the Gran Premio Carlo Pellegrini, one of the Argentinian classic races, the following day.

A twelve-race card began at one o'clock in the afternoon, and the first of my seven rides was in the opener. At that time the racecourse Tote was operated by hand, and such was the volume of betting that the times between races got longer and longer. Before we knew it darkness had descended, and on came the lights, but the big race did not get under way until 11 p.m., by which time 103,000 people had crammed into the track. My horse ran badly in the Pellegrini, but I won on my last ride of the night, and was relieved to be able to change and leave the course. It was ten past one in the morning!

Brazil was much hotter, which did not help the atmosphere at the racetrack: small, sharp and sandy, it was situated close to a bay full of dead fish, which during the prevailing spring tide gave off the most dreadful smell. I rode in Brazil for three days (one winner) before setting off for South Africa for the International Jockeys event at Pietermaritzburg, where the visiting team included Maurice Philliperon and Yves Saint-Martin from France, Gianfranco Dettori from Italy, Bill Shelton from New Zealand, Glynn Pretty from Australia, Hikozo Sugai from Japan, Fernando Toro from Chile, and myself and Geoff Lewis from Britain.

The defending South African team was made up of a representative jockey from each province, plus the overall champion of South Africa, a diminutive apprentice named Michael Roberts. 'Muis' was then only seventeen, but would become the greatest jockey South Africa ever produced and champion jockey in England in 1992. Back in 1971 he was confined during his apprenticeship to the Jockeys' Academy, an establishment at the Summerveld Training Centre midway between Durban and Pietermaritzburg. So strict were the Academy's rules that, champion jockey or not, Michael had to be in by nine o'clock every evening, and so was unable to stay long at the many social functions laid on for the teams.

My cousin Fred Rickaby, who had met us on our arrival in South Africa and for whom I had several rides while in the country, was married to a leading journalist, a wonderful woman named Molly Reinart: a brilliant writer, she was also a staunch opponent of apartheid and made no effort to conceal this in the weekly articles she wrote for the country's leading Sunday newspaper.

On the race day the jockeys had a wonderful reception from the vast African crowd, but they were a furlong down the track, in stands segregated from the members and paddock area.

After returning to Britain for a quiet Christmas, in January 1972 I was off again for yet another international jockeys' competition, this time in Hong Kong – the brainchild of Jimmy Lindley, then an official of the Royal Hong Kong Jockey Club. My cousin Bill Rickaby (who in 1971 had suffered terrible injuries in a car crash, from which he never fully recovered) had been closely involved in the colony's smooth transition from amateur to professional racing, but although I had visited several times I had not ridden there until now. Happy Valley, built on the only piece of flat land on Victoria Island and surrounded by towering apartment blocks, was then an exceptionally sharp track with a run-in of just one and a half furlongs (it has since been enlarged), and although I managed to steer my three mounts around safely, none of them managed to win.

Then it was back to zig-zagging around the globe – to Perth and Adelaide in Australia before heading north again in February to Singapore, where the Queen made an official visit. In honour of this occasion the racecourse staged the Queen Elizabeth II Cup, which I was delighted to win on Jumbo Jet, trained by Ivan Allan. Ivan had taken out his licence only the year before, following the death of his father, and was to become a close friend as well as owner of one of my favourite horses, Commanche Run.

From Singapore we headed south again to Auckland, where as I cantered to the start of the New Zealand International Invitational Stakes on the six-year-old mare Sailing Home (bred, owned and trained by a wonderful old lady named Miss Joyce Edgar-Jones), the stands into which 12,000 racegoers were crammed began to rock with laughter.

What had tickled their fancy was my riding style. Australian and New Zealand jockeys in those days tended to ride with much longer leathers and lower in the saddle than their European counterparts, so I stuck out like a sore thumb with my short leathers and bottom in the air. But I had the last laugh: they cheered me back after the mare had won by a neck.

(The matter of my riding style has exercised many people over the years, but the explanation is really quite simple. As Flat jockeys go I am very tall, and so in order to achieve the right mix of comfort in the saddle – which is a great deal to do with balance – and effectiveness in getting down to drive my horse as forcefully as I can, the bottom goes higher in the air than is usual with other, shorter, jockeys.)

Back again to Singapore – but by then the start of the Flat at home was on the horizon, and I had to turn my mind once again to the Classics.

I had chosen to ride Crowned Prince rather than Roberto in the 1972 Two Thousand Guineas, and along with most of the rest of the racing world thought that his three-year-old debut in 1972, in the Craven Stakes at Newmarket, would be a formality. He started at 9–4 on, but showed absolutely no response when let down and asked to race a quarter of a mile out, and finished fourth behind a horse of Noel Murless's named Leicester. My view after that race was that he could still win the Guineas if he were right on the day, but ten days after the Craven, following a work-out on Yarmouth racecourse, Bernard van Cutsem announced that the colt would never run again, due to a respiratory condition. He retired to stand at Airlie Stud, close to Dublin.

It is easy to be wise after the event, but I never really liked Crowned Prince. Although he had terrific ability, and used to flow over the ground like few horses I'd ridden, I never trusted him.

Now, though, I had to find a ride for the 1972 Two Thousand Guineas. It was too late to get back on Roberto, but Bill Marshall – a wonderful trainer with whom I had enjoyed a great association over the years – asked me to ride his colt Grey Mirage. In the event Bernard van Cutsem won the Two Thousand Guineas after all with Crowned Prince's deputy High Top, a first Classic victory for an up-and-coming young jockey named Willie Carson. Runner-up was Roberto, with Grey Mirage well down the field.

A controversial game of jockeys' musical chairs was now beginning.

Roberto had been ridden in the Two Thousand Guineas by the popular Australian jockey Bill Williamson – known in some circles as 'Weary Willie' on account of the world-weary expression which tended to be his usual countenance – and Bill would again have the ride in the Derby. By 1972 I had ridden in the Derby nineteen times – every year since 1951 except 1961 and 1962 – and had won the race five times, and the story 'What Will Lester Ride?' had become a traditional part of the build-up to the big day. This year speculation was even more rife than usual, for with Crowned Prince sidelined and Roberto unarguably Bill Williamson's mount, there was no obvious candidate for me. My name was linked in the newspapers with several different horses – about none of whom I had actually been approached – and as the race got nearer it seemed that my most likely mount would be Vincent's second string, Manitoulin.

Vincent asked me to go over to Ballydoyle to give the horse a gallop, so after racing at Sandown Park on the Tuesday of the week before the Derby, Susan and I set off in a small plane, landing just before dark in the paddock behind the house at Ballydoyle. Early next morning I put Manitoulin through his paces. It was soon clear to me that the colt was not a patch on Roberto, and I boarded the plane for the return trip to England feeling very dejected. Over the next few days the gloom was lifted by good overseas winners – including the Spanish Oaks in Madrid on Delfica and my first (and only) Prix du Jockey-Club (French Derby) on Hard To Beat – but the lack of a real chance in the big one at Epsom was still depressing.

Then the picture suddenly changed.

On 27 May Bill Williamson had a fall from a horse named The Broker at Kempton Park, leaving him with injuries which, while nasty at the time, did not look like putting in jeopardy his Derby ride on Roberto. But as the day of the big race got nearer, doubts about his fitness increased.

Roberto was owned by the Ohio-based construction magnate John Galbreath, who was also the owner of the Darby Dan Farm, one of the leading studs in Kentucky, and – significantly – of the Pittsburgh Pirates baseball team. In this last role he believed, quite reasonably, that he knew something about the fitness or otherwise of sportsmen, and once he had convinced himself that there was no way Bill Williamson could be fit enough to do Roberto justice at Epsom, despite Bill's own insistence that he would be, Mr Galbreath instructed Vincent to put me up on the horse.

News of this leaked out, and the press exploded with indignation, blaming everybody in sight – notably, of course, me – for another disgraceful example of L. Piggott jocking off a fellow rider in order to grab the plum mount. On the Monday night before the race on the Wednesday a meeting was hastily convened between Bill, Vincent and Mr Galbreath, followed by a press release the following morning confirming that I would be riding Roberto.

On the Tuesday, Bill, by then passed one hundred per cent fit by the Jockey Club doctor, rode at Salisbury in an attempt to prove his complete recovery, but Galbreath was adamant – as, of course, he had every right to be. He insisted that, as owner of one of America's most successful baseball teams, he knew all about how injuries could impair an athlete's performance, and when I think back on how hard I subsequently had to ride Roberto in the Derby, you could see that he had a point.

All in all, Galbreath seemed to me to approach a difficult situation very fairly. He wanted to give his horse the best ride possible in the most important race of the colt's – and indeed his owner's – life, but he was aware of the distress which this would cause Bill Williamson, and offered him the same cut of the winning prize money as I would get in the event of Roberto's landing the race.

There was undeniably a strange atmosphere at Epsom on Derby Day. The papers had been full of the last-minute switch, with letters from readers almost unanimously painting Galbreath, me and even Vincent as villains, and the Chairman of the Betting Levy Board, Lord Wigg, going on the record with expressions of disgust. Matters were made worse by Bill Williamson being quoted as having claimed that there had been no Monday night meeting, saying that he had simply been informed by phone of the change, and adding that he would definitely not settle for the ride on Manitoulin.

While by this stage of my career I had become philosophical about being torn apart by the press, I still felt a measure of resentment as I walked Roberto across the downs to the Derby start. At no point had I approached Vincent or Galbreath about shoving Bill off the horse and getting the ride myself, and the owner was perfectly entitled to get the best jockey available for his horse. And if Bill really were fit enough for the big race, why had he not been able to ride at all until the day before?

After all the palaver, it was quite a relief when the stalls for the 193rd Derby Stakes crashed open and we were on our way. Pentland Firth took the field along at a good early pace, and as usual I tried to keep my horse handy. Coming round Tattenham Corner we were about eighth, with Rheingold just on our outer, and once into the straight the race shook down into a three-way battle between Roberto, Rheingold and Pentland Firth, with my fellow the meat in the sandwich. Pentland Firth gave Roberto a hefty bump before falling away beaten, which left Roberto and Rheingold locked together and battling for the line, Roberto on the inner, Rheingold on the outer, neither giving an inch. The course at Epsom has a marked camber in the straight, where it is common for horses on the outside to lean in on rivals nearer the inside rail, and this is exactly what happened as we fought out that finish. Several times Rheingold leaned in on Roberto and delivered hefty bumps – to such effect that we were a neck down inside the final furlong, and I really had to get to work.

People have made a great deal of the way I laid about Roberto with the whip in the closing stages of that race – and certainly had that finish been under today's whip guidelines I could have expected a long suspension – but the fact is that at the time I really needed to get after Roberto, and I could not do so as Rheingold was leaning on me and repeatedly bumping my horse. I couldn't hit Roberto properly – I didn't have the room!

In the last hundred yards I managed to get Roberto balanced again, and with necessary recourse to the whip got him to peg back Rheingold. We crossed the line together, and although initially I thought I'd not got back up, I had no doubt that we'd get the race after a stewards' enquiry, as Rheingold's leaning on me had been so blatant.

Since I did not think we had won I unsaddled on the track rather than taking Roberto into the winner's enclosure (which of course is one reason why I did not get a rapturous reception on returning to unsaddle), and went back into the weighing room to be greeted with the very unsurprising news that an enquiry had been announced. The result of the photo declared Roberto the winner by a short head, but it was another twenty minutes before we were confirmed the winner after the enquiry had left the placings unaltered.

Bill Williamson gave no particular reaction when I returned to the weighing room after the Derby, and in the circumstances it was good to see him back in the winner's circle later in the afternoon – twice: he rode the winner of the race immediately following the Derby, and then capped that by landing the last. The crowd's rousing reception after both these victories doubtless reflected their great sympathy for his having missed out on what would have been his only winner of the Derby, but racing can be a hard game, and I saw no reason to feel bad.

After all those shenanigans it was pleasant to settle back into a quiet period – though for me it was too quiet, with winners hard to come by, and I was trailing Willie Carson and the late Tony Murray in the jockeys' table, my cause not helped by a four-day suspension handed out in Paris.

Roberto went for the Irish Derby, but, as had been the case with Sir Ivor and Nijinsky, Vincent's stable jockey had the ride back for all races in Ireland. This time Johnny Roe was on board, but Roberto (who started favourite, with my mount Ballymore second market choice) had had a very hard race at Epsom, and it was little surprise to see him run poorly, beating only two home when finishing behind Steel Pulse, trained by my old rival Scobie Breasley and ridden by none other than Bill Williamson.

For some reason the press had got hold of the idea that I was going to retire in 1977, and although I had no specific plans to do so, Susan and I decided in 1972 to set in motion the building of our own yard in Newmarket, an idea we had long been mulling over. Looking to the future, this was a logical step to take.

At that time the Jockey Club were leasing plots of land alongside the Heath off the Hamilton Road, not far from the Rowley Mile stands, and as these were quickly being snapped up we put in a proposal to build our yard there. Apart from setting up our own training facilities, we wanted to keep ponies for Maureen and Tracy – both of whom were by now riding regularly at Pony Club level – and that was impossible while we were still living in the town.

We had put time and care into planning the layout of our yard, and here the extensive international travel which we had undertaken over the years bore fruit, as we were able to incorporate many ideas we had seen in action in America, Australia and elsewhere. The comfort of the horses and staff was a prime consideration, so we finally settled on a hundred-box complex under one roof – the 'American barn' system, rather than the traditional English arrangement of boxes around a yard – incorporating tack room, feeding area, offices and all the necessary ancillary facilities. This H-shaped building was to run east to west, and was accompanied by four staff bungalows and a large covered arena for breaking yearlings and for winter exercise in bad weather. This left us plenty of room for paddocks and for building a new house for ourselves when the yard had been completed.

Those plans were for the future. For the present, there was a feast of high-class racing in prospect, and I was asked to ride the Italian Derby winner Gay Lussac in the King George VI and Queen Elizabeth Stakes at Ascot in late July.

A couple of weeks before the race I flew to Milan to ride the colt in a gallop at the San Siro racetrack. I was impressed by the horse – and also by the tall sixteen-year-old boy who rode his galloping companion, who seemed an excellent horseman. His name was Luca, and he was the son of Gay Lussac's trainer Sergio Cumani. In the event Gay Lussac started second favourite at Ascot but in finishing fifth to the mighty Brigadier Gerard failed to impress. The same can hardly be said of his trainer's son, who moved to Newmarket and is now one of the top trainers in the land.

The month after the Ascot race brought an unwelcome continuation of the musical chairs.

Roberto had been a dismal failure at The Curragh, but there was a possible explanation to add to his simply feeling the after-effects of his drubbing at Epsom. He could not go right-handed, and always disappointed when racing in that direction. Left-handed, he was a different horse altogether, and a very big race run the 'correct' way round for him was now on the horizon in the shape of the newly instituted Benson and Hedges Gold Cup at York. At one time this had been billed as the rematch between Brigadier Gerard and Mill Reef, each of whom had been achieving great things since they had met in the Two Thousand Guineas in 1971, but Mill Reef had suffered a setback (before the injury which finished his career) and as the race approached it seemed more and more like a benefit for Brigadier Gerard, then unbeaten in fifteen races and fresh from his Ascot victory.

Although Roberto was a possible runner, Vincent – as so often, very careful to ensure that conditions were perfect for his horse before committing himself – was not certain about the colt's participation. So when I was offered the ride at York on Barry Hills-trained Rheingold, who since the Derby had brilliantly won the Grand Prix de Saint-Cloud, in which I and the odds-on favourite Hard To Beat came only third, I had to take it. Apart from the evidence of the Saint-Cloud race that Rheingold had kept his form, I had little doubt that York's flat, galloping track would suit this long-striding horse far better than the undulations of Epsom.

Then, the week before the race, by which time I was committed to Rheingold, Roberto was named a definite runner, with crack American-based jockey Braulio Baeza (who actually hailed from Panama) being flown in to ride – another example of Mr Galbreath's individual approach to jockeys for his horses.

Despite not being able to partner my most recent Derby winner I felt sure that Rheingold was the one to be on, though I did not realistically expect either of the Epsom first two to beat Brigadier Gerard, who by anybody's standards was a great horse. His owners John and Jean Hislop would not hear of defeat, and why indeed should they?

Five runners went into the stalls at the ten-and-a-half-furlong start: Brigadier Gerard, Roberto, Rheingold, Gold Rod (who had run the Brigadier to a length in the Eclipse Stakes) and Bright Beam. The instant the stall doors opened Roberto was out like a scalded cat – 'He must have been stung by a bee,' said Jean Hislop later – and within a few hundred yards Baeza had laid down his challenge: catch me if you can. By halfway Rheingold was flat to the boards, and the only runner still on the bit was Brigadier Gerard. Close home the truth dawned: Roberto was not stopping, and the Brigadier was not catching him. Roberto just kept on galloping, and Brigadier Gerard was beaten for the one and only time in his eighteen-race career: both horses broke the track record. Gold Rod was third and Rheingold a deflated fourth – though I subsequently learned that an infected cut on his leg ten days before the race had interrupted his preparation, and in any case his greatest hour was still to come.

Roberto was not my only Classic winner in Britain for Vincent in 1972, as in September I landed my seventh St Leger on Boucher. This huge horse, who had worked brilliantly at Ballydoyle early in the season and who we always felt had a great deal of class, had progressed steadily over the months, and with Roberto being aimed at the Arc became the main O'Brien hope for Doncaster. The ground for the St Leger was softer than I would have liked, but I knew that Boucher would have no problem staying the trip, while his two main rivals, Oaks winner Ginevra and Irish Derby winner Steel Pulse, both had question marks over their stamina, and there was no pacemaker in a field only seven strong.

The race did not start well for Boucher: we were very slowly out of the stalls and ten lengths down before we knew it. But the complete lack of pace in the early stages of the race meant that I could make up the ground without being too hard on the horse, and in no time we had caught up. The race did not start in earnest until the straight, where Boucher ran on well to beat Jimmy Lindley on Our Mirage by half a length.

The following day saw the running of one of the key Arc trials, the Prix Niel at Longchamp. Baeza was again over to ride Roberto, while I was on my Prix du Jockey-Club winner Hard To Beat. Playing Roberto at his own game, I went to the front from the moment the stalls opened and the Derby winner could never catch me – which made me wonder what might have happened had Hard To Beat come to Epsom. Hard To Beat and Roberto met again in the Arc, where Roberto – again ridden by Baeza – finished one and a half lengths in front of us when seventh to San San.

The end-of-season phase of 1972 had its moments, including a victory in the Duke of Edinburgh Stakes at Ascot in October on Sea Pigeon, a very nice two-year-old of Jeremy Tree's, owned by Jock Whitney. This colt would go on to run unplaced in the 1973 Derby behind Morston, but it was as a hurdler that he became one of racing's legends, winning the Champion Hurdle in 1980 and 1981 and establishing himself as one of the most popular horses the sport has ever seen. Come to think of it, in my time I have ridden winners of all three of jumping's great races: triple Grand National winner Red Rum, dual Champion Hurdle winner Sea Pigeon, and Cheltenham Gold Cup winner Norton's Coin, whom I rode for his trainer Sirrell Griffiths in the Queen Alexandra Stakes at Ascot in 1991.

But if the year had its ups, its final down was the loss of my jockeys' title. After eight consecutive years at the top I had to give best to Willie Carson, who was champion with 132 winners. Tony Murray was second with 122, then Edward Hide on 105 and L. Piggott on 103. There were very plausible reasons why I had not managed to hold on to my title – principally that I was spending more and more time at Ballydoyle – but none the less it was a blow to be dislodged from the top of the tree.

Globe-trotting that winter started in Marseille. Then to Laurel Park for the Washington International, in which my mount Jumbo Jet, whom Ivan Allan had sent all the way from Singapore, fell when the horse in front went down. Both horses and both jockeys were unharmed, but it was a long way for Jumbo Jet to travel for such an outcome.

Then Pietermaritzburg again – and an unhappy episode when one morning Susan woke up with her face all swollen: mumps! Maureen and Tracy had contracted mumps several weeks before the trip, and Susan (who had not had the condition, although I had, as a child) had been assured by the doctor that the incubation period meant it would be quite safe for her to travel. He was wrong.

We made plans to withdraw from that day's planned trip around stud farms and agreed with Gavin Brown, secretary of the Pietermaritzburg Club, that we would quietly slip away from the club and return to Fred and Molly Rickaby's where we had been staying. However, when we got downstairs the rest of our party was there, and horrified to learn of Susan's condition as most of the visiting lads had not had mumps either. Back at Fred and Molly's – which we reached eventually after the exhaust had fallen off the ancient Mini they had lent us – Susan was banished to a remote part of the garden while the rest of us ate lunch. The doctor advised her to stay put for a week, but we decided to return home as scheduled: luckily the plane was half empty so we could get seats well away from the other passengers and hide her condition.

She recovered in time for Christmas, which the family spent in Trinidad – reached via a brief riding stop-over in Venezuela. On Christmas morning I rode work at the Trinidad racecourse, just across the road from our hotel in what amounted to a public park called The Savannah, and racing itself took place on Boxing Day – a far cry from the traditional Boxing Day fixtures back home!

From Trinidad we moved to Jamaica, where we stayed in Kingston with our friend Jack Ashenheim. Jack was a steward of the Jamaican Jockey Club, and before we left for the races he took me aside for a quiet word. Looking rather sheepish, he explained that the racing authorities had been suspecting some skulduggery among the local riders, and that spot checks of equipment might be carried out, so I was not to be taken aback if asked to submit to a search.

Sure enough, before the seventh race of the afternoon all the jockeys were required to dismount, remove our helmets for inspection and hand over our whips. It transpired that there was one particular jockey the stewards had their eye on, as he was riding a suspiciously high number of winners, and it was him that they were really trying to catch. All kinds of theories were put forward, from electric shocks in his whip to a similar device located under his saddle, but nothing was ever found and he continued to ride winners for years. The explanation – which perhaps they'd never thought of – was that he was a very good jockey.

The 1973 season in Britain began in what was now the traditional Piggott way: defeat in the Lincoln Handicap, despite riding the favourite Jan Ekels.

By then the yard we were having built in Hamilton Road was not far from completion, and the press were convinced that I was on the verge of retirement. Stopping race-riding, though, was the last thing on my mind, not least because Vincent had some very promising three-year-olds lined up for 1973. In the early part of the season the stable star appeared to be Thatch, the property of one of Vincent's newer owners, the American steel tycoon John Mulcahy. As a two-year-old Thatch had been unbeaten in Ireland, though he finished only fourth when I had ridden him in the Prix Morny at Deauville. He came out as a three-year-old to win the Phoenix Park Classic Trial brilliantly, but things did not go our way in the Two Thousand Guineas: he was a much better horse on fast ground, and on Guineas day the going came up soft and he could manage no better than fourth behind 50–1 outsider Mon Fils, a first Classic winner for trainer Richard Hannon.

My Derby mount this year was Cavo Doro, the horse I had bred by sending my mare Limuru to Sir Ivor. Though brave in his battle to the line with Morston, Cavo Doro began to hang at the crucial moment and was beaten half a length. It was a huge thrill to have bred as well as ridden the runner-up in the Derby, and I'm convinced that but for the firm ground at Epsom that day Cavo Doro would have won.

Morston never raced again, and Cavo Doro was never again as good a horse: the Derby finished him off.

The day after the 1973 Derby the enigmatic Roberto was back at Epsom, and my theory that he was an infinitely better horse going to the left than to the right was borne out by our easy victory in the Coronation Cup: he simply hacked up in the manner of the extremely good horse that, when conditions were right, he was.

His next planned outing was the Eclipse Stakes, which I had to miss on account of a suspension incurred at the Newmarket July Meeting. That year the Eclipse was to be run at Kempton Park as Sandown was having its splendid new stand built, and Geoff Lewis, my replacement on the horse, went down to the track the day before to try the horse out. Roberto did not work well and Geoff and Vincent decided the ground was too soft and withdrew him. But when you come to think of it, Roberto could not have won the Eclipse, as Kempton is a right-handed course . . .

Back from suspension, I rode twelve winners in eight days and was soon well into the swing of things, especially on Irish Oaks day at The Curragh in mid-July.

Vincent produced a particularly nice debutant that afternoon in the shape of the two-year-old Cellini, a Round Table colt who had cost $240,000 as a yearling and won his maiden in the colours of my old friend Charles St George. Charles often named his horses after painters and sculptors: Lorenzaccio and Giacometti are others that come to mind, though I have to say I'm no great authority on art history!

In the Irish Guinness Oaks itself I rode L'Eaulne, owned by another old friend Sourien Vanian, but along with the rest of the field we were demolished by the finishing speed of a filly ridden by Bill Pyers and trained in France by Maurice Zilber. The filly's name was Dahlia, and a week later she announced her arrival on the international stage she was to grace for years with another sensational performance to land the King George VI and Queen Elizabeth Stakes at Ascot – which I, who in later races would have the privilege of riding this great mare, witnessed from a respectable distance on Roberto.

A few days later the whole family decamped to the Sussex coast, where we took a house by the sea for the Goodwood July Meeting – which in 1973 was a particularly good one for me, with victories on Thatch in the Sussex Stakes, and Dragonara Palace in the Richmond Stakes, and a noble performance in the Stewards' Cup by Mrs Engelhard's big black horse Home Guard, who carried the crushing burden of 9 stone 13 pounds and was beaten a head by Paul Cook and Alphadamus.

At this time more and more of my regular riding – as opposed to the winter trips or the Sundays in France – was taking place abroad, which brought with it certain practical problems, the most pressing among them the matter of the weighing-room valet, for with all the travelling I was doing it was essential for my riding gear to be kept in top condition.

Many racing fans, however keenly they follow their favourite horses or jockeys, do not give a second thought to the equipment which is an essential part of the jockey's trade, nor to the vital importance of keeping it in working order. In England we have a marvellous bunch of valets who clean and maintain our saddles, boots and breeches, and ensure that when we go to weigh out the equipment is of the right size for the weight we have to do. They travel from meeting to meeting, taking with them the gear belonging to the jockeys they look after, and it is down to the valets to check that the stitching on stirrup leathers and girths is secure and that the trees (frames) of the saddle are not fractured. All jockeys owe them a very great deal.

For many years I was looked after by the Hales family: first Ernie, then his boy 'Son', and then Son's own sons Paul and Mick. They, along with my later valet Brian Yorke, operated mainly in the south and at the biggest northern meetings, while another who has valeted for me over the years had been Des Cullen, at one time a weighing-room rival as one of the top lightweight jockeys of the post-war period.

Abroad the situation with valets has been very different. France and Ireland were fine, because I was riding there so much during the 1960s and 1970s that I left a complete set of everything in each country. In South Africa, to which I became a regular visitor, every jockey was allocated a lad from the apprentice school who would look after him. There were no such luxuries, however, in Australia, where even these days each jockey has to look after himself and his tack, making sure that everything is clean and in safe working order.

At The Curragh on 18 August 1973 – the twenty-fifth anniversary of my first ever winner on The Chase at Haydock Park – Vincent O'Brien launched yet another Ballydoyle two-year-old towards stardom. His name was Apalachee, and although he was bred along similar lines to Cellini – they were both by the American sire Round Table and their dams were related – the comparison went no further. Cellini was quite small. Apalachee was massive, with a huge stride which he put to good use on his debut appearance that afternoon, winning the Lee Stakes by six lengths. Like Thatch, he ran in the colours of John Mulcahy, and he and Cellini really gave me something to look forward to in 1974.

But there were exciting two-year-olds to be ridden in France as well as Ireland, for me none more so than Nonoalco, with whom I teamed up for the Prix Morny at Deauville. This really lovely colt by Nearctic was trained by the great François Boutin and had been ridden on his winning first appearance by the stable jockey and brilliant apprentice Philippe Paquet, whose life was to be so tragically shattered by a fall during a gallop in Hong Kong a few years later. Nonoalco's owner was the glamorous Mexican film actress Maria Felix, a huge celebrity in France.

In the Prix Morny the colt just bolted in, and I told François he had a true champion in his stable – then redoubled the praise after Nonoalco had flattened a good field in the Prix de la Salamandre at Longchamp in such style that he was quoted favourite for the 1974 Two Thousand Guineas.

Meanwhile some of the established stars were still earning their corn.

Roberto was due to run again in the Benson and Hedges Gold Cup at York a year after his sensational victory in 1972, and this time I was looking forward to riding him. Then it started to rain, and a round of jockeys' musical chairs even more convoluted than before the 1972 race started off.

Vincent called me on the Monday – the day before the race – to say that the ground was not too bad and Roberto was still on course, but I made contingency plans to ride Harry Wragg's horse Moulton should the Ballydoyle horse defect – as I rather thought he would – with Geoff Lewis standing by to step in on Moulton should Roberto run. Just to add to the confusion, the syndicate headed by Henry Zeisel which owned Rheingold told me they wanted me to ride their horse in the race again – as I had in 1972 – if I became free to do so. In particular, they were looking for a jockey who would be available to ride Rheingold both in the Benson and Hedges and in the Prix de l'Arc de Triomphe, and the colt's regular rider Yves Saint-Martin had indicated that while he could take the mount at York, he was unlikely to be free for the Paris race.

At 1 p.m. on the day of the race Roberto was announced a non-runner, and my problems began. Geoff Lewis was perfectly relaxed about riding Moulton so I plumped for Rheingold, though I harboured reservations that he had had a very hard race against Dahlia at Ascot (when ridden by Yves Saint-Martin), and that the lack of pace in the small field at York would not be to his advantage.

The trouble was that no-one had thought to tell Yves Saint-Martin that he was not after all required for Rheingold, and when he turned up in the weighing room at York – having flown across from Deauville – to discover that the ride had been taken by his old friend L. Piggott, he was not best pleased and exploded in Gallic fury. Even I had to sympathize.

My sympathy was wearing thinner shortly afterwards, however, as the race itself could not have worked out worse for me. There was, as I had feared, very little pace early on, and to compound my problems Rheingold felt very lacklustre and never really fired. Worst of all, Moulton, whom I could have ridden, won! No doubt Roberto, had he run, would have trounced the lot of them, but such speculation did not prevent the banner headlines proclaiming yet another Piggott 'jocking off' story with a sting in its tail.

For two seasons Rheingold had been, for one reason or another, a horse close to my heart. He had lost out in that frantic Derby finish with Roberto and been my ride in two controversial runnings of the Benson and Hedges Gold Cup. Then he transformed himself into one of my favourite horses ever by giving me my first victory in what is arguably Europe's greatest race, the Prix de l'Arc de Triomphe at Longchamp.

By the time of the 1973 running I could not put the Arc among my top races, the defeats of Park Top and Nijinsky being especially painful recollections. But if past experience of any race has never put me off – the next running is always more important than the last – there was no questioning that Longchamp is a tricky course to ride, and until I had won its biggest race there was something of that track that remained to be conquered. Indeed, I would place the mile and a half at Longchamp as one of the most difficult courses in the world for a jockey to read properly. It is different from anywhere else I've ridden, and its primary problem is the succession of half turns into the straight before you reach the straight proper, the run from the final turn being a fairly sharp two furlongs. (In fact, there are two winning posts at Longchamp, as many a visiting jockey – not excluding myself – has discovered to his cost and embarrassment!)

When I studied the declarations for the 1973 Arc I could honestly not see Rheingold winning. There was a very big field – twenty-seven runners – and a strong line-up, including the previous year's winner San San, my old friend the 1972 French Derby winner Hard To Beat, and a trio of formidable fillies in the shape of Dahlia (that year's King George winner), the great French filly Allez France (like Dahlia, a three-year-old), and Hurry Harriet, who two weeks later would sensationally beat Allez France in the Champion Stakes.

Rheingold had won on his two previous visits to France in 1973, and Barry Hills assured me that the horse had made phenomenal progress since I had ridden him at York, where he was obviously amiss. I rode Rheingold in his final piece of work before the Arc and he seemed a different horse from the one he'd been at York, so it was with increasing optimism that we set off for Paris.

In a field of that size it was vital to keep reasonably handy, as when beaten horses start to fall back on the downhill run towards the straight a runner trying to make a forward move can meet all manner of traffic problems. But Rheingold knew how to look after himself, and as we straightened up for the line I was in the perfect position, about two lengths off the leaders. I knew that he wasn't going to get beaten once he took off – and when he went, he just flew! Allez France and Hard To Beat were trying to launch their challenges, but once Rheingold had stormed clear they had no chance of getting to him, and he won by two and a half lengths from the filly.

The scenes in the winner's enclosure were amazing. Henry Zeisel, in whose colours Rheingold ran although the horse belonged to a group of owners (including Charles St George, who had bought into him just before the Derby), was a colourful Austrian whose usual headgear was a Tyrolean hat with a feather in it. By the time I steered Rheingold into the unsaddling area of the Longchamp paddock – a great thrill, after my first Arc – the hat had long gone, and Henry was ecstatic. It was glorious bedlam – certainly one of the greatest moments of my riding life – and a memorable day was rounded off when Sparkler, trained by Susan's brother Robert since Sam Armstrong had retired, won the Prix du Moulin.

I marked Rheingold's particular place in my affections by choosing him as one of the horses to figure in a painting by the best equestrian artist of the time, Richard Stone Reeves. An American, Dick had spent most of his life among horses, and his work – almost photographic in style – had the knack of capturing a special feature of each horse he painted, making it instantly recognizable. He was represented in England by Patrick Robinson, whom I knew as the owner of the occasional racehorse, and the pair of them approached me with the idea of a composite painting of the five greatest horses I had ridden.

What a choice to have to make! After a great deal of consideration I finally came up with:

Crepello – my first Two Thousand Guineas and second Derby winner

Petite Etoile – brilliant from three to five years

Sir Ivor – the bravest and most intelligent of horses

Nijinsky – an equine genius

Rheingold – the horse who broke my long-standing Arc hoodoo

The result, painted in oils on board, features the five in characteristic poses. I have the original, and a limited edition of prints was issued, to each of which I was asked to put my signature: so I went along to Patrick Robinson's London flat, where he had arranged for a friend to hold the prints flat while I signed them. That friend turned out to be the American film star Lee Remick, who was filming in England at the time.

A week after Rheingold's Arc I was back in Paris, but it turned out to be a less happy occasion. In the Grand Criterium I was beaten a nose by Bill Pyers on Mississippian, then had a hefty fine slapped on me for misuse of the whip after Bill complained to the stewards that I had hit his horse. We had indeed come very close, and I think that Bill, unaware that he had won, lodged the objection on the off-chance of getting the race.

Again I failed to head the jockeys' table, finishing the season second to Willie Carson, and well beaten, but the prospects of Classic success in 1974 looked even rosier after Vincent's star juveniles Cellini and Apalachee had won the Dewhurst Stakes and Observer Gold Cup respectively: the latter was especially gratifying, as we easily beat Bill Pyers on Mississippian – no accusations of hitting his horse this time!

Some pundits were getting very excited indeed about Apalachee, but I had my reservations. Even as a two-year-old, he was a giant of a horse with a devouring stride, but he couldn't quicken in the manner of all the really top-class performers: rather, he would kill off the opposition with the sheer power of his gallop, which his rivals simply couldn't live with. This meant, though, that he would always be vulnerable to a horse with a real turn of foot. He won the Observer Gold Cup easily enough but ran green and on the whole was not impressive, and I wondered whether such a big individual could improve significantly over the winter.

Before I would find out, it was time for our travels again.

First stop South Africa, for the Bull Brand International Stakes featuring a field of international jockeys including myself, Willie Carson, Joe Mercer and Tony Murray from Britain, and the great star of the domestic riding scene, Michael Roberts – who won the race on Sledgehammer, trained by my cousin Fred Rickaby.

That afternoon was stiflingly hot, in the high eighties, and halfway through the programme some of the visiting jockeys were beginning to wilt. I lost four pounds in two hours, Tony swore he had shed thirteen pounds in two days, and the sweat was seeping through Willie's breeches.

By the time of the last event on a nine-race programme I had ridden two winners and was hopeful of adding one more on a horse named Yarmouth, trained by my cousin. As soon as the stalls opened I took up the running, and was swinging along in front when I saw a man on the track wave a flag, then duck under the rail as I approached. I began to ease up, but then, glancing across at the local jockey Johnny McCreedy, racing upsides me, saw that he was still going strong, and a peep over my shoulder told me that the others were as well. Thinking it must be some form of protest I kept riding, but a couple of furlongs out Yarmouth packed up, leaving Alfred Gibert to win from Willie Carson.

As we walked our horses off the track an announcement came over the loudspeaker: 'No race. Would all trainers please retain their horses at the course.' It transpired that two of the fourteen stalls had failed to open, but the starter had not seen this, and some seconds had elapsed before his assistant had been able to make him aware of what was going on. He then raised his flag and the signal was picked up by the flagman down the track, who did likewise, but the only person who took any notice was Michael Roberts, who pulled up and turned back towards the start.

There was pandemonium in the weighing room, with the jockeys, by now in a state of serious dehydration, ordered to stand by for a re-run – and outside eleven sweating, heaving horses with the same ordeal in prospect. Freddo Gibert, who spoke very little English, was already in the shower, and when I managed to explain the situation to him he nearly had a fit.

One rumour going the rounds was that the starter was known to suffer from an active thirst which, by the last race in that heat, he had been trying to quench – but whether that was the case or not, the idea of re-running the race was mercifully soon dropped.

From South Africa we moved to Rhodesia – where the highlight of our visit was a wonderful trip to a game reserve – and we left for home with a suitcase full of avocado pears (then very difficult to find in England) from the garden of our friend Benny Lobel: they provided a novel addition to the lunch parties we had at home during the December Sales.

En route to New Zealand in February we stopped off at Palm Springs in California for a meeting with Vincent and Jacqueline O'Brien, John Mulcahy and the bloodstock agent Tom Cooper, who over the years had been responsible for acquiring many of Vincent's best horses. The purpose of this meeting – which involved many hours sitting around in the sun, and eating in the evenings in the finest local restaurants – was to evolve a strategy for the coming season which would prevent Cellini and Apalachee having to race against each other. Although the former ran in the name of Charles St George and the latter carried Mulcahy's colours, both men owned part of each horse, along with a number of other shareholders including Robert Sangster.

Susan and I were staying in a house near Vincent's, a short drive from Jack's Thunderbird Hotel, and security in this playground of the rich was extremely tight. We had to carry identification to show to the guards at the entrance to our 'housing estate' – and, having been allowed to pass, had to drive over a barrier which, after the wheels of the car had passed over it, shot up to form a line of metal spikes. Jacqueline O'Brien, returning from a shopping trip, had driven over the barrier and was approaching the security guard when she remembered something else she should have bought in town and put the car into reverse. Before the guard could stop her, she had slashed the car's rear tyres on the spikes.

Poor Vincent had his own troubles, this time involving the remote control for the garage door: he had driven halfway in when the door descended onto the roof of the car, making a horrible dent.

Sometimes horses seem much more controllable than modern technology.

Also in Palm Springs at the time was another bloodstock agent, the flamboyant Billy McDonald. A native of Northern Ireland, Billy had lived in California for years – originally as a car salesman selling Jensen Interceptors and Rolls-Royces. He invited us up to Santa Barbara to visit a friend's stud and for me to 'sit on a couple of two-year-olds' – but when we arrived there were not just a couple but sixteen! A photographer was on hand to snap me on each one, and a few weeks later an American racing magazine was full of these photos, under the headline: 'Billy McDonald Brings Lester Piggott To California.'

The farm manager at that stud was Monty Roberts, now famous for his unique method of breaking in horses almost by word of mouth, and since then Monty and his wife Pat have been close friends.

Our eventual destination was New Zealand, where we went to Te Rapa for a Jockeys' Invitational Race: here I won on Kaufmann for owner–breeder Sid Munro, who had landed New Zealand's biggest hurdle race with the horse.

We were staying in the Waikato area, and close by were hot springs and geysers, which provided a novel way of losing weight. Although the sulphur stank, sitting in the hot mud was a nifty way of shedding a few pounds!

9

The mid-Seventies

The upshot of those sun-baked discussions at palm Springs was that Apalachee, rather than Cellini, would form Vincent's main attack on the Two Thousand Guineas, and the spring of 1974 was dominated by the prospect of that giant horse pulverizing his opponents up the Rowley Mile.

Early in the season I flew to Ballydoyle to ride work on Cellini and Apalachee, and was very happy with what I found. Both had matured impressively over the winter, and both gave me a great feel, confirmed when they made their respective seasonal debuts: Apalachee made mincemeat of some high-class opponents in the Gladness Stakes at The Curragh and became an even hotter favourite for the Two Thousand Guineas, and though Cellini had to work harder to land the Vauxhall Trial at Phoenix Park the following week, we were pleased enough with him.

Vincent then decided to get another race into Cellini before his main early-season target, the Irish Two Thousand, so the colt went to The Curragh for the Tetrarch Stakes, this time winning cosily – though he still idled with me when hitting the front.

That same day at The Curragh marked the beginning of a significant change in racing when Mary Dowler, apprenticed to Seamus McGrath, became the first lady rider in the British Isles to beat the men in a Flat race. Progress towards allowing ladies to ride on equal terms with men had been slow since the Jockey Club rules had been changed to allow women to ride professionally, and the first race for ladies only did not take place until

May 1972, when Meriel Tufnell made the history books by winning the inaugural running at Kempton Park. Since that hesitant start girls riding in races have come to be an accepted part of the scene, but with the occasional exception it's very difficult for them to make it into the big time. This is certainly nothing to do with lack of dedication or determination, and I tend to attribute it to the basic physical differences: girls simply cannot be as strong in a finish as their male counterparts.

There had been rumours going round that Apalachee had some problem with his wind, though I had no idea where that notion came from. Nevertheless, come Two Thousand Guineas day he was understandably a very hot favourite at 9–4 on to beat eleven opponents, among them two good horses that I had ridden in the shape of the French-trained Nonoalco and Charles St George's Giacometti.

Perhaps all the hype surrounding Apalachee was beginning to convince even me, as before the race I had put my reservations on one side and begun to think that he couldn't be beaten. In the early stages I held him up; then, when I asked him to go on two furlongs out nothing happened, and he faded to finish third behind Nonoalco and Giacometti, beaten two and a half lengths by the winner.

The first questions Vincent asked me when I returned to dismount were: 'Did he make a noise? Was there something wrong with his breathing?' But I had to report that there was no sign of any wind trouble. He simply did not pick up as he should have, and that was that.

Apalachee's defeat in the Two Thousand Guineas was one of the great burst bubbles of racing in recent years, but deep down I think that people just wanted to believe he was a wonder horse before they had the evidence. Those of us who are close to horses know in the bottom of our hearts how good they are, and sometimes you allow yourself to become convinced that they're better than you really know them to be.

Cellini likewise disappointed, though in his case expectations had not been so high. In the Irish Two Thousand Guineas at The Curragh he never gave me any feel at all, and just fell apart when I asked him to pick up: he finished third behind Furry Glen and Pitcairn, and the softness of the ground that day was not sufficient excuse. Cellini was simply not as good as we'd hoped, and any thoughts of aiming him at the Derby were hastily dropped.

I felt very disappointed, but Jeremy Tree's marvellous nine-year-old sprinter Constans gave me a boost by winning the Prix de Saint-Georges at Longchamp for the third time. After that the old man ran just once more before returning to France to spend the rest of his days as hack and family pet to the great trainer Alec Head.

But gloom returned the following day at Windsor. I had just the one ride, Campanologist for Fulke Johnson Houghton, and he was five lengths clear of his field when, right on the line, for some inexplicable reason he tripped up. I fell off, lucky to avoid being trampled by his pursuers, and was incensed to hear the announcement that the judge had decided that I had fallen off before the post and had awarded the race to the runner-up. There was a simple way to adjudicate on this – the photo-finish – but as luck would have it the camera had broken down, so it was all down to the judge, whose decision that I had to lose the race was final.

Following Cellini's disappointment at The Curragh, Vincent had little choice but to consider running Apalachee at Epsom, and I went over to Ballydoyle to work the colt over ten furlongs, with the good four-year-old Hail The Pirates giving him weight. The upshot of the trial was sadly conclusive: Apalachee didn't stay, so Epsom was out. Vincent then announced that the horse would be trained for the St James's Palace Stakes at Royal Ascot over one mile, but personally I doubted that he would ever run again. I was right. Apalachee never saw another racecourse, and was shipped off to stud at Gainesway Farm in Kentucky.

In the event Vincent ran Cellini in the St James's Palace, but he could only run second to Averof, and like his stable companion was retired to Gainesway.

What a contrast to the plans we'd hatched in the California sunshine! By the middle of the season both Apalachee and Cellini had finished with racing, and Apalachee's defection from the Derby had left me without a mount again.

Then Maurice Zilber, the volatile Egyptian-born but French-based trainer whose major patron was the American oil magnate Nelson Bunker Hunt, phoned to offer me the Derby ride on Mr Hunt's Mississippian. Naturally I accepted, although I knew perfectly well that the horse was usually the ride of Bill Pyers, and that Bill would be none too pleased to find himself removed. Nor was he, and over the next few days the papers were full of his threats – which included blowing up Mr Hunt's oil wells and, much more serious, giving me a black eye. To add fuel to the fire, Maurice Zilber preposterously denied approaching me at all, which put me in an extremely bad light.

Maurice then performed a U-turn and confessed that he had indeed approached me about riding Mississippian, but said that he would also be running Blue Diamond in the race, and Bill would ride that colt. Then yet another twist: Zilber yet again denied my engagement for Mississippian in the Derby – and finally Bunker Hunt announced that he did not want Mississippian to run in the Derby at all: the horse would go for the Prix du Jockey-Club at Chantilly four days later, and Bill Pyers would ride him!

There seemed to be an epidemic of 'jocking off' at the time – by no means all of it involving me – and whereas some took a deeply moral line about it, it is part of a jockey's job to get on to the best horses, and if that involves ruffling a few feathers, so be it. Nowadays, with jockeys' agents burning up the phone lines day and night, it seems perfectly in order for there to be a scramble for rides: back then we were supposed to act more decorously.

Nor were jockeys calling all the shots. Sometimes – as in the Mississippian case – the toing and froing could be not only exasperating but potentially costly, as you could miss a decent ride while waiting for the connections of a better one to come to a decision. And I have to say that Maurice Zilber could be downright impossible in the matter of riding plans: you never knew for sure that you were riding his horse until you got up on it in the paddock – and even then it would not have surprised me to find another jockey up there!

So after all that messing about, there I was again, horseless in the Derby, and my mood was not improved by an eight-day suspension doled out at Longchamp for the not uncommon mistake there of stopping riding at the first winning post when the finish of the race was at the second! The horse who got me into this little local difficulty was Garzer – and appropriately Susan and I bumped into the horse's owner Herr Boss and his wife while I was seeing out my suspension, after the Derby (the rules had been changed that year so that a suspension started nine days after the offence), at the Hotel du Cap in Antibes, a lovely hotel perched on a rocky point overlooking the Mediterranean.

My Derby problem had been resolved when Henry Cecil came to the rescue with Arthurian, on whom I'd won at Newbury earlier in the season. As some of the fancied horses in the race had stamina doubts I thought we had a chance, but it was not to be my year. Snow Knight, ridden by my good friend Brian Taylor, won at 50–1.

Another hiccup in my decidedly unsmooth summer occurred the next day when I flew to Chantilly to ride Moulines in the Prix du Jockey-Club. After accepting that ride I was offered an alternative in the shape of Caracolero, but thought it proper to decline as I was already committed. And the way things were going for me at that time, it was inevitable what would happen: Caracolero won at odds of 41–1. Mississippian, ridden by Bill Pyers, was fourth, and I finished eighth on Moulines. I was subsequently engaged to ride Caracolero in the Irish Derby at The Curragh, but he could never get in a blow and finished well down the field behind English Prince.

But it was not all gloom, and one horse with whom I was developing a great partnership was Gerry Oldham's wonderful stayer Sagaro, trained in France by François Boutin and without doubt the greatest long-distance horse I ever rode. On 30 June, the day after the Irish Derby, I went to Paris for the Grand Prix de Paris, feature race on a day which for many people formed the pinnacle of the French racing season. Morning dress was *de rigueur* and the sport of the highest calibre, with the Grand Prix itself, then run over nearly two miles, always a superb race. Sagaro had much more speed than the average stayer and no matter how long the race could produce a dazzling turn of foot in the closing stages, and he won the Grand Prix in great style from Bustino, who had run a fast-finishing fourth to Snow Knight in the Derby and who would go on to win the 1974 St Leger before finding his own special place in racing history in the famous 1975 King George against Grundy.

Those two great French fillies Dahlia and Allez France had both been kept in training as four-year-olds and were dominating the older middle-distance generation. Yves Saint-Martin had been riding both, although his contract put him on Allez France in the event of their clashing, and since both were being trained for the King George VI and Queen Elizabeth Stakes at Ascot at the end of July, the ride on Dahlia was offered to me by Maurice Zilber. And this time he meant it.

I was nearing a personal milestone as the day of the big race approached, and by the start of racing on Saturday 27 July was just two winners short of a career total in Britain of 3,000 – though I realized I still had a fair way to go before getting anywhere near Gordon Richards's British record of 4,870.

Roussalka in the Princess Margaret Stakes, second race on the card, looked a good thing to bring up number 2,999, leaving Dahlia to score the 3,000th in the big race – but I had reckoned without Olympic Casino, my ride in the first race of the day, who duly won, as did Roussalka, thereby providing the 3,000th and robbing Dahlia of double glory!

In the event Allez France did not run in the King George, and Dahlia sailed home with the greatest of ease, never coming off the bit, beating the Queen's One Thousand Guineas and Prix de Diane winner Highclere to become the first horse ever to win the King George twice. She was a wonderful mare, along with Petite Etoile and Park Top one of the three best fillies I ever rode. As tough as old boots, she was none the less highly strung, and could get very worked up before a race, but she was a real professional – as she showed on her next appearance after Ascot, when she went to York for the third running of the Benson and Hedges Gold Cup and won decisively from Imperial Prince and the Derby winner Snow Knight. We were then narrowly beaten in the Prix du Prince d'Orange at Longchamp, and a proposed trip to ride her in the Man O' War Stakes at Belmont Park, New York, was scuppered by my doctor, who pronounced that a transatlantic flight at that time could rupture my sinuses. So I had to cry off, and she won (ridden by Ron Turcotte, for ever associated with the incomparable Secretariat): I don't know which hurt more – the sinuses or missing a valuable winner!

My sinuses were soon back in working order, and I was able to fly to Toronto to ride Dahlia in the Canadian International Championship at Woodbine, where Snow Knight was again among her opponents.

Each racing authority seems to have different rules, and I thought that I had come across most of them. At Woodbine I discovered I was wrong.

Since Dahlia tended to get wound up at the start before a race, I often used to get off her and walk her round until it was time to get her loaded into the stalls. At Woodbine that day I dismounted as usual, and was surprised to see the starter rushing towards me, shouting. I couldn't hear what he was on about, and asked him to repeat it, at which point he became irate and demanded that I get back on Dahlia immediately – even insisting that I lead her back to the spot where I had first got off. By European standards this sounded daft, but it appeared that the spirit of fair play in Canada demanded that every runner carry its allotted weight for the same length of time, and for that reason no jockey is permitted to dismount after leaving the paddock. If a rider falls off on the way to the start, he is required to remount at the precise point where he and the horse parted company. You live and learn.

In the race itself Dahlia turned in a brilliant display, hugging the rail and then shooting through a gap to win and break the track record.

She stayed in North America for the Washington International at Laurel Park, which she had won as a three-year-old in 1973, when ridden by Bill Pyers. I was hopeful that we could end our season of memorable partnership on a high, but racing at the top level since April may have taken its toll even of this tough customer, and she ran below par to finish third behind Sir Michael Sobell's Admetus, trained in France by Jack Cunnington.

Dahlia was kept in training as a five-year-old in 1975 and I continued to ride her whenever possible, including in the King George VI and Queen Elizabeth Diamond Stakes, when after a characteristic display of mulishness at the start she finished third, five lengths adrift of that pulsating contest between Grundy and Bustino but with plenty of top-class horses strung out behind her.

Bustino, trained by Dick Hern and ridden by Joe Mercer, could win only by blunting the undoubted speed of the Derby winner Grundy, and Major Hern consequently hatched a plan which would ensure a blistering gallop from the word go, with two pacemakers in the form of the good handicappers Kinglet and Highest blazing the trail. As a result this race felt like the fastest mile and a half I have ever ridden – and Dahlia, who always pulled in her races, did not pull that day!

She met Grundy again the following month, when landing her second successive Benson and Hedges Gold Cup. All the attention on this race has focused on the eclipse of Grundy, who clearly did not give his true running after his arduous effort at Ascot and would never run again, but that emphasis has tended to downplay Dahlia's wonderful achievement. Looking at the race beforehand it seemed there was nothing that would go on and make the pace, so I decided to dictate from the start on the mare. I knew she stayed much further than the ten and a half furlongs of the race, so in the circumstances making all the running seemed the obvious thing to do. The strategy worked to perfection, Dahlia winning comfortably from Card King. It was the only race she won all season, from eleven starts.

Grundy's jockey Pat Eddery, son of the Irish rider Jimmy Eddery whom I had so narrowly beaten when winning the 1957 Oaks on Carrozza, was on the crest of a wave in the mid-1970s, and became champion jockey for the first time in 1974, beating me by 148 to 143 after a fine struggle over the closing weeks.

The late phase of this season had featured me as the 'Piggott-in-the-middle' as riding plans for the Arc were finalized. Yves Saint-Martin, injured in a fall a few days before the big race, was not sure to be fit in time to partner the great local heroine Allez France, and her owner the art dealer Daniel Wildenstein asked me to ride her. Dahlia had been withdrawn from the race (and in any case I never thought she was at her best around Longchamp) and Sagaro, brilliant as he was, would surely be tapped for foot in the final furlong of an Arc, so I was very pleased at the prospect of riding the hot favourite for Europe's richest race.

The plan did not work out: at the last minute Yves was declared fit and took the ride on Allez France, his considerable pain alleviated by a shot of novocaine half an hour before the race. Although he was unable to be his usual forceful self in a close finish, his great filly beat Comtesse de Loir by a head. I ended up on good old Mississippian, who finished ninth of the twenty runners.

At that period my home winners seemed to have dried up somewhat, allowing Pat to establish his lead in the title race, but there were still some classy horses to ride, notably Charles St George's Giacometti, who won the Champion Stakes at Newmarket. What a wonderfully consistent racehorse Giacometti was! Unbeaten at two, placed in three Classics as a three-year-old, he was a tough and versatile horse to whom all types of going came alike, and it was extraordinary that the Champion Stakes was his first victory of the season.

On the domestic front, Maureen and Tracy were both growing up rapidly, and both becoming increasingly interested in horses and riding – though at this stage Maureen was much the keener. Even before the yard in the Hamilton Road was finished, she kept her pony Sport in one of the old stables on the property, but she was outgrowing him and graduated to a fifteen-hand gelding named Kilkenny. We had long encouraged both girls to ride, and they both showed a natural aptitude for the saddle, under the tuition of the local riding-school owner Ann Hammond.

With the training yard completed, we had begun work on our new home – named Florizel like the old one, which we had leased to an Irish-based bloodstock agency – and moved in a couple of weeks before the start of the 1975 Flat season.

On a site well away from the road we had built a single-storey house around the essential swimming pool, with four bedrooms, three bathrooms, a large lounge, a den for the girls, an office for Susan (whose business was in full swing) and one for me. Flower beds surrounded the circular parking area outside the front door, and over the years shrubs, trees and evergreens have almost hidden the house from the road.

I had no plans to start training in the foreseeable future, so the yard itself we leased to Ben Hanbury. Among his intake of yearlings in 1974 had been five for the Kashmiri shipping tycoon Ravi Tikkoo, who had hit the big time when his Steel Pulse won the Irish Derby in 1972 and was expanding his racing interests. After I had won the 1974 Gimcrack Stakes at York on his colt Steel Heart he told me that he wished to purchase yearlings at the forthcoming Deauville sale which would be sent to be trained by Ben at our yard. Nobody must learn of these plans, but Ben and I were to select five of the best yearlings we could find at Deauville and purchase them through Susan's bloodstock agency. Tikkoo himself would not appear, but wanted to be contacted while on holiday with his family in Switzerland.

The big week in Deauville was always a wonderful experience, and this year we were delighted by an invitation from Sourien Vanian, an owner with François Boutin who had become a great friend, to stay with him at the house he had rented in the town: he suggested we bring the girls as they were in the middle of their school holidays, but although Tracy came over, Maureen was so involved in various horse shows at home that she could not tear herself away!

The week began with a wonderful gala dinner to which Susan and I had been invited by Maria Felix, who swept into the room swathed in a magnificent sapphire blue dress decorated with feathers and dripping with jewellery. She was then nearer sixty than fifty but certainly did not look it, and the crowd parted like the Red Sea as she was escorted to her table by the *maître d'*, the rest of us following in her wake.

The following day Ben Hanbury and Susan's partner Cormac McCormack arrived from England. The prospect of training the cream of Deauville's yearlings must have gone to Ben's head, as one morning we heard peals of laughter from the room opposite ours which he and Cormac were using as their base. Apparently Ben had mistaken a bedside lamp made out of an old-fashioned telephone for the real thing: grabbing the handset, he was pumping away at the 'cranker' and cursing 'bloody French operators' before Cormac recovered his composure and put him right.

Mindful of Ravi Tikkoo's insistence that no-one must know on whose behalf we were buying, we crept round the sales complex like conspirators, arousing much curiosity. Every day Susan had to go to the Normandy Hotel to phone Tikkoo in Switzerland and report in: after hearing her views of the day's selections, he would give her a bidding limit for each lot.

A filly I had bred was coming up at Deauville that week, and since a condition of the sale dictated that all yearlings sold must be named in advance of the auction, we had christened this filly Maroukh – which happened to be the name of Ravi Tikkoo's wife. Naturally we hoped that this name would catch his eye in the catalogue, but it seemed not to do so. However, Susan had quite a turn one morning when her sister-in-law came up and said: 'I've just seen Maroukh.' Thinking the Tikkoos had paid an unannounced visit to the sale, she exclaimed, 'Where?' – only to be told, 'In stable number 105'!

The purchases were duly made, and the five yearlings made their way to Eve Lodge.

As the 1975 season started I felt yet again that I had a great chance of breaking my Lincoln Handicap hoodoo, this time on a horse named Talk Of The Town, trained at Newmarket by Neville Callaghan. But the fates had clearly decided that I was not to win that race, and it is strange the lengths they went to: Neville duly sent the declaration to run to Weatherbys but it never arrived there, so the horse could not run.

After the previous year's foray at the Deauville sales, Susan had bought several more yearlings for Ravi Tikkoo, and one of these, Brave Panther, trained by Ben Hanbury and ridden by L. Piggott, became the first winner from the new yard at Eve Lodge when successful at Newmarket on 17 April.

But there were serious industrial relations problems besetting racing, and these broke the surface on One Thousand Guineas day.

During the early months of 1975 there had been rumblings of discontent among stable staff concerning pay and conditions, and although the majority of people working in racing had a large measure of sympathy for the lads – without whom the sport could not operate at all – little was being done to address their grievances. So a strike was called, and the response brought some of the biggest stables, especially those in Newmarket, to a virtual standstill.

On One Thousand Guineas day some 200 stable lads staged a sit-down on the course before the first race, but were cleared off in time for it to be run. They were back before the second, and as we went to post they attacked us, pulling Willie Carson off his horse. Bruce Raymond and I were making our way down together, and as the mob advanced I shouted 'Charge!' Off we went, through and over the demonstrators, to get to the start, and meanwhile Willie had remounted and galloped back up the course to the front of the Members' Stand, where he shouted to racegoers: 'Well, what are you waiting for?!'

Chaos ensued, with a large section of the crowd clambering over the fences and under the rails onto the course to confront the strikers, and a battle broke out. It was a few minutes before the police were able to intervene and calm matters down.

Eventually the second race was run, thirty minutes late, and the programme then continued without further interruption – though another demonstration before the Two Thousand Guineas two days later delayed the start of that Classic and dictated that the race be started not from the stalls themselves but by flag just in front of them.

With the strike crippling many Newmarket yards, both Susan and Maureen were helping Susan's brother Robert Armstrong by riding out two lots for him each morning, along with various friends – among them Nicky Henderson, now one of the top National Hunt trainers.

On the Sunday morning following the Guineas meeting it was business as usual. Susan and Maureen went to Robert's yard while I headed for Heathrow to catch a plane to Paris, where I had rides at Longchamp. On arrival in France I followed my usual routine of dropping in on Sourien Vanian on my way to the track, as his apartment was only five minutes from Longchamp and as a big owner in France he usually had the low-down on the opposition. After a plate of smoked salmon, a glass of champagne and a cup of thick Turkish coffee, I made a move, as I had a ride in the first race. Just as I emerged into the street Sourien called me back from the upstairs window: Susan was on the phone, from Newmarket Hospital. The horse she had been riding out for Robert that morning had bolted, its saddle had slipped, and she had taken a fall which had left her with a broken pelvis. She sounded in reasonable shape, so we agreed that I would fulfil my Longchamp commitments and get back as soon as I could.

When I returned that evening and reached the hospital the news was not too bad, though Susan would have to stay in for about a week, so Maureen and Tracy had been sent to stay with Nellie and Len Hobden. Back at the new house I somehow managed to set off the burglar alarm, which at that time had not yet been connected to the police station. I was unable to stop the bell ringing, and eventually had no choice but to telephone Susan in the hospital so that she could go through with me the procedure for turning it off. But still it wouldn't stop ringing, and eventually she suggested that I call her brother Robert, who is more mechanically minded than the rest of us.

'No problem,' he said, 'I'll be right round and we'll shoot it!'

He arrived with his air rifle and proceeded to fire at the box containing the infernal bell, situated halfway up the chimney stack. But even a succession of blasts from Robert's rifle would not stop the ringing and it continued – until some while later it just ceased of its own accord.

A few days later Susan was discharged from hospital, and once she'd come home we realized some of the advantages of living in a bungalow. The lounge of Florizel took up almost one whole side of the house, and instead of a solid wall we had had installed huge sliding glass doors which looked out onto the swimming pool. Near these we positioned a hospital bed for Susan, and Carlyn Wyndham, a trained nurse and friend of the St Georges, also a great racing fan, was only too happy to come and spend a couple of weeks in Newmarket looking after the convalescing Susan.

Some years previously, when Maureen was one, her godfather Charles St George had given her a kitten – a tortoiseshell female which we had had spayed and christened Tiddles. She had been joined in 1972 by Puff, a fluffy black male with blue eyes. Naturally when we moved into Florizel we kept a close eye on both cats, but Tiddles disappeared, and despite the presence of Puff, Maureen and Tracy missed their old pet and feared that old age might have caught up with her.

Ben Hanbury had two marmalade cats – both males (Ben said) – named Jake and Oscar, and when Oscar started putting on weight rapidly there could be only two explanations: he was either exceedingly greedy, or pregnant. It turned out to be the latter, and at the end of April 1975 Oscar gave birth in the box of one of Ben's charges, a beautifully bred but unsound horse belonging to Ravi Tikkoo who spent most of his time confined to barracks. Three tabby kittens appeared, to the great delight of Mr Tikkoo's horse, Maureen and Tracy, and by the middle of May the youngsters were regularly brought over to Florizel for Susan – still unable to get about – to admire. The kittens climbed up the curtains, scratched the furniture and were nowhere to be found when it was time for them to return to the yard. Eventually one of them – Ollie – took up residence with us, while the others kept coming round to the back door with their mother Oscar for any food that might be in the offing.

Two months after her disappearance Tiddles returned, so we then had three resident cats and two part-timers. It was all too much for the black furry fellow Puff, who after a while left – only to turn up two years later a couple of houses down from where we used to live. He was returned to us, settled down nicely and lived for many years.

By the end of May Susan was up and about on crutches, her progress only slightly hampered by an extraordinary change in the weather. After a mostly fine and warm May, on 2 June 1975 – two days before the Derby – it snowed in Newmarket: it was quite cold and the flakes settled overnight, not clearing till mid-morning.

As the 1975 Derby approached the identity of my ride was as usual giving rise to a good deal of speculation. Charles St George had a lovely grey colt named Bruni which had finished a good second in the Predominate Stakes at Goodwood, and asked me to ride him at Epsom. Since Vincent O'Brien had no intended runners I was happy to accept, but a complication arose.

For the Oaks I was expecting to choose between two of Jeremy Tree's fillies: Juliette Marny and Brilliantine. Then I won the Prix Saint-Alary at Longchamp for Maurice Zilber on Nelson Bunker Hunt's Nobiliary, who became a third Oaks possibility. But immediately after the Longchamp race Maurice, contrary as ever,

186

announced that Nobiliary would probably run at Epsom – not in the Oaks but in the Derby, on the understanding that he could get either myself or Yves Saint-Martin to take the ride.

I have to admit that I thought Maurice had finally gone mad. Nobiliary was a filly out of the top drawer, but I couldn't seriously consider her good enough to take on colts of the calibre of the leading Derby fancies Green Dancer and Grundy, and decided to stick with Bruni. In the event I was quite wrong: Nobiliary ran a sensational race in the 1975 Derby to finish runner-up to Grundy, while my mount Bruni was way back in fourteenth place.

Even with Nobiliary out of the reckoning, my ride in the Oaks was not decided until three hours before the race itself, when I finally came out in favour of Juliette Marny over Brilliantine: the racecard that day had my name against both fillies. The ground had firmed up since the start of the meeting, which was in Juliette Marny's favour, and I had suggested to Jeremy Tree that blinkers might help galvanize her and keep her mind on the job in hand. Although weak in the betting market and starting at 12–1, she responded wonderfully, taking the lead two furlongs out and quickly putting daylight between herself and her rivals. She won by four lengths from Val's Girl to give me my first English Classic since Boucher in the 1972 St Leger.

It felt good to be back riding Classic winners, and within a few weeks I felt even better after equalling my 1965 record with eight wins – four of them for Vincent O'Brien – at Royal Ascot.

After all that hectic activity I felt I'd earned a rest, so we took a week off and spent a few days in the South of France, where we met up with film producer Nat Cohen – who had owned the 1962 Grand National winner Kilmore – and his fellow film mogul Sam Spiegel, lunch with whom one day on Spiegel's yacht moored off Cannes was much enhanced by the excellent company of Yul Brynner.

Back to business: Maurice Zilber asked me to ride Nobiliary in the Irish Oaks, and in the same race Vincent wanted me on board his filly Tuscarora. But I felt like staying loyal to Juliette Marny, who had been so impressive at Epsom, and was glad that I did, as after a tough struggle with Tuscarora she got home by a neck, with Nobiliary two lengths further away in third.

A few days after riding Dahlia behind Grundy and Bustino in the King George I went over to Évry, the course near Paris's Orly Airport which had then been functioning for a couple of years, and rode a treble for Malcolm Parrish. Malcolm, for whom I rode often, was originally from Brighton; the son of a bookmaker, he had made his money from carpet warehouses in France and had then burst upon the French racing scene, buying a yard in Lamorlaye and using the services of one of the best bloodstock agents in the business, George Blackwell, to buy him yearlings – the objective being value for money rather than spending the top dollar. His approach worked brilliantly, and during the mid-Seventies I enjoyed a great deal of success in France on the Parrish horses, who ran in the pink and mauve colours of Malcolm's French wife Denise, known to everyone as 'Sniff'. They lived in a wonderful house in Gouvieux, close to Lamorlaye, and somehow Malcolm managed to run his carpet business while simultaneously organizing the training and racing of his increasing string.

It was back to 'what will Lester ride?' speculation before the St Leger. Vincent had a very strong candidate in the shape of King Pellinore, who had won the Blandford Stakes at The Curragh, and I was expecting to ride him. But the announcement that Bruni would run started speculation that I might switch to him, as there was some doubt as to whether King Pellinore would take part were the ground to come up heavy, as at one time seemed likely. In the event the going was to Vincent's liking, King Pellinore ran, and both Vincent and I thought he would win – so we were rather disappointed when he finished second, ten lengths behind the runaway winner Bruni!

Despite being beaten, I was delighted for Bruni's jockey Tony Murray, trainer Ryan Price, and especially for my friend Charles St George. The fact that I could have ridden Bruni I just had to push to the back of my mind.

I did at least finish St Leger day on the right note, winning the last on Calaba, one of my favourite horses of this period. I'd first teamed up with Lord Fairhaven's mare when she was a four-year-old the previous year: together we won five consecutive races in 1974. Until Doncaster she'd had a disappointing 1975, but regained her form when beating Shantallah in the Great Yorkshire Handicap over the St Leger trip of a mile and three-quarters, and won twice more before the end of the season. Unfashionably bred, tall and angular, Calaba had a great engine coupled to limitless determination and courage. When she retired, Lord and Lady Fairhaven gave me a beautiful figure of the Colossus of Rhodes carved in coral, standing astride a silver ship.

Yet for all the Classic rides and big-race memories, and for the award that year of the OBE (which I no longer hold), 1975 will for ever stick in my memory as providing one of the most bizarre victories of my entire riding career.

Back in South Africa for the Bull Brand International at Pietermaritzburg, history looked like repeating itself in a quite uncanny way. As in 1973, the last race of the day suffered from a malfunctioning of the starting equipment. I was riding the favourite, a horse called The Maltster trained by Basil Cooper, whose brother Tom was probably the best and certainly the nicest bloodstock agent of all time, and a man who died far too young.

The field was loaded into the gate and ready to go when The Maltster stuck his head into the next-door stall. I shouted at the starter (amazingly, the same man who had been officiating over the 1973 fiasco) but he took no notice and let the runners go, with the result that I lost ten lengths and, I thought, any chance of winning. Once I'd extricated The Maltster's head we set off in pursuit of our rivals, with me pausing only to voice to the starter my opinion of his skills: he heard my greeting and took it rather unsportingly, but there was no time to worry about the consequences, as the rest of the field were still way ahead of us and we had to concentrate on hauling them back. To my surprise, we gradually began to catch up, and as we entered the long straight I began to feel rather more optimistic. When I asked The Maltster to quicken he went through the pack of horses like a knife through butter, and got up to win by a length.

The crowd went mad – and so, in a different way, did the starter, who reported me to the stewards for swearing at him. They imposed a fine but I decided to lodge an appeal: the hearing was hastily arranged for Durban a couple of days after the race, and I took along Eugene Sannan, a solicitor who was also a prominent racehorse owner. He argued my case and the fine was quashed.

More shenanigans awaited on our Far East trip in January 1976.

I was riding in the last at Sha Tin, in Hong Kong, and in the first the following day at Bukit Timah in Singapore, where I had a good ride for my friend Ivan Allan in the Lion City Cup, the premier sprint of the season there. Problems with the flight – which should have been a simple matter of three hours – meant that we could not travel until the morning of the Lion City Cup, and once we finally boarded the plane we had to sit and wait on the tarmac for another half hour. I was becoming very anxious that I would not get to Bukit Timah on time, and asked Susan to negotiate with the steward about getting us a quick exit once we'd landed: we were in economy, and her efforts got us moved up to first class, nearer the exit.

At the old Singapore airport of Payer Lebar (now Changi) there were no jetways: you disembarked down steps, crossed a short strip of tarmac and then went up a ramp into the main terminal building. The plan was for me to rush straight through, to be met by Ivan Allan's driver, who would whisk me off to the races while Susan would collect the luggage and take a cab to our hotel, coming on to the races later.

Sebastian Coe himself could not have beaten me down those aircraft steps and up that ramp; but at the top of the ramp was the Health Desk, where you were supposed to show your vaccination certificate, and then Passport Control – where passengers from an earlier flight had already formed long queues. I hared past both desks and straight down to Customs, where I showed my riding gear – stuffed into a plastic bag – to the friendliest-looking official and charged out to the waiting car. Some distance behind me, Susan was explaining to various enraged officials what was going on, and only narrowly escaped arrest herself.

By the time she arrived at the racecourse I'd already brought home one winner and was looking forward to my ride in the Lion City Cup on Blue Star, whom Ivan had purchased in England the previous summer and for whom he had a very high regard. I had a break of three races before the Cup, and after that hectic journey was having a doze in the weighing room when I was told that Susan wanted to see me: her lunch with the head of racecourse security Mr Zein had been interrupted by the arrival of three officials from Immigration, to arrest me! I was ushered into the racecourse secretary's office, where it was agreed that I could ride Blue Star, after which the interview would be resumed.

Blue Star duly did the business, just holding on in a close finish, and I suppose that the immigration officials drew the line at dragging off the hero of the hour in handcuffs: I was ordered to report to their headquarters the following morning, when I would face possible deportation and a ban on entering Singapore in the future.

A friend who lived locally gave me the name of a top lawyer (who, handily, was a racing fan) and he came with me to plead my case – so successfully that the immigration officials decided that no further action would be taken. Mercifully, that was the end of the matter, though on reflection I suppose I took a big chance doing what I did, as there were armed police all over the place in Singapore, and they might have been in the mood to shoot first and ask questions later!

That was not the end of our Far Eastern dramas. A fire in our hotel in Kuala Lumpur caused mass evacuation, and at the racetrack at KL I took a heavy fall from a horse called Uncle Ivor. When I got back to the hotel I was stiff and sore, so phoned Susan – who by then was back in Singapore. She suggested I tie my pyjama cord to the door handle and pull hard on it. If it hurt I'd probably broken a rib. I did as she recommended, and it did hurt; but I decided to fill myself with painkillers and carry on with my rides the next day. This turned out to be a mistake, so I flew back to Singapore, where the Turf Club doctor diagnosed a broken rib and a bruised lung and advised me not to ride for a fortnight. That ruled out the onward trip to New Zealand, and as soon as I was fit we returned to Newmarket to get me in shape for the new season.

It was to be a slow start. Not until the Craven Meeting – well into April – did I ride a winner: Charley's Revenge for Susan's brother. My second was in the Craven Stakes itself on Charles St George's three-year-old colt Malinowski, who won in such style that Vincent O'Brien was very keen on his chance in the Two Thousand Guineas.

A couple of weeks before that Classic, it was time for the now customary jockeys' merry-go-round.

Vincent started having second thoughts about running Malinowski – the horse was comparatively inexperienced and, as a son of Sir Ivor, bred to get further than the one mile at Newmarket – and this triggered speculation that I would ride either Manado, trained in France by François Boutin, or Loh for Reg Akehurst: I had ridden both horses as two-year-olds. If Malinowski were to take his place in the line-up, then Yves Saint-Martin would ride Manado and Pat Eddery would be aboard Loh. Yves was on the easy list following a fall, but at the beginning of Guineas week declared himself fully fit and ready to ride Manado; and, to make matters even more confused, my name was also linked with Gentilhombre, trained by Neil Adam, and Ryan Price's pair Whistlefield and Duke Ellington.

Pat went into print with the declaration that he would ride Loh, then Reg Akehurst denied all knowledge of this; the upshot was that Malinowski did not run and I rode Loh, which brought me fearful stick in the press. Even Willie Carson managed to stick his oar in: as Loh was leaving the paddock he suddenly stopped dead, at which Willie was heard to cackle, 'Send for Pat Eddery!' In the race itself Loh ran well below his best and finished unplaced behind Henry Cecil's Wollow – a second successive Two Thousand Guineas victory for Frankie Dettori's father Gianfranco.

I had a much happier time in the Derby, but again the build-up to the race was dominated by the press's obsession with riding plans.

When I was approached by Nelson Bunker Hunt to ride Empery, on whom I had finished fourth in the Poule d'Essai des Poulains – the French Two Thousand Guineas – there were howls of protest: Piggott is at it again! Bill Pyers had come third on the colt in the Prix Lupin, which was won by his stable companion Youth, and was widely expected to keep the ride at Epsom, but for once was fairly philosophical about being removed.

In all honesty Empery did not look like having a winning chance. He was not even Bunker Hunt's best three-year-old, being clearly inferior to Youth, who was being aimed at the Prix du Jockey-Club as it was felt that he would be less likely than Empery to act around

Epsom. And although Empery was a nice enough horse – a free-going type with a good stride – he did not look like having much of a chance against Wollow, a high-class performer so far unbeaten in four races as a juvenile and two at three, who would certainly win if he stayed the trip. At this time I was writing a weekly piece in the London *Evening Standard*, and the headline to my Epsom preview summarized my view bluntly: 'I Think I'll Need A Gun To Stop Wollow.'

In the event I didn't need a gun, and although Empery was not the longest-priced of my nine Derby winners (that distinction goes to Never Say Die at 33–1), in some ways he was the most surprising.

There were twenty-three runners, with the betting market headed by even-money favourite Wollow. That Empery shared second favouritism with Norfolk Air, ridden by Ron Hutchinson, and Oats, ridden by Pat Eddery, on 10–1 indicates how widely this was viewed as a one-horse race. In truth, the Classic crop of 1976, Wollow apart, were a pretty moderate bunch.

Empery gave me a beautifully smooth ride, laying handy off the pace then moving up to lie a close fourth as Vitiges led us into the straight. Clearly the whole key to this race was to exploit any chinks in Wollow's stamina, and as soon as we had straightened up for home I started gradually to stoke Empery up for his maximum effort. He was not a horse with a great turn of foot and would have no answer to any late challenge from the favourite, so as we entered the final furlong I put him under pressure and asked him to go past the leader Relkino. He did so, showing an acceleration which I had not expected of him, and at the line was three lengths to the good.

Relkino was second, Oats third, and Wollow, who palpably failed to get the trip, not far back in sixth.

This was my seventh Derby, which put me clear of Jem Robinson and Steve Donoghue, both of whom had ridden six (though two of Donoghue's were in wartime substitute races at Newmarket rather than at Epsom), and made me the winning-most jockey in the history of the race. I do not as a rule get too worked up about records, but this was one of which I was especially proud.

Nelson Bunker Hunt was at home in Dallas on Derby day, celebrating his twenty-fifth wedding anniversary, but his daughter Elizabeth, a student in Paris, was there to lead Empery in, and after unsaddling we went with Maurice Zilber up to the Royal Box for a glass of champagne with the Queen and the Queen Mother – almost making me late for the next race, which I won on Mr Nice Guy. And the following day I landed the Coronation Cup on Jeremy Tree's Quiet Fling.

Despite these Epsom successes, in terms of the jockeys' championship things were not going at all well. Empery in the Derby had been only my twentieth winner of the whole season, and I was way down the list in the title race. Yet I couldn't complain about the quality. At Royal Ascot the brilliant Sagaro won his second consecutive Gold Cup, absolutely hacking up from Crash Course and Sea Anchor. There was a downside to the Royal meeting, though, with Ryan Price profoundly unimpressed that I'd managed to get beaten on Bruni in the Hardwicke Stakes.

I was back on Empery for the Irish Derby, but we were no match for an even better French challenger in the shape of Malacate, owned by our old friend Maria Felix, trained by François Boutin and ridden by Philippe Paquet. In an all-French finish Empery, who started odds-on favourite, was beaten two and a half lengths.

Originally the intention had been to train Empery for the Benson and Hedges Gold Cup at York, but a leg injury prevented his running there. Maurice Zilber told me the horse could not be fit in time for the St Leger and suggested I try out the stable second string, Campero: I did so but could not consider him Classic material, so when Henry Cecil asked me to ride his colt General Ironside I accepted.

Then – surprise, surprise! – Zilber started his tricks again, announcing to the press that Empery would run at Doncaster, that I would ride him, and that were that plan to be shelved then I would switch to Campero. Henry went mad and threatened to find another jockey for General Ironside, but I managed to calm him down. Come St Leger day I was indeed on General Ironside, Bill Pyers rode Campero – we were both well beaten behind Daniel Wildenstein's colt Crow – and, as expected, Empery did not run. Nor did the Derby winner ever run again – a good horse, but a long way off a great one.

Greatness, however, was just what we thought we were glimpsing that autumn in a two-year-old trained at Warren Place by Noel Murless, with whom over the decade since our split I had maintained a close and relaxed relationship.

Noel, by now sixty-six, was not in the best of health and had announced his intention to retire at the end of the 1976 season: I had ridden his Jumping Hill to win the Royal Hunt Cup at Ascot, and much had been made of the fact that this was his last winner at the Royal meeting. But for a while it seemed that the retirement plans could be put on hold, as in March there had arrived at Warren Place from California a two-year-old so good that Noel pronounced he might postpone putting his feet up in order to train this horse for the Classics.

The colt, a well-grown dark brown horse by Mill Reef's sire Never Bend, was named J. O. Tobin. We gave him plenty of time to get acclimatized, and for weeks before his racecourse debut in the Fulbourn Maiden Stakes at the Newmarket July Meeting the grapevine had been humming with word of this new superstar. He ran away with that first race in the manner of a tip-top performer, and the sky seemed the limit.

One morning soon after that race I galloped J. O. Tobin on the Limekilns, one of the most famous gallops in Newmarket. It is a wonderful place on which to work a horse, with close-knit turf avoiding any jar on the delicate legs of a young Thoroughbred, and is bordered by two main roads. I asked Susan to drive alongside as we galloped and check the colt's speed, and although we were far from flat out I was intrigued to learn from her that J. O. Tobin had been clocking over 43 miles per hour.

But I was not surprised, as the great thing about this horse was his stride. I can only describe him as having an action like a panther, clawing at the ground and devouring it with a huge enthusiasm for his task. When you changed your hands on J. O. Tobin and asked him to pick up, he seemed to stretch and get lower to the ground, and his acceleration was amazing. But like many great horses he was nervy and temperamental, and Noel and I knew that we would have to be very careful with him if we were to realize his undoubted potential.

His next outing was in the Richmond Stakes at Goodwood, which he won easily, and then it was off to the St Leger meeting at Doncaster for the Champagne Stakes, one of the top two-year-old events of the year. Here he was just sensational, cruising up to the filly Durtal on a tight rein inside the final furlong and then producing an explosive turn of foot to go four lengths clear. On that running I have to put J. O. Tobin alongside My Swallow as one of the best two-year-olds I've ever ridden.

Had J. O. Tobin called it a day for the season after that, he would undoubtedly have been winter favourite for the Two Thousand Guineas. Noel revealed to Peter O'Sullevan in the *Daily Express* his idea about postponing his retirement, though Warren Place had already been made over to his son-in-law Henry Cecil, and J. O. Tobin's owner George Pope, who was based in California, had stated that following Noel's retirement he would no longer have any horses in England. Noel's idea was to rent a small yard in Newmarket where he could continue as Pope's private trainer while training the colt for the Classics, but before any final decisions were taken J. O. Tobin would have one more outing, in the Grand Criterium at Longchamp in October.

The home crowd that day were not impressed by the reputation of the English challenger and made an odds-on favourite of their own star, the brilliant Blushing Groom. Owned by the Aga Khan and trained by François Mathet, Blushing Groom had won several big two-year-old races in France and was clearly an exceptional colt – but so, we thought, was our fellow.

I was slightly concerned about J. O. Tobin beforehand, as he looked a little less robust than usual and felt ill at ease, and when in the final furlong I pressed the button and asked him to race in earnest, nothing happened. Blushing Groom, who was indisputably a brilliant racehorse, shot clear of us to win by four lengths, and we were even pipped for second by an outsider named Amyntor.

It was a disaster. Noel's retirement plans were brushed off and reinstated and J. O. Tobin was sent back to California. There he continued to race, and not without distinction: among his successes in the USA was a victory in the 1977 Swaps Stakes at Hollywood Park, where he had that year's Triple Crown winner Seattle Slew sixteen lengths behind him.

Two particularly memorable moments back on the home front marked the end of the year. In October I rode that grand old stayer John Cherry, owned by Jock Whitney and trained by Jeremy Tree, to hack up in the Cesarewitch at Newmarket under the crushing – and then record – burden of 9 stone 13 pounds. John Cherry wore blinkers to help him concentrate but was as genuine as the day is long, and for a handicapper over extreme distances had a remarkable turn of foot. I won several races on him – including the Chester Cup in 1976 – and he remained one of my favourites.

And then there was a horse named Tinsley Green, on whom I won the Ticehurst Stakes for two-year-old fillies at Lingfield Park on 2 November 1976. An obscure horse in an obscure race, but a particularly emotional moment for me as she was the last winner ever trained by Noel Murless, who retired in the position he had held for so long, the complete master of his profession. It was over twenty years since I had first taken the job as stable jockey at Warren Place, and I had won seven Classics and countless other big races on the great horses which the yard sent out with such regularity.

Finishing only seventh in the jockeys' table with eighty-seven winners (Pat Eddery was again champion) provided a downbeat end to a great year. But one of those eighty-seven was the Dewhurst Stakes on a flashy chestnut horse who would make 1977 a very special year.

The Sangster years

The first offspring of Northern Dancer – winner of the
Kentucky Derby and Preakness Stakes in 1964 – to make
any great impression in Europe was of course Nijinsky
(from the stallion's first crop), but it was not until
the mid-1970s that the Northern Dancer bloodlines
became widely influential, mainly through the buying
power of Robert Sangster, who was fast emerging as
a big owner on a global scale.

Robert – whom I had known for many years and for
whom I had ridden often – had taken the decision to
move into the business of stallion syndication in a big
way, having inherited a fortune through his family's
Vernons Pools business. He had had horses in training
for many years, initially with Eric Cousins, and more
recently had maintained sizeable strings both with
Vincent and with Barry Hills at Lambourn. His sphere of
influence had stretched to Australia, where he acquired
more than just horses: he met Susan Peacock, wife of the
politician Andrew Peacock, who owned a top racemare
named Leilani in whom Robert was after a share, and in
due course it was Susan and no longer Christine who as
Mrs Sangster was leading in the winners.

For his new bloodstock venture Robert joined forces
with Vincent and with Vincent's son-in-law John
Magnier, a new force to be reckoned with in Irish
bloodstock breeding, and together they decided that
the foundation stone of their operation should be
buying into the key American bloodlines: Vincent
would train the horses to win Classics and other big
races, and then these champions would be syndicated

to stand as stallions at the Coolmore Stud in County Tipperary, not far from Ballydoyle, which they were to build up over the next few years until it became the largest stallion station in Europe.

The first syndicate included Robert Sangster, John Magnier, Alan Clore (son of Sir Charles Clore), the late Simon Fraser (son of the Scottish landowner Lord Lovat), Vincent himself and various others, and in July 1975 Vincent, Robert and John headed off for the Keeneland Sales with a budget of $3 million to spend on the best yearlings they could find. With them they took along Tom Cooper, who then headed the British Bloodstock Agency in Ireland, P. P. Hogan – an astute Irish horseman who had bought for Robert in the past – and top vet Bob Griffin. After a week of hard grind they returned to Ireland with twelve yearlings on whom they had spent almost $1,800,000; among them were Artaius, Be My Guest, Cloonlara and The Minstrel.

My first race on The Minstrel was the Larkspur Stakes – named after Vincent's first Derby winner – at Leopardstown in September 1976, his second outing following a winning debut under Tommy Murphy at The Curragh. Bred in the purple by Northern Dancer out of a half-sister to Nijinsky (which made him a three-parts brother to my Triple Crown winner), The Minstrel was not a big horse, and his colour – bright chestnut with four white stockings – would have put off many a purchaser ready to believe old wives' tales about the unreliability of flashy chestnuts (though the recent exploits of Grundy had gone a good way to dispel such prejudices). Vincent, however, knew exactly what he was looking for in a horse and was not one to be put off; he had always been very keen on The Minstrel, going to just over $200,000 to secure him at Keeneland.

After the Larkspur Stakes I could see why Vincent so liked the colt. Like many of Northern Dancer's offspring he may have been on the small side but was very compact and tough, and I was impressed by the way he knuckled down to the task of racing, winning nicely.

It was then time to test him against the cream of the two-year-old generation, so he came across to Newmarket to run in the Dewhurst Stakes. Starting 6–5 favourite, he took up the running over a furlong out and kept on well to win by four lengths from Saros. The Classics beckoned.

First, though, time for our usual winter jaunt, and in January 1977, as soon as Maureen and Tracy were back at school, we set off for Australia.

I had been asked to ride at a special race meeting to help celebrate the 150th anniversary of the founding of Albany, in Western Australia. Albany is situated on the most southerly point of the state, and understandably the weather was at first very cool; but the hospitality, as always in Australia, was extremely warm. The Governor of Western Australia and his wife came down for the races, as did the chairman of the Turf Club Sir Ernest Lee-Steere and his wife Jackie, old friends of ours. If the racecourse itself was a little basic – what the Aussies call a 'picnic meeting' – the atmosphere was wonderful, with the whole town turning out, and I was delighted to ride a winner on the locally trained Master Atom.

There was, however, one problem with regard to travel arrangements: I wanted to ride in Singapore the following day, and the flight times didn't seem to work out. But Swan Breweries, co-sponsors of the Albany race meeting, put their Lear jet at my disposal, arranged for an immigration officer to be on board to clear me as we flew up to Perth to catch the Qantas flight to Singapore, and even persuaded Qantas to hold that flight back half an hour so that I could make the connection. With a police escort, Susan and I were driven along the bumpy road from the racetrack as the crowd waved their goodbyes – it's the nearest I ever got to feeling like royalty! – and the special travel arrangements worked like a dream: I flew off to Singapore while Susan went on to Melbourne.

It was worth all the hassle, as Blue Star won the Lion City Cup in Singapore for the second year running, and

I then went to Hong Kong for the annual International Jockeys' Race – which I also won, on the favourite Glenmalin.

Our next port of call was sunny California, where I had been asked to go and ride by J. O. Tobin's owner George Pope, who had brought all his horses back on Noel Murless's retirement. In addition there were a few of John Mulcahy's horses from Ballydoyle out there, so there seemed to be the prospect of plenty of rides.

Susan had rejoined me in Hong Kong, from where we flew to Los Angeles. Out on the track early the next morning, I put a few horses through their paces before repairing to the course canteen, where I found 'Cockney' Cliff Lines, who for many years had been Noel Murless's chief work rider. He had accompanied J. O. Tobin to the USA after the French débâcle and had stayed on, as the horse would simply not have anyone other than 'Cockney' around him.

But I was annoyed to discover that the prospect of rides was not as rosy as I'd thought. Jumping Hill, on whom I'd won the Royal Hunt Cup in 1976, was due to race in a few days' time, but Willie Shoemaker had been booked. Worse, J.O. Tobin would not be ready to run for a while. Also out there was Bruni – but he had picked up a virus and was on the sick list.

In the circumstances I decided there was no point in staying around California, so I called Ivan Allan and arranged to return to Singapore, where I rode six winners over two weekends and then, having ascertained that I would not be needed back home at the very beginning of the 1977 Flat season, stayed on until the end of March.

There was one horse above all that I was looking forward to riding when I did get back. The Minstrel's first race as a three-year-old in 1977 came in the Two Thousand Guineas Trial at Ascot: the going was hock-deep but The Minstrel ploughed through it to win well enough, and the Guineas was still firmly on the agenda.

On the same day at Ascot, however, his stable-mate Cloonlara, a filly for whom the sky was thought to be the limit and who was at the time a warm favourite for the One Thousand Guineas, disgraced herself in the fillies' trial. A daughter of Sir Ivor, Cloonlara was unbeaten after three races as a two-year-old, and although I had not ridden her in any of those I knew that she had a reputation for being rather wayward. Her race at Ascot was the fourth on the card, by which time the ground on the round course – on which this seven-furlong event was being run as the straight course was too waterlogged for use – was so cut up that the stewards decided to dispense with the starting stalls. Instead, the race would be started by flag.

Cloonlara broke well, but a false start was called so we had to return to the starting point and try again – at which point she planted herself and simply refused to move. When the starter eventually lost patience and let the others go she still refused to budge, and took no part in the race.

I returned to howls of protest from the sparse crowd (this was the day when the eyes of most of the racing world were on Liverpool, where my erstwhile partner Red Rum was winning his third Grand National), and the starter and I were both carpeted by the stewards: they accepted my explanation that I did not consider that the starter had given her enough of a chance to line up, but nothing could be done to change the result.

Despite that display of contrariness, Cloonlara still started favourite for the One Thousand Guineas at Newmarket a few weeks later. I tried to make the running on her, but when she was collared by Mrs McArdy two furlongs out she lost interest, and did not take kindly to being rousted along, eventually finishing fourth. Back at Ascot for the Cork and Orrery Stakes at the Royal meeting, she again disgraced herself by dumping me on the way to the start and then being withdrawn after refusing to enter the stalls. She showed no such mulishness at the start of her only subsequent race, the Prix de la Porte Maillot at Longchamp, but again could finish only fourth. It is always sad when a good racehorse is brought down by temperament – as was undoubtedly the case with Cloonlara – but once the resolution has gone there's usually very little you can do to get it back.

The Minstrel had no such mental problems, but after Ascot it took him a while to regain the winning thread. He ran third behind Nebbiolo (whom I had ridden earlier in the season in the Vauxhall Trial Stakes at Phoenix Park) and Tachypous in the Two Thousand Guineas, and was then beaten a short head in the Irish equivalent after a desperate struggle with Pampapaul: a subsequent stewards' enquiry failed to reverse the placings.

One aspect of The Minstrel about which I was learning rapidly was his courage, and I became convinced that in spite of those reverses we should persevere with the original plan of taking him to the Derby. Vincent was doubtful, thinking it might be better to wait for the St James's Palace Stakes at Royal Ascot, but I was sure that this beautifully balanced colt would act well around Epsom: 'If you run him, I'll ride him' was my suggestion, and as soon as Vincent had agreed there was, for once, no further speculation about which horse I would be on in the big race.

It was a good Derby field that year. In addition to The Minstrel, Vincent also ran Valinksy and Be My Guest (ridden respectively by Geoff Lewis and Edward Hide), but the very hot favourite was Blushing Groom, who since slamming J. O. Tobin the previous autumn had established himself as a star three-year-old when winning the French equivalent of the Two Thousand Guineas, the Poule d'Essai des Poulains at Longchamp. Shortly before the Derby, Blushing Groom had been syndicated to stand as a stallion in Kentucky at a valuation of $6 million, and he started favourite for the race at 9–4, with The Minstrel 5–1 and the third market choices Lucky Sovereign and Nebbiolo out at 12–1.

The connections of Blushing Groom were very confident of success, to the extent that Charles Benson, man about town and a good friend of both Robert Sangster and of Blushing Groom's owner the Aga Khan – and also at that time racing correspondent of the *Daily Express* – booked a private room at Annabel's for the celebration party, requesting the Aga's colours of red and green for the table settings.

The only apparent chink in the favourite's armour was the usual Derby factor, stamina: if he stayed, he would win; if he didn't, he probably wouldn't.

Derby Day was bright and sunny, the going officially good but riding quite fast. As yet further testimony to his training philosophy of leaving nothing to chance, Vincent stuffed The Minstrel's ears with cotton wool when saddling him, just in case the elongated pre-race parade caused him to boil over. Although probably the toughest horse I ever rode, the chestnut shared with most of the Northern Dancer stock – including The Minstrel's three-parts brother Nijinsky – the tendency to get a little temperamental at times, and on Derby Day Vincent was taking no risks.

We arrived at the start cool enough – in fact, the horse was so relaxed that he missed the break and in the early stages was a little farther back than ideally I would have wished. But gradually, and without rushing, we worked our way into the right position for the swing down into Tattenham Corner, and at the turn into the straight we were just behind Willie Carson on Hot Grove, who was tracking the leader Milliondollarman. Like every other jockey still in contention I was very aware of where Blushing Groom was, but as we came into the straight he was three or four lengths behind us, Henri Samani careful not to make too much use of a horse with a question mark over his stamina.

In the straight, Willie and Hot Grove got first run, and with Blushing Groom now mounting his challenge the race was between the three of us. But with a quarter of a mile still to go it was clear to me that Blushing Groom had reached his limit, so I forgot about him and concentrated on tackling Hot Grove.

Having won the Chester Vase on the colt in May, I was familiar enough with Hot Grove to know that he would be a tough nut to crack, but here The Minstrel's courage really came into its own.

That he always raced with his ears flat back sometimes gave the impression to spectators that he was trying to duck the issue, but nothing could be further from the truth: it was just his way of expressing his determination, and now he responded magnificently to the whip as I rode him out to catch Hot Grove. I was very hard on the colt – how could I deny that? – but his willing response was marvellous, and gradually we wore down Hot Grove throughout the final two furlongs, The Minstrel finally getting his head in front just before the post to win by a neck.

It had been a magnificent race, and I was full of admiration for my horse, who had given his all and never flinched. What a tough customer!

And what a resourceful fellow Charles Benson could be. As the disappointed Aga Khan flew home to come to terms with Blushing Groom's defeat, Charles phoned Annabel's to change the booking for that evening's party to the name of Robert Sangster – and the table settings to the green, blue and white of Robert's colours! It was some party that night.

Unfortunately I could not add the two other big races of Derby week to my haul, as Quiet Fling was beaten by Exceller in the Coronation Cup, and the Oaks was a disaster.

My ride was Durtal, a fine filly owned by Robert Sangster and trained by Barry Hills. Although she had been firmly put in her place by J. O. Tobin at Doncaster the previous autumn, her three-year-old form had been good enough for her to go into the Oaks as hot favourite.

But she never got to the starting stalls. Cantering back past the stands after the parade she was pulling very hard, which caused her saddle to slip, and as we turned the bend near the entrance to the paddock the saddle went right round underneath her and I came off. Terrified, she bolted, dragging me behind her with my foot stuck in the stirrup, and headed for a fence with concrete uprights, a familiar enough feature of British racecourses before safety regulations mercifully replaced them with plastic poles. When we hit the upright the impact broke the aluminium stirrup iron, freeing my foot, but Durtal impaled herself on the splintered wood of the fence, narrowly missing puncturing a main artery. She was eventually caught and calmed down, and lived to race again, while I, a little shaken, was taken back to the ambulance room, where I recovered well enough to ride the winner of the last – Elland Road for my brother-in-law Robert Armstrong.

In Durtal's absence, the Oaks was won by the Queen's grand filly Dunfermline – Her Majesty's second victory in that Classic, following my win on Carrozza back in 1957.

Despite that horrific accident I looked like having a great summer, with The Minstrel being aimed at the Irish Derby and King George; but first Royal Ascot had a special treat in store when Sagaro, in the final race of his career, became the first horse ever to win the Ascot Gold Cup three times, strolling home five lengths ahead of Buckskin. He really was a magnificent stayer, as good as any I rode, and his turn of foot was, for a long-distance performer, phenomenal. And to cap a memorable Royal meeting – seven winners, three of them for Vincent – dear old John Cherry landed the odds when easily winning the Queen Alexandra Stakes from Shangamuzo.

The Minstrel duly won the Irish Derby from Lucky Sovereign, despite veering over towards the stands in the closing stages and surviving both a stewards' enquiry and an objection from Frankie Durr on the runner-up, but in the next race, riding a horse named Glencoe Lights, I was brought down to earth with a hefty bump: as we left the stalls one of my stirrup leathers broke, but despite being unable to give my mount a proper ride I

One of the easier wins of my career, on Shergar in the 1981 Irish Derby. *Liam Healy*

Gallant Special winning the Richmond Stakes at Goodwood, 1982. *Gerry Cranham*

Ardross (white cap) just fails to get to Yves Saint-Martin and Akiyda in the 1982 Prix de l'Arc de Triomphe. *Gerry Cranham*

Twenty-eight up! A new Classic record as Commanche Run holds off Steve Cauthen and Baynoun in the 1984 St Leger. *Gerry Cranham*

Storm Warning landing the Scarborough Stakes at Doncaster, 1985. *Gerry Cranham*

The first winner of the comeback: Nicholas at Chepstow on 16 October 1990. *Bernard Parkin*

The cream on the comeback, as Royal Academy (number 1) gets up to pip Itsallgreektome in the Breeders' Cup Mile at Belmont Park, October 1990. *George Selwyn*

My thirtieth English Classic: Rodrigo de Triano goes clear of Lucky Lindy (Mick Kinane) in the 1992 Two Thousand Guineas. *Gerry Cranham*

After winning the Swedish Derby in 1992 on Tao. *Hakan Hansson*

My last Royal
Ascot winner:
College Chapel
after the 1993
Cork and
Orrery Stakes.
John Crofts

Get me to the church on time: leaving Florizel with Maureen on 4 March 1989. *Camera Press/Srdja Djukanovic*

At home with Tracy after the Gulfstream Park fall.
Sunday Express/Mason

Jamie Piggott, aged twenty months

My father with three later generations of his family at the christening of Sam Haggas in March 1993. *Idols/Adrian Houston*

Mary-Anne Haggas and her doting grandfather, photographed by Patrick Lichfield. *Camera Press*

Looking to the future, 1994. *George Selwyn*

managed to stay on board for the whole six-furlong trip before landing heavily on the deck just after the winning post – little the worse for the experience, except for annoyance and a few bruises.

Having landed my seventh Eclipse Stakes on Artaius, another of the 1975 Keeneland acquisitions, who would go on and win the Sussex Stakes at Goodwood, I was ready to ride The Minstrel in his first race against older horses in the King George. It was a typically high-class field, with 1975 and 1976 St Leger winners Bruni and Crow, Coronation Cup winner Exceller and Prix du Jockey-Club winner Crystal Palace among The Minstrel's main rivals. A 20–1 outsider was Orange Bay, trained by Peter Walwyn and ridden by Pat Eddery in the Grundy colours of Dr Carlo Vittadini, who had been third behind Pawneese and Bruni in the race twelve months earlier but had shown little to date in 1977. And yet Orange Bay it was who not only proved The Minstrel's chief danger but played a major part in a wonderful finish, for me every bit as good as the 1975 King George between Grundy and Bustino – but then I won this one, so perhaps I'm biased!

As at Epsom, The Minstrel started slowly, but I gave him time to find his rhythm and on the turn into the short Ascot straight we were still about sixth. Orange Bay was making the best of his way home and I had to put The Minstrel under severe pressure to get to him. Once he had done so, and then gone half a length up, I thought that was that, but Pat and Orange Bay fought back with great tenacity and we had a humdinger of a battle to the line, The Minstrel just getting the better of a great struggle by a short head.

After that race The Minstrel's racing career was cut short. He was being trained for the Arc, but then import restrictions to North America – where he was due to stand as a stallion – following an outbreak in England of a disease called equine contagious metritis meant that he was hastily packed off in September.

It's a pity that he did not have the opportunity to prove himself even further in the Arc, as in some ways he was the ideal horse for that rough-and-tumble of a race, but The Minstrel achieved enough to put him right up there with my all-time favourites: gutsy, resilient, a horse who really got his head down and raced. I often wished there'd been a few more like him!

As The Minstrel's racing career was coming to its premature end, that of another Ballydoyle three-year-old was about to blossom. Alleged, a son not of Northern Dancer but of another influential American sire Hoist The Flag, had been bought by Robert Sangster as a two-year-old in California for $175,000, which turned out to be a wonderful bargain.

As a juvenile he had run just once, winning a small race at The Curragh by eight lengths under Tommy Murphy, and Tommy rode him again on his three-year-old debut at Leopardstown, where he started at 3–1 on and duly won. His next outing was in the Royal Whip at The Curragh, where he faced opposition of a much stiffer order than he'd encountered before. I rode Valinsky, a son of my 1966 Oaks winner Valoris, and the third of Vincent's trio was the 1976 Irish St Leger winner Meneval. I had not at this stage ridden Alleged, though in a piece of work at Ballydoyle earlier in the year I had been impressed by him when riding Valinsky – so I was not hugely surprised when at The Curragh he and Peadar Matthews, a Ballydoyle work rider, cruised past us in the closing stages to win at 33–1.

I wasn't going to pass up the chance of riding this star in the making next time out, and together we duly landed the Gallinule Stakes at The Curragh.

Next stop for Alleged was that traditional St Leger trial, the Great Voltigeur Stakes at York, where he turned in an extraordinary performance to go clear of his rivals – who included Classic performers such as Hot Grove and Lucky Sovereign, runners-up to The Minstrel at Epsom and The Curragh respectively – with a stunning burst of speed halfway up the straight. He won by seven lengths, but it felt like three times that.

After that performance Alleged, who was by then unbeaten in five races, looked a certainty for the St Leger (he started at 7–4 on), but found one too good for him in the form of the Queen's Oaks winner Dunfermline, who, under an inspired ride from Willie Carson, wore us down inside the final quarter mile after we had taken up the running early in the straight and made for home. I received a fair amount of criticism for the way I rode Alleged at Doncaster, the complaint being that I made too much use of him and thus laid us open to a challenge from behind – to which I can only reply that I rode him in just the same way at York and don't recall any grousing then! More to the point, Dunfermline on St Leger day was an exceptional filly, and behind the pair of us there was a huge gap back to the third horse Classic Example.

Up to and including the St Leger, Alleged had run in the colours of the Californian tycoon Bob Fluor, but Robert Sangster bought a major share in the horse after the Classic, and it was in his familiar silks of emerald green, royal blue sleeves, white cap, emerald green spots, already so prominent that season on The Minstrel, that Alleged went into the stalls at Longchamp to face twenty-five rivals in the Arc.

The St Leger defeat had done little to dent the public's regard for Alleged – nor should it have done – and he started favourite at pari-mutuel odds of nearly 4–1, with Crystal Palace, Dunfermline, Orange Bay, Crow, Malacate and the New Zealand horse Balmerino all attracting support in a typically strong international field.

The early pace was slow so, having no doubts about his stamina, I decided to send Alleged on and dictate matters from the front. Vincent had not wanted me to set out to make the running, but I couldn't see where the pace was going to come from, and there's no point in complaining after the event if the race is not run to suit you. Alleged was always a very relaxed horse, and I had no worries about not being able to keep him happy in front, so off I went. Towards the top of the hill, after the field had passed the small wood known as the Petit Bois, I smartly stepped up the pace in an effort to get his rivals off the bit – a quick foot down on the accelerator – and by the time we were nearing the straight Alleged had them all flat to the boards. He just kept on galloping like the great horse I knew him to be, and although Balmerino and Ron Hutchinson made a spirited attempt to get to us close home we were always holding them, in the event winning by one and a half lengths. Dunfermline, who had robbed Alleged of his unbeaten record in the St Leger, was fourth.

For once after a Piggott ride in the Arc there were more bouquets than brickbats – but then tactical races like that always seem like a master-stroke when you win. In the Arc you have to be lucky, but riding Alleged in that way made luck less of a factor than it would have been had I tried to bring him from off the pace, making one frenzied effort up the final straight in the usual manner of the French jockeys. The glass of champagne which I enjoyed with the O'Briens and Sangsters in the box of the President of France, Valéry Giscard d'Estaing, tasted very good.

By the time he returned to Longchamp a year later to attempt to become the first horse since his great-grandsire Ribot in the 1950s to win the Arc in successive years, Alleged had run only twice more. He won the Royal Whip at The Curragh again in May, but the race jarred him up, and firm ground through the next couple of months saw the big midsummer races such as the King George go by without him. His main target had always been a second Arc, and patience has always been one of Vincent's greatest virtues, so we waited with him and sent him to Longchamp for his prep race in the Prix du Prince d'Orange – where he left us in no doubt about his well-being by beating the track record.

A serious gallop on the horse at Ballydoyle a week before the race put him spot on, and as Alleged travelled to Longchamp four days before the Arc, accompanied by Vincent's travelling head lad Gerry Gallagher and a hundredweight of oats to satisfy the horse's prodigious appetite, we were full of confidence.

So were the punters, who sent him off hot favourite. Unlike the previous year the ground had been softened by rain, so tactics which involved a sudden burst of acceleration were of dubious use, and there was a tiny doubt that he might not like the ground that soft. Without wanting an exact repeat of the 1977 tactics, I knew I had to have him handy to avoid trouble coming down towards the straight, so kept him right up with the pace all the way and then pushed him on to go clear after the final turn. Without needing to use the whip, I allowed him to coast home by two lengths from Trillion, a great French filly who would become even more famous as the dam of Triptych. (Trillion was ridden that day by the legendary American jockey Willie Shoemaker, who had been narrowly beaten that year in the Derby at Epsom on Hawaiian Sound. After the Arc, Trillion's trainer Maurice Zilber made the curious observation that he thought Willie was too small to ride her!)

This was an easier victory for Alleged than in 1977, and it thrilled the huge Longchamp crowd, some of whom ran after him as we returned to unsaddle and pulled out his tail hairs as souvenirs of a great racing occasion. Hemmed in as he was by the usual Arc day crush and jostle, Alleged might have got upset by such an assault, but he took it all wonderfully in his stride.

Which is more than can be said for his rider's family. Maureen, by then seventeen, had been pursuing with increasing enthusiasm her interest in three-day eventing, and on Arc day Susan and Tracy had driven across to the Midlands to see her compete at Meriden. The event finished early, and on the way home the three of them stopped at a hotel near the M1 to watch the race on television – and made such a racket, cheering and jumping up and down as Alleged came to the front, that the hotel manager had to come and investigate the cause of the disturbance!

The possibility of Alleged going for the Champion Stakes was shelved, and he was retired to stud at Walmac Farm in Lexington, Kentucky, at a valuation of $16 million.

Although he never won a Classic, Alleged's achievement in winning the Arc twice puts him right up among the greats of the post-war era, and I would certainly have to rank him among my top five. He was a wonderful horse to ride: you could do anything with him in a race, ride him from the front or from off the pace, and he had a gloriously relaxed attitude. As he matured he developed more pace – Vincent had an extraordinary knack of getting more speed into his middle-distance horses as they got older – and had the ground not gone against him in the summer of his four-year-old career, he'd have won everything.

But not all the Sangster–O'Brien horses had the same measure of success as The Minstrel or Alleged, and one of those who ultimately has to go down as a disappointment was Try My Best.

Another fine-looking son of Northern Dancer out of a Buckpasser mare, Try My Best was unbeaten in three outings as a two-year-old in 1977. In his first two races in Ireland, both of which he won exceptionally easily, he was ridden by Tommy Murphy, and I did not team up with him until the Dewhurst Stakes at Newmarket in October. He won that with great authority from Sexton Blake and Camden Town – both of whom would prove high-class colts – and went into winter quarters giving me plenty to look forward to over the cold months ahead.

Travel to warmer climates during those months took in Penang's New Year meeting, then Ipoh, a border town in the north of Malaysia which is probably the best racetrack in the country, then to Singapore for the Lion City Cup meeting, where I rode six winners, including my third successive victory in the big race:

Blue Star had retired, but I scored the hat-trick on Gentle Jim, trained by Garnie Bougoure, who was a familiar jockey in Europe in the early 1960s and had ridden such horses as Noblesse and Ragusa for Paddy Prendergast. That run of success was capped by eight winners in Kuala Lumpur before the winning streak ground to a halt in Hong Kong.

Our journey home was broken at the invitation of Essa bin Mubarak al Khalifa, one of the first of the big Arab owners, who had asked me to go and take a look at the new racecourse in Bahrain, the first Middle Eastern country to build a modern track. Situated some ten miles from the capital Manama, the course was an amazing sight – grass growing in the middle of the desert, and the stands being erected by a team of British engineers. The night before we left Essa gave a party for us in a large tent in the desert, where we sat on the ground on rugs and ate a very good dinner: not a sheep's eye in sight, thank goodness!

Back home, the Classic hopes were being brought along. I missed the Lincoln for once in order to go to Phoenix Park to ride Try My Best on his seasonal debut in the Vauxhall Trial Stakes, in which he came with a smooth late run to cut down his opponents and earn an even-money quote for the Two Thousand Guineas, and only 5–2 for the Derby.

And yet my most pleasing victory that spring came in the maiden race which opened the Craven Meeting at Newmarket, which I won on Gold Prospector, trained by my brother-in-law Robert. By that wonderful performer Gold Rod – owned and bred by Lottie Dickson – Gold Prospector had a doting fan in Tracy, who spent a great deal of time at Robert's yard. The Newmarket win gave Tracy huge excitement, which was trebled when Gold Prospector's owner–breeder Ronnie Driver invited her to lead her beloved 'Goldie' into the winner's enclosure. (Ronnie had almost turned Gold Prospector's dam Prairie Girl into a polo pony, but changed his mind, and Gold Prospector was her first foal. As I write, Goldie is still in active service as stable pony at Robert's.)

The gallops at Ballydoyle were sodden during the run-up to the Guineas, so Try My Best was transported to the racecourse stables at Newmarket ten days before the race in order to finalize his preparation, and when he lined up on the day against eighteen opponents there was no reason to suspect anything particular amiss. One factor about which we could not be sure was the going. Try My Best had not encountered soft ground as a juvenile and had not pleased every expert on his seasonal reappearance at Phoenix Park when the going had more cut in it than he was used to.

On Two Thousand Guineas day the going was officially soft, but his failure cannot be attributed to the ground: the truth is that the writing was on the wall a very long way from home, and he simply felt like a dead horse underneath me. There was nothing for it but to stop riding, and the even-money favourite trailed in a tailed-off last of the nineteen runners – a collapse in many ways more sensational than that four years earlier of Apalachee, who at least finished third.

We were all devastated by the complete eclipse of Try My Best, and nonplussed that such a good horse – which he clearly was – could turn in such a miserable performance. Subsequent tests showed up the early stages of an infection, of which there would be no outward sign until the horse had been put under the stress of racing, and it transpired that a virus had got its grip on Ballydoyle: although the two-year-olds showed symptoms of coughing and nasal discharge, the older horses showed the effects only when racing.

The intention to train Try My Best for the Derby was shelved after he had disappointed in a home gallop and he never ran again. Retired to Coolmore Stud, he proved quite a successful sire, his best son to date being Last Tycoon, winner of the William Hill Sprint Championship at York and the Breeders' Cup Mile at Santa Anita in 1986.

With Try My Best out of the picture, I had a choice to make for the 1978 Derby – which seemed on paper a very open race – between Vincent O'Brien's Inkerman, who had won the Gallinule Stakes, and Hawaiian Sound, owned by Robert Sangster and trained by Barry Hills. I picked Inkerman, and I picked wrong. Vincent's colt beat only a couple home, while Hawaiian Sound, to partner whom Robert flew the great Willie Shoemaker over from the USA, was beaten a head by the late burst of Greville Starkey on Shirley Heights.

The Epsom Summer Meeting proved a complete blank for me in 1978, but Royal Ascot had its great moments, including Jaazeiro's victory for the O'Brien–Sangster combination in the St James's Palace Stakes, and Solinus, a magnificent sprinter trained by Vincent, on whom I had won the Coventry Stakes at the meeting the previous year, winning the King's Stand Stakes in impressive style by four lengths.

In the same month two wins on one horse at different meetings at the much humbler venue of Lingfield Park brought special satisfaction, for the winner in question was the wonderfully versatile Attivo, owned by one of my greatest friends, journalist and broadcaster Peter O'Sullevan. These were Attivo's first races since breaking his hip in an accident while schooling over hurdles two years before.

Back with the O'Brien winner-producing machine, Solinus confirmed his status as the best sprinter of his generation when winning the July Cup at Newmarket – causing Vincent to describe him as one of the best sprinters he had ever trained – and Jaazeiro won the Sussex Stakes at Goodwood almost without drawing breath. Solinus then consolidated his position as a sprinter right out of the top drawer when winning the William Hill Sprint Championship (now the Nunthorpe) at York, and at the same York August meeting I took advantage of Willie Shoemaker's being unavoidably detained in the USA to win the Benson and Hedges Gold Cup on Derby runner-up Hawaiian Sound.

At the end of the 1978 season – when I finished fifth in the jockeys' table with ninety-seven winners, well adrift of Willie Carson, champion on 182 – I set off on my travels as usual, initially to Pietermaritzburg in South Africa for another International Jockeys day, and then, after Christmas, to Hong Kong.

In the colony the new racecourse at Sha Tin had recently been completed. Several years before I had flown over the proposed site when Sir Douglas Clague, then Chairman of the Hong Kong Jockey Club, had unveiled the plans for the new course to the press, and looking down from the helicopter to the cold sea below it was impossible to envisage how a modern, state-of-the-art racecourse could ever emerge from those depths.

But it could. First, a large area of the sea was reclaimed, and the new land allowed to settle. Then the track was laid out, and experts brought in from all over the world to advise on the best type of grass to use: several different strains were sown in blocks and monitored for suitability. Accommodation was built for a designated number of trainers and for the stable lads, and for the horses themselves there was stabling in air-conditioned multi-storey blocks, with equine swimming pools, an equine hospital and every possible facility. In Hong Kong racing, they were doing nothing by halves.

The stands, with seating for thousands and replete with restaurants and boxes, completed what has to be one of the very finest racecourses in the world, and early in January 1979 I got my first chance to ride there.

I kicked off right away with a winner and clocked up a couple more at the other Hong Kong racetrack, Happy Valley, before coming unstuck back at the next Sha Tin meeting: no winners, and a £500 fine. Riding American Eagle for trainer Frank Carr, I was on the rails when Grasshopper Green, ridden by top French jockey Philippe Paquet, came alongside and then ducked in towards me. I thought I was going to end up over the rails, so my immediate reaction was to push the horse's head away with my left – that is, my outside – hand. All very nimble, but it looked bad on the patrol film, and the stewards were not impressed.

In Singapore I failed to win a fourth consecutive Lion City Cup, then, while in Kuala Lumpur for the Chinese New Year meeting, we decided to make a trip into the mountains to Genting Highlands. We set off by scheduled helicopter service and on landing about fifteen minutes later were struck by how cold it was up there – not surprisingly, as the altitude was such that we could see the clouds going by directly outside our hotel room. The hotel management invited us as their guests to a dinner and show, but although the dinner was fine, the show was all in Chinese, and the only bit we could appreciate was the juggler.

It was difficult to sleep as bus after bus ground to a halt under our window to disgorge hundreds of revellers, who formed a kind of conga line and weaved to and fro, singing a merry Chinese New Year song which was rather lost on us.

The next morning we staggered down to breakfast and commented to the management on how the place was filling up. 'Oh yes: at least twenty thousand more people will be arriving today!', we were informed proudly – at which point we suddenly remembered a pressing engagement back in KL, thanked the manager for his hospitality and headed back by road, as conditions made it impossible to fly. It was a relief to return to the stifling heat and comparative quiet of the city and just lie in the sun by the pool at the Regent Hotel.

I'd totted up a very healthy nineteen winners during that trip, and returned to England eager to get on with the new season.

At the beginning of 1979 the story of my impending retirement was yet again in the press. Why certain journalists should have been so obsessed by this theme I don't know, but for the immediate future the story was well and truly laid to rest by the announcement that I had come to a fresh agreement with Vincent

O'Brien whereby I would continue to ride for him for at least another two years. At the same time, much more sensational news broke: Robert Sangster was bringing over the American whizz-kid jockey Steve Cauthen – dubbed 'The Six Million Dollar Man' over there in tribute to the phenomenal earnings won by his mounts in 1977 – to ride those of his horses based in England with Barry Hills.

I made a very slow start to 1979, but this time I was not obsessed with chasing titles and so was not too worried. By the time evening racing commenced in mid-May I had ridden only five winners in England, and only another four in Ireland and France – though these included Trillion, whom I had ridden often the previous year and who now showed she was still in top form by winning the Prix d'Harcourt at Longchamp and running second to Frère Basile in the prestigious Prix Ganay. Classic success came with Godetia, owned by Robert Sangster and trained by Vincent O'Brien, in the Irish One Thousand Guineas at The Curragh (later supplemented by the Irish Oaks on the same filly).

Although the Sangster bandwagon was still very much rolling, signs of things to come were in evidence with the gradual arrival of Arab owners on the European racing scene. Mahmoud Fustok, from the Lebanon, a powerful owner in France who had the majority of his horses in training with Maurice Zilber, offered me a retainer which, given my commitment to Robert Sangster, I had to decline, while in England Khalid Abdullah – a Saudi prince, though on the racecourse he preferred to go under the unassuming designation 'Mr' – was beginning to make his presence felt. With ex-trainer Humphrey Cottrill as his racing manager and Jeremy Tree as his main trainer, Mr Abdullah got off to a good start in this country, and I rode both his Known Fact – who would go on to win the 1980 Two Thousand Guineas on the disqualification of Nureyev – and Abeer when they won their maiden races in the spring of 1979.

That summer was notable for the 200th running of the Derby, when I found myself in the happy position of being able to accept an invitation to ride for the Queen. Her Majesty had never owned a Derby winner – her Aureole had been second to Pinza way back in 1953 – but in 1979 seemed to have a very live chance in the shape of Milford, a Mill Reef colt trained by Major Dick Hern.

Milford had been second twice as a two-year-old and won both his starts at three, including a facile victory in the Lingfield Derby Trial which put him right into the Epsom picture and gave Major Hern's stable jockey Willie Carson a sticky problem.

Good as Milford undoubtedly was, the Major had one better in Sir Michael Sobell's Troy, who had won the Classic Trial at Sandown Park and the Predominate Stakes at Goodwood. Willie plumped for Troy in preference to the Queen's runner – which in former times would no doubt have landed him in the Tower – and Her Majesty sent for me. Robert Sangster and Vincent O'Brien had a candidate for the race in the shape of Accomplice, but graciously released me from my commitment to ride him – making it clear that this was only on account of the Royal connection.

The combination of the 200th Derby, the Queen and L. Piggott seemed to strike a sentimental chord with punters, who gave Milford a good deal of support, but the colt turned out to be rather one-paced, and like the rest of the field had no chance once Troy got into top gear and powered his way into the lead. Willie had made the right choice: Troy won by seven lengths.

Yet again Royal Ascot provided me with a feast of winners, notably a four-timer on Gold Cup day which included the big race itself on Henry Cecil's great stayer Le Moss. I got the ride because Joe Mercer, Henry's stable jockey, had elected to ride stable companion Buckskin, and Le Moss turned the race into a procession, coming home seven lengths clear in great style. Le Moss was essentially a lazy horse who needed to be stoked up and kept about his business, but once rousted up he could really go.

That Royal meeting saw the first award of the Ritz Club Trophy to the leading rider of the meeting. The brainchild of Phil Isaacs, managing director of the Ritz Club in the basement of the Ritz Hotel in London, the trophies are now presented to the top jockey at Royal Ascot, the Cheltenham Festival, the Goodwood July Meeting, the York August Meeting and the Grand National meeting at Aintree, with substantial donations being made by the Club on each occasion to racing charities. The Queen Mother made the inaugural presentation to me on the Saturday (the 'non-royal' Ascot day which follows the four-day fixture), and I now have no fewer than ten of these beautiful trophies.

Had there been a presentation to me at Longchamp on the Sunday after Ascot, the crowd would doubtless have grabbed the trophy and broken it over my head, as that day I collected a four-day ban and caused a riot. I rode Trillion into second place in the Prix d'Ispahan, only for the stewards to step in and declare that she and the third horse – Opus Dei, ridden by my old Hong Kong sparring partner Philippe Paquet – had interfered with two other runners. They altered the placings and suspended us both for four days, but what really enraged the local punters was that forecast bets involving Trillion were ruined. All hell broke loose, with matters becoming so serious that the next race had to be delayed. Hundreds of people, hurling bottles and cans, invaded the paddock and threatened to storm the weighing room, and the only way to calm them down was to show repeated re-runs of the race on the racecourse television sets. Eventually they grudgingly agreed that a sort of justice had been done, and racing resumed.

The silver lining for me in this particular cloud was that my suspension allowed me time to pay my first ever visit to the tennis championships at Wimbledon and see at the very top level a game I've enjoyed since those early days on our tennis court at Letcombe Regis.

Maureen was becoming ever more involved in her eventing, and for some time had been learning the skills from one of the top event riders, Alison Oliver. She had been chosen to join the British Junior Team after the final trials early in August, but just before she was due to depart for the championships at Punchestown, not far from The Curragh, disaster struck: her horse Barney went lame and a degenerative disease of the foot was diagnosed, so Maureen had to withdraw. She was understandably devastated, as she had worked so hard at her chosen sport, and opportunities to represent your country do not come along very often.

In a sense, of course, a jockey is representing his country every time he rides overseas, in which case I'm not sure how much credit I brought the home flag with a bizarre incident at Deauville in August. Riding African Hope in the Grand Prix, I was tracking the eventual winner First Prayer in about fifth place as we turned into the straight. Alain Lequeux's mount Jeune Loup, on my inner, was under pressure, and as I passed him his whip accidentally caught mine and knocked it out of my hand. I was going much better than Alain, whose horse seemed to be back-pedalling, so I just grabbed his whip out of his hand and gave African Hope a couple of cracks: he responded to finish second, just ahead of Jeune Loup, who can't have liked the whip, as instead of dropping out he had run on again once Alain was empty-handed!

The Deauville crowd – who as a rule are much more relaxed than racegoers on the Paris tracks – thought all this a huge joke, and hooted with laughter. But the stewards did not see the funny side of it, upgrading Jeune Loup to second, demoting African Hope to third and handing me a hefty twenty-day suspension.

This sort of incident was not uncommon in the years before the camera patrol, but nowadays very little escapes the lens of the camera, and as soon as I'd made the switch I knew I was going to be in trouble.

The suspension brought about by that moment of inspiration started immediately after a four-day ban following a careless riding conviction on Thatching at York, so with a decent amount of time off in prospect Susan and I headed for the Côte d'Azur, which was much quieter than when we usually went there in midsummer, and after a week in Antibes we flew to Malaga.

But once back in the saddle – with Tracy's beloved Gold Prospector my first home winner after my return – I found myself heading north rather than south, for the All-Stars Jockeys Festival in Stockholm at the end of September: Joe Mercer, Willie Carson, Pat Eddery, Steve Cauthen and I all travelled to Sweden for this event and the afternoon was a huge success, 10,000 racegoers packing into the track and the Tote takings hitting a Scandinavian record.

I clinched the All-Stars Jockeys title in a photo finish, but poor old Willie Carson was in the wars: one of his mounts had trodden on his big toe, and his wafer-thin leather riding boots afforded little protection against such violence. Willie spent the afternoon with his left leg horizontal, assuring everyone in sight that he would be perfectly fit enough to partner the great Troy in the following week's Prix de l'Arc de Triomphe. And so he was, though Troy could finish only third behind Three Troikas and Le Marmot. My mount Trillion ran her usual game race to come fifth.

By this time attention was switching to Classic prospects for 1980, and as far as the O'Brien–Sangster team was concerned our main hope seemed to lie with the handsome chestnut colt Monteverdi, who as a son of Lyphard was a grandson of the ever-influential Northern Dancer. Unbeaten in three races in Ireland, Monteverdi followed the course of most of Vincent's top two-year-olds over the years by coming to Newmarket for the Dewhurst Stakes.

He gave me an extraordinary ride. Going clear of his field in the final furlong, he suddenly swerved so violently to the left that I thought we were in danger of crashing into the stands rails. I took the only course of action open to me – swiped him on the side of his face with my whip. Startled, he flung his head in the air, but my unusual manoeuvre had exactly the desired effect, as he then ran straight as an arrow to win by two lengths from the subsequent Irish Derby winner Tyrnavos.

He had won all right in the end, but I was perplexed. He was not an inexperienced horse, and we were racing well away from the crowd when he swerved – so why had he done it? Despite serious doubts about his steering or his resolution – or both – Monteverdi became favourite both for the Two Thousand Guineas and for the Derby.

One two-year-old in 1979 about whose resolution I could have no doubts whatsoever was Moorestyle, owned by Moores International Furnishings Ltd and thus one of the first horses whose name advertised a company. Trained by Robert Armstrong, Moorestyle had been bought by Susan extremely cheaply as a yearling for 4,000 guineas, which given his later achievements has to be one of the great bargains of recent years. He won two out of four as a juvenile – the important Convivial Maiden Stakes at York, where he hacked up, and the Doncaster Stakes, in which he responded like a champion once I asked him to quicken.

As the season came to a close, with Joe Mercer champion jockey for the first and only time and me back in sixth (tolerably good, considering all the time off with suspensions), I had two interesting partners to look forward to in 1980, Moorestyle and Monteverdi. I knew which I trusted the more.

First, though, time for another busman's holiday, this time at the vast Meadowlands track in New Jersey, where they race five evenings a week throughout the winter. On a freezing cold night Yves Saint-Martin joined Joe, Willie, Pat and me to represent Europe against a home team consisting of Steve Cauthen, Jorge Velasquez, Angel Cordero, Don McBeth and, from Canada, Jeff Fell. A huge crowd watched the Americans beat us hands down – Velasquez winning all three of the international races. I didn't score a single point, but at least racing took place

– unlike the previous week in South Africa, where I had been accompanied by Maureen on another international jockeys' competition at Turffontein. It rained and rained, until racing finally had to be abandoned.

On that downbeat note ended both the year and decade. For me the Seventies had been marvellous. What did the Eighties hold?

For the most part, I'm glad I didn't know.

On my usual winter travels to the Far East early in 1980 I was accompanied by a BBC film crew making a documentary about me: they followed me from Singapore to Hong Kong and then back to Kuala Lumpur for the Chinese New Year meeting, but although they had plenty of opportunity to film me in action, I had only four winners.

From there we went to New Zealand, where on my first visit to Ellerslie racecourse in Auckland I rode four winners, including a horse named Arbre Chene. His trainer Peter Cathro had been killed only ten days earlier in a freak accident when a two-year-old he was leading into a horsebox lashed out. The licence had been passed to his young assistant Clive Bennett, who saddled the horse with the help of Cathro's widow Colleen, and when we won the reception was overwhelming. The old horse also met a sad end: taken to Melbourne for a big race, he died of colic and is buried in that city in the pets' cemetery. Susan and I still get a Christmas card from his owner–breeder Kathleen Moore.

We then went north to the Bay of Islands, where a fishing trip intended to provide film of me landing a big one did not quite work to plan: I caught nothing, so we arranged to borrow a marlin which had been caught by someone else, and I was photographed on the quayside alongside the poor thing, and credited with having landed it!

From New Zealand we flew to California. I had ridden many times over the years at the gloriously scenic Santa Anita course, but had never until this trip managed a winner there, and what better time to put that right than in front of the BBC cameras? My winner was Madam Markievicz, trained by Tommy Doyle, who during the late 1940s had worked as a stable lad for Susan's father Sam Armstrong. Having been one of the first to make the unusual and giant step from being a stable lad in England to a trainer in the USA, Tommy had been a huge success.

The 1980 home season began quietly. Vincent O'Brien, ever upgrading and developing his facilities, had established for his overseas runners a private taxi service in the form of a new flying horse-box. A runway had been put in beside the gallops for the Skyvan, painted in Robert Sangster's racing colours, and from then on travelling times were cut dramatically, with consequent benefits for the horses' well-being.

Not that shorter trips would necessarily improve Monteverdi's frame of mind. He had not developed as much through the winter as I had hoped he would, and on his first outing – in the Trial Stakes at Phoenix Park – could only finish second, though his defeat was generally put down to the soft going. He then came second to Final Straw in the Greenham Stakes at Newbury, and this time there was serious cause for concern: I'd had to ride him very hard even to get second, and there was definitely a suspicion that he wasn't putting his heart into his work. The doubts I had had about him after the Dewhurst looked like being justified, and it was time for a rethink: we decided to miss the Two Thousand Guineas and head the colt for the Irish version. We also decided to fit him with blinkers.

Neither the change of target nor the blinkers did much good at The Curragh. Monteverdi simply did not try at all, and when I got off him after he'd finished fifth behind Nikoli I was so annoyed with the horse that I burst out to Vincent: 'He's useless.' I did not regret that remark. Monteverdi was one of the most unpleasant horses I ever rode, a clue to his nature being that he had very short ears. Long ears on a horse are often the sign of genuineness; the opposite interpretation can be read into short ears, and Monteverdi had the shortest of any of the O'Brien horses I rode. Furthermore, he had a mean look to him. He was, in short, a brute. But my timing of telling Vincent he was useless admittedly could have been better, as that comment was picked up by the press and published widely – not the ideal situation for Vincent, whose skill at increasing and then maintaining the value of his charges, with a view to their stallion careers, was now at a premium. That remark was the beginning of the end of my long association with Ballydoyle.

There was no doubt that things had changed since the days of Sir Ivor and Nijinsky. The name of the game now was stallion values, and this put Vincent under considerably more pressure than before. Results were needed, and needed far more quickly than previously. A huge amount of money had been invested in the whole Coolmore operation, and a very great deal was at stake. Failure to produce big winners would result in heads rolling. Mine could well be one.

An additional element in the strain between Vincent and myself at this time was his perception of my attitude towards home gallops: he was quoted as saying that when I rode work at Ballydoyle I did so more to suit myself by finding out how good the horse was, rather than to suit him.

It was a tense time, but there were still races to be run, and we decided to let Monteverdi take his chance in the Derby. We left off the blinkers and he started third favourite, but ran another awful race and finished fourteenth behind Willie Carson on the wonderfully brave Henbit, who cracked a cannon bone during the race and still ran on to win. But the Derby apart, I had a marvellous Epsom, eight winners bringing me another Ritz Club Trophy.

In the King George and Queen Elizabeth Diamond Stakes I came second to Ela-Mana-Mou on Ian Balding's lovely filly Mrs Penny, on whom earlier in the season I'd won the Prix de Diane – the French Oaks – at Chantilly, and the fact that I'd gone for her in the Ascot showpiece rather than for Vincent's runner Gregorian inevitably sparked rumours of a rift. The fact was that by the time the decision was made to run Gregorian I was already committed to Mrs Penny, but none the less the rumours were not so far wide of the mark.

In August 1980 the break came, with the announcement that Pat Eddery would be moving from Peter Walwyn to ride for Robert and Vincent. They felt they needed somebody who would be able to ride for them in Ireland whenever they had a runner, and for me that was just too much of a commitment, so they were obliged to find somebody else – and they could hardly have done better than Pat.

Joe Mercer, who was then riding for Henry Cecil, and with whose powerful string behind him he had become champion jockey in 1979, would move to Peter Walwyn, who trained at Lambourn, much closer to Joe's home near Newbury. All this left Henry without a jockey, and me without a retainer.

Charles St George, who by then was one of Henry's biggest owners, asked me if I was interested in taking the job at Warren Place. I could think of no good reason why not, and after meeting Henry and Charles we came to an agreement. It had struck me in the past that Henry did not seem to keep his jockeys for any great length of time, but I was coming up for my 45th birthday and felt that I would not need too long anyway. The position as Henry's stable jockey was certainly the plum riding job in England, and to be connected with Warren Place would mean spending a great deal less time in transit than during the years when I was constantly flying across to Ballydoyle, a level of travelling I found tiresome.

The decision, once it had been made, came as a great relief. Now I could concentrate on riding big winners, and on chasing Willie Carson for the jockeys' title. I won the Ritz Club Trophy at the York August Meeting and was associated with some exceptionally nice two-year-olds, including the brilliantly fast filly Marwell, on whom I won the Molecomb Stakes at Goodwood and later the Cheveley Park Stakes at Newmarket, and a beautifully built Great Nephew colt with a great big white blaze, owned by the Aga Khan and trained like Marwell by Michael Stoute, whom I rode to victory on his highly promising debut at Newbury in August. His name was Shergar, and he confirmed this promise in his second race when runner-up to Beldale Flutter in the William Hill Futurity at Doncaster.

Moorestyle had gone from strength to strength as a three-year-old, winning the Free Handicap at Newmarket before finishing runner-up in the Poule d'Essai des Poulains. In all he won seven of his nine races that year, including the July Cup, the Vernons Sprint Cup, the Prix de l'Abbaye, the Challenge Stakes and the Prix de la Fôret, and it was entirely appropriate that he should have been voted Horse of the Year by a panel of racing journalists. He was a terrific horse, kept in the prime of condition through a very long season by Susan's brother Robert Armstrong, and has to be up there with the best sprinters I ever rode.

When Moorestyle won the Challenge Stakes at Newmarket in mid-October he was part of a five-timer (including my first winner for Henry Cecil under the new arrangement – a walkover on Main Reef, but they all count!). This reduced the gap between Willie and myself to just five, but despite landing the Cesarewitch on that grand stayer Popsi's Joy I was still eight wins down with just six days of the season to go – at which point overseas riding commitments rather put paid to the idea of a late challenge. I couldn't complain, though, as one of those commitments was to partner the Arc runner-up Argument in the Washington International, and after racing behind the leading three until well into the straight, he went on for an easy win.

That was followed by yet another International Jockeys Championship in the USA. These events tend to attract a rather lukewarm reception when held in Britain, but overseas everyone enters into the spirit and I've always had a great time when taking part in them. Naturally a good deal hinges on which jockey is drawn to ride which horse, so nobody takes the results too seriously; but they do provide a wonderful opportunity for racegoers in one country to see the top performers from other countries – often other continents – in action, and I'm all for them.

This time the European team of myself, Willie Carson, Gianfranco Dettori, Joe Mercer, Greville Starkey and Yves Saint-Martin faced a home team including Steve Cauthen – who had made such a great impact and won himself so many friends since moving to England the previous year – and the new young star Cash Asmussen. At Meadowlands we raced under floodlights – which the Europeans were then not used to – before moving across the country to Bay Meadows in California. The home team took the championship, but I kept the flag flying for the visitors by winning the individual competition.

A real treat on our California trip was a visit to the Los Angeles home of Berry Gordy, part-owner of Argument but better known in the world outside racing as founder of the Tamla Motown record label which launched Stevie Wonder, Diana Ross and so many other great singers.

For jockeys, the telephone has always been a mixed blessing: if it doesn't ring, you're not getting the rides, and if it rings constantly you get fed up with the sound of it. But just occasionally the telephone becomes a real menace.

Over the years I have received any number of death threats – as on the day Nijinsky won the St Leger – and simply learned to ignore them as the work of cranks. Some came over the phone, some in letters, but by far the worst instance was a lady whose persistent pestering of me culminated in a court case in October 1980.

She had begun calling some years earlier, initially just now and again, and her routine then would be simply to put the phone down when Susan or I answered, as if she'd got a wrong number. Then the regularity of the calls increased, and sometimes she would put her phone near the vacuum cleaner or radio. At other times she would just scream. Occasionally she would hurl abuse down the line at me.

One day a letter arrived, with a London postmark, enclosing a photo of herself. Her deranged look, and the increasing frequency of the calls, led to our calling the police, who tracked her down to the house of a retired diplomat and his wife, where she was employed as a cleaner, all the while using their phone to call and bother us.

In March 1980 she was convicted at Newmarket Magistrates' Court, and fined £100.

For a while that was that, and we thought we would hear no more of her. Then in August the same year the calls started up again, and the following month she paid us a visit. She had taken a taxi all the way from London, and had told the driver that I would pay the bill. Susan answered the door to find a wild-eyed woman standing there: as soon as she spoke, Susan realized who it was, slammed the door and called the police – who arrived a few minutes later to find the lady leaning on the doorbell and screaming abuse.

She was charged again, and appeared in court in October, where she claimed to be in telepathic communication with me, saying that I willed her to make the calls. Her sentence was to be bound over for a year, fined £10 and referred to a London psychiatric hospital.

You would have thought that that really would be the end of the matter, and for a while it was. Then she started calling again: she had been discharged from the hospital, and blamed Susan and me for her condition. During one call she said she would be coming up to Newmarket with a friend named Stanley, and claimed already to have paid a visit without our knowledge, taking the keys to Susan's car: Susan's car keys had indeed gone missing, so we were now very perturbed. She did come, and the police were waiting for her. On her they found a Stanley knife.

We didn't hear from her again, and understood that she was back in hospital. Later we learned that as soon as she was discharged again she went to the nearest railway station and threw herself in front of a train.

I I

Back to Warren Place – and into 'retirement'

As a prelude to the 1981 season at home, I took part in an International Jockeys' Competition in South Africa – Durban followed by Johannesburg – where I took the individual title, beating local hero Michael Roberts by one point, then rode a couple for my brother-in-law Robert Armstrong at Cagnes-sur-Mer before arriving back in Newmarket for yet another new challenge, at my old stamping ground of Warren Place.

Quite apart from the quality of rides which I knew I would get from the association with Henry Cecil, one of the great attractions of the job was that it was in Newmarket itself, and after years of travelling life would be somewhat less hectic: I was, after all, forty-five, and beginning to think more seriously about when I would hang up my riding boots and start training.

In these circumstances, Henry was a particularly good trainer to work for as he was not constantly asking me to go to far-flung racecourses: there was always someone else, one of his band of excellent back-up jockeys, who could take on those rides.

I had ridden for Henry many times over the years since the 1969 Eclipse Stakes at Sandown Park, when having been replaced on Park Top by Geoff Lewis I took the ride on Wolver Hollow for the little-known first-season trainer H. R. A. Cecil, and proceeded to beat the great mare – who admittedly had a terrible run – by two and a half lengths.

Wolver Hollow was one of the horses Henry had taken over from his stepfather, the great Royal trainer Captain

Cecil Boyd-Rochfort, on the Captain's retirement in 1968, and he was based at Boyd-Rochfort's old yard of Freemason Lodge and then Marriott Stables until moving into Warren Place in 1976 on the retirement of Noel Murless (whose daughter Julie he had married in 1966).

During the time Noel Murless had been at Warren Place it was normal for a top trainer to have around fifty horses in his yard, but Henry was one of the first in Newmarket to build up a three-figure string, and when he moved up from Marriott Stables he had to make big changes at Warren Place, using all the old boxes and converting existing buildings (including garages) to provide others. Many of Noel's staff had remained – among them Jim White, who had been with him since he first started training in 1937. When Henry took over Jim was more or less retired, but he still lives at Warren Place, and now makes toys in his spare time.

Henry's head lad was Paddy Rudkin, who had been with Teddy Lambton before joining Henry soon after he set up on his own, and the two had a wonderful working relationship which was reflected in the astonishing success of Henry's horses – the trainer of a very large string places great reliance on his head man – and which came to an end only when Paddy moved to Dubai to set up as a trainer on his own account, in which he has been notably successful.

Like all the great trainers, Henry Cecil has a knack of knowing exactly what is right for every inmate of his yard. He is exceptionally patient, and would never ever fall into the trap of running a horse too quickly: he will always wait until the horse tells him it is ready (the 1993 Derby winner Commander In Chief, who did not run at all as a two-year-old, is a case in point), and whatever the pressures will never rush a horse. In many ways Henry lives on his nerves, but he has long been a brilliantly instinctive trainer who always puts the interests of his horses first.

Not surprisingly, given the number of horses in training there, I spent a great deal of time each week at Warren Place. Henry's habit was to take his horses out later than other trainers, with the first lot pulling out around 8 a.m., which meant that the yard did not stop for breakfast until about 9.30. (If he has to work a particularly good horse he tries to get out earlier, as it is crucial to take advantage of the decent ground early in the morning – especially at certain times of the year when many horses are working over the same gallop.)

Warren Place oozed class that spring of 1981, and I was looking forward to rich pickings.

By the time the season was a week old I had already notched up a treble at Leicester, but it was not to be expected that the best Cecil horses would start appearing until around the time of the Craven Meeting at Newmarket in mid-April. Our first winner under the new arrangement came with Belmont Bay, owned by Daniel Wildenstein, at Newbury on 11 April, and the following week a treble on the third day of the Craven Meeting included a genuine Classic prospect when Jim Joel's Fairy Footsteps took the Nell Gwyn Stakes.

Jim Joel, by then 86 years old, was one of the greatest owners of the century, his colours of black, scarlet cap a familiar sight both on the Flat and over jumps: by 1981 he had owned a Derby winner in the shape of the 1967 victor Royal Palace, and in 1987 would add the Grand National with Maori Venture. He had already won the One Thousand Guineas in 1944 with Picture Play, and in Fairy Footsteps, a compact, appealing filly by Mill Reef who had run away with her third race as a juvenile, he seemed to have a very live prospect of another success in the race.

Her main target for the season, however, was the Oaks – for which her breeding seemed to suggest she was more suited than the One Thousand Guineas – and Mr Joel was especially keen to land the Epsom fillies' race, as it was the one English Classic he had ever won, his West Side Story being beaten by the shortest of short heads in 1962.

But Fairy Footsteps was really burning up the Newmarket gallops in the spring of 1981, and her victory in the Nell Gwyn Stakes over seven furlongs indicated that she had a live chance in the One Thousand. As she continued to please us at home our confidence grew, but then something happened to her jockey.

In the week between the Craven Meeting and the Guineas meeting fell the three-day Epsom Spring Meeting, on the Thursday of which – exactly one week before the One Thousand Guineas – I was riding a five-year-old named Winsor Boy in a five-furlong sprint handicap. Everything was going perfectly normally as we went into the starting stalls, but just as we came under starter's orders a couple of the other runners started fiddling about, and the starter did not let us go instantly. Winsor Boy, keyed up and ready to explode out of the gate like most experienced sprinters are at the moment of starting, tried to jump off before the gates opened, panicked and went down on his knees, trying to wriggle out under the stall gates. I was down on his neck waiting for him to jump off and not prepared for this, and as he writhed his way out he dragged me with him.

My back was badly scraped against the bottom of the gate, and as my head was dragged under, my right ear was all but torn off: it was just held on by a thread at the base of the ear, and the medical staff quickly put a bandage on my head to hold it in place until they could get me to hospital. (Winsor Boy himself had sustained injuries which necessitated his immediate destruction.) Throughout all this I did not lose consciousness, but my back was hurting badly and the racecourse doctor had me put into a scoop stretcher so that I did not have to be lifted by hand. (The back protector which is now a mandatory part of a jockey's equipment would certainly have alleviated – even if not eliminated – my injuries.)

An ambulance took me to Roehampton Hospital, to where a top plastic surgeon, Patrick Whitfield, had been rapidly summoned, and after X-rays to confirm that the rest of me was in one piece, he started to operate: an hour and thirty-two stitches later his handiwork was complete, and by the time I came round, about midnight, my ear was beginning to heal.

Having been in London during that day and hearing the news from the Jockey Club doctor Michael Allen, Susan, who had rushed to the hospital with Charles S George, spent the night sleeping on two chairs pushed together next to my hospital bed.

The following day (when I missed three winners I'd been booked to ride – a painful experience in itself!) the hospital was thronging with journalists. Susan managed to persuade them that I was being kept in for another night so they might as well go away and come back in the morning; then after they had departed I was slipped out of a back door.

I still had every intention of riding Fairy Footsteps in the One Thousand Guineas. Although my ear was still very sore, a greater worry was my back, which continued to be so painful that I knew I had to get specialist treatment on it as soon as possible. On the way home from Roehampton to Newmarket I went into central London to see Johnny Johnston, a leading osteopath who had treated me in the past, and after an examination he told me that I'd pulled all the ligaments in my back. This news did not come as a complete surprise as I was as stiff as a board and could hardly bend at all, so in order for Johnny to get me back in working order I returned to him every day for the next few days, and gradually my back started to loosen up.

The One Thousand Guineas was on the Thursday, and early that week it was very much touch and go whether I would be ready or not. I decided I had to put my fitness to the test by riding at Ascot on the Wednesday, so booked three rides: Lady Be Mine was unplaced when odds-on favourite in the first and Rabdan – trained by Robert Armstrong – runner-up to Columnist in the Victoria Cup, but I was not feeling too good and gave up the third of my booked rides as I did not think I could do the horse justice – and, annoyingly, it won!

On Guineas morning I was still feeling pretty stiff, but after riding out first thing I decided I was well enough to go ahead – one factor in the decision being that Fairy Footsteps was a very easy filly to ride. With a special attachment fitted to my riding helmet (perforated for sound and ventilation) to protect my damaged right ear, I warmed up for the big race with two rides (one third, one unplaced) before Henry gave me the leg-up on Fairy Footsteps.

It was a high-class field. Despite obvious question marks over the fitness of her jockey, Fairy Footsteps was a hot favourite at 6–4, with the flying filly Marwell, trained by Michael Stoute and ridden by Walter Swinburn, second choice and Tolmi, ridden by Edward Hide, third in the market; among the outsiders on 50–1 was Paul Kelleway-trained Madam Gay, of whom I would be seeing more.

Since stamina would certainly be Fairy Footsteps's strong suit, and she had such a relaxed attitude towards her racing, I decided to try to make all the running and expose the stamina limitations of some of her main rivals – notably Marwell, who on breeding and style of racing was most unlikely to stay. So I took my filly into the lead on the far side of the track immediately after the start, kept her going at a reasonably brisk pace, and then gradually stepped up the speed as we approached the final quarter of a mile. With a furlong and a half to go they were lining up behind to take Fairy Footsteps on and I had to put her under pressure, but she responded magnificently when Tolmi looked like heading her, and stuck on up the hill to win by a neck, with Go Leasing another neck away third and Marwell just behind in fourth. It had been a great race, and had brought me my twenty-fourth Classic in England.

In the Two Thousand Guineas on the Saturday I rode Kind Of Hush, and finished way behind Greville Starkey on To-Agori-Mou, but the following race, the five-furlong Palace House Stakes, brought a worse outcome. Valeriga, a good sprinter trained by Luca Cumani, was a very difficult horse indeed who on more than one occasion had dropped his jockey in the paddock. This habit had led to his tending to be mounted on the racecourse itself, but before the Palace House Stakes the trainer decided that in view of my recent fall it would be safest if I did not mount Valeriga until we were down at the start. The day before the race he outlined this plan to the stewards, who refused to allow it. On the Saturday morning he asked again, but still they refused. Despite that reaction Luca decided that Valeriga was too volatile to take the risk, and I was driven to the start by car while the horse was led down. This display of defiance led to Luca and I being fined £400 each, and Valeriga – who despite his waywardness was a classy and genuine horse once under way in a race – could finish only fourth.

We all knew Fairy Footsteps to be a filly with guts, but perhaps her race in the Guineas took more out of her than we'd appreciated as next time out, stepped up in distance to ten and a half furlongs in the Musidora Stakes at York *en route* to her date at Epsom, she could finish only third behind Condessa and Madam Gay. For a while we still harboured hopes of getting her to the Oaks, but a piece of work about two weeks before the race convinced us that she was making no progress – indeed, she was going backwards – and she was retired to the paddocks.

The disappointment of being beaten in the Musidora Stakes on Fairy Footsteps was softened by the victory, in the Yorkshire Cup two days later, by probably the finest horse I ever rode for Henry Cecil: Ardross. He was as tough a performer as any horse I've ridden, a real workman who would just never give up, and a joy to partner.

By 1981 he was five years old, having been trained earlier in his career by Kevin Prendergast – son of Paddy – in Ireland. The previous year he had bolstered his eputation by running a close second to Le Moss in the three big Cup races – Ascot Gold Cup, Goodwood Cup and Doncaster Cup – beaten by three-quarters of a length at Ascot and a neck at both Doncaster and Goodwood. I had ridden him during the back end of that season when winning the Jockey Club Cup at Newmarket and running third behind Gold River in the Prix Royal-Oak (the French St Leger). That winter he was sold to Charles St George and sent to Henry Cecil, and with Le Moss (who had been trained by Henry) now retired, Ardross looked odds on to be at the top of the staying tree in 1981.

Despite possibly being in need of the race, he opened his campaign at York in brilliant style by beating Nicholas Bill three lengths, and was then primed for his attempt at emulating Le Moss by winning the stayers' triple crown at Ascot, Goodwood and Doncaster.

Meanwhile there were the summer Classics.

In the Derby I turned down offers to partner Robellino and Sheer Grit in order to ride Shotgun, owned and bred by Guy Reed, but knew that we had not much chance against Shergar, whom I had ridden on both his outings as a juvenile and who at three had won his two trial races in spectacular fashion. He now proceeded to annihilate his rivals in the Derby, winning by the record margin of ten lengths, with my mount Shotgun a respectable – if distant – fourth.

Three days later the absence of Fairy Footsteps from the Oaks did not hurt so much after I had won the race anyway on Blue Wind, owned by Mrs Bertram Firestone and trained in Ireland by Dermot Weld. This was Dermot's first English Classic, but – not for the first time in Classic history – the race was a trifle overshadowed by resentment that I had been brought in to replace the stable jockey, in this case Wally Swinburn, Walter's father. Had Wally kept the ride and won the Oaks, the Epsom Classics of 1981 would have gone to a father-and-son team, but the offer to ride Blue Wind – she had been beaten a short head in the Irish One

Thousand Guineas – was not one to pass up, and she won in sensational style: I kept her well back in the early stages as Leap Lively set a fast pace, then brought her quickly past her rivals into the lead with a quarter of a mile to go, and she went further and further clear to win by seven lengths from Madam Gay. In one newspaper she was described as leaving the rest of the runners straggling home in single file, like a field of exhausted four-mile steeplechasers.

My third fillies' Classic of the year was gained just eight days later when Epsom runner-up Madam Gay – still a maiden despite good form in top-class races – won the Prix de Diane (the French Oaks) for Paul Kelleway, the irrepressible Newmarket trainer who in his time as a jump jockey had won the Cheltenham Gold Cup on What A Myth. Not only did she slam her Chantilly rivals by four lengths, she beat the course record into the bargain.

Royal Ascot provided another bonanza, with five more winners to add to my tally at the greatest fixture of the Flat year. Just as Cheltenham is the pinnacle of the jump racing calendar, so Royal Ascot has a very particular buzz for the Flat fraternity, and throughout my riding life it was the one meeting which gave me a special thrill, and that extra surge of anticipation before every race.

Ardross won the Gold Cup in a facile manner, but the meeting had its sad side for the Warren Place contingent when our candidate for the Jersey Stakes, Age Quod Agis, never got to the race. On the Newmarket gallops the previous morning he had stumbled and thrown his work rider – ex-lightweight jockey Willie Snaith – before careering off around the Heath. He had calmed down and started to make his way back towards the stables when he collided with a car. The horse, though badly concussed, survived, but the driver of the car was tragically killed. (The working areas of the Heath are now fenced off to minimize the risk of such an accident happening again.)

One Royal Ascot incident which affected me indirectly, and very much to my advantage, was when Walter Swinburn got himself into hot water with the stewards over his riding of Centurius in the King Edward VII Stakes and found himself hammered with a suspension which would keep him off Shergar in the Irish Derby at The Curragh. Michael Stoute, Shergar's trainer, approached me, and I didn't have to ponder too long before accepting.

Shergar gave me my fifth victory in the premier Irish Classic, and I have hardly ever had a simpler ride: he so outclassed his opponents that he was literally never out of a canter to beat them. There is no doubting that during the summer of 1981 Shergar – who followed up his Irish Derby victory by winning the King George, reunited with Walter – was a great horse, one of the greatest we've seen during my career. He could finish only fourth in the St Leger, but he must have been going off by then.

One aspect of Shergar which inhabitants of Newmarket got to know well was that he could get very fresh, and in that mood would do his best to get loose on the gallops – often succeeding with frightening consequences. I remember one particular time when our lads found him walking – alone – down the road which runs by Warren Place. They brought him in, put him in a stable and – having recognized him from his distinctive large white blaze, as well as from the Stoute yard rug he was still wearing – phoned his home stable to report him safe and sound. The lad who came to collect him said that Shergar had got loose on the Limekilns and had been galloping all over the Heath.

The chance to ride Shergar as a three-year-old (albeit only once) was typical of a year in which my rides were full of quality, both for Henry and for outside stables – the latter category including such star turns as Shergar himself, Madam Gay, Blue Wind, Moorestyle and Two Thousand Guineas winner To-Agori-Mou, on whom I won the Queen Elizabeth II Stakes at Ascot in

September while his regular jockey Greville Starkey wa suspended.

Moorestyle had a year of mixed fortunes. On his firs outing at York he spread a plate – lost a shoe – befor the race, and had another buckle during it; on his nex outing he was outpaced by Marwell in the July Cup One morning between those two races Moorestyle wa: minding his own business out at exercise in Newmarke when he was suddenly cannoned straight into by Beldale Flutter – winner of the previous year's William Hil Futurity and at the time of the incident a leading Derby candidate – who was enjoying a riderless cavort around the Heath. Poor Moorestyle was left bruised and battered, but when he returned to the racecourse he won the Prix Maurice de Gheest at Deauville, walking all over the opposition and breaking the track record even though we were easing down at the line. He was then beaten when reverting to five furlongs in the William Hill Sprint Championship and ran a marvellous race to come second – beaten only half a length – to To-Agori-Mou in the Waterford Crystal Mile at Goodwood, but ended his career with three glorious victories in the Diadem Stakes at Ascot, the Challenge Stakes at Newmarket and the Prix de la Foret at Longchamp. In all I won thirteen races on him. What a horse he was!

As for Madam Gay, she provided me with a ride in the inaugural running of the Arlington Million at Arlington Park, in the suburbs of Chicago, and ran a wonderful race to finish third behind that legendary American gelding John Henry, who beat The Bart by a short head. Paul Kelleway was convinced that the heavy ground had been against his filly, even though she had been fitted with special plates, and a week later she was back in action at Longchamp in the Prix Vermeille, where she again finished third. Plans to run in the Arc were scrapped, but in any case my Arc ride was always going to be Ardross.

Having duly completed his cup treble at Goodwood and Doncaster with the greatest of ease, Ardross went to Longchamp in good form, and although we knew that he was basically a stayer, he had such a turn of foot that we were hopeful he would acquit himself well. He did, but not as well as I had expected, and in finishing fifth behind Gold River I was aware that I had made too much use of him, and should have dropped him right out. A year later our performance would improve.

Along with the quality came the quantity (including, in September, a five-timer – four for Henry – at Yarmouth), and for the first time in many years I was back with a real chance in the jockeys' championship. The bookmakers were mindful of the advantage enjoyed by any jockey who had at his disposal the fire-power of Henry Cecil's yard – Joe Mercer, after all, had won his one and only championship in 1979 when stable jockey at Warren Place – and had made me odds on for the title, but by the middle of the season I was locked into a fair old tussle with Willie Carson. Then, in the Yorkshire Oaks at York in August, Willie had a crashing fall when his filly Silken Knot broke a leg: Willie sustained a fractured skull, several fractured vertebrae and a broken wrist, and for him the season was over, which handed the jockeys' championship to me on a plate, though not in a way that I would have wished. All things considered, Willie came out of that horrific fall well, considering that the Jockey Club's medical officer Michael Allen stated that it was only his helmet, which had two large cracks in it, which saved his life.

The same could not be said of poor Joe Blanks, a young jockey who had not survived a fall at Brighton the previous month. Not long out of his apprenticeship and with thirty career wins to his name, Joe was the victim of one of race-riding's more serious occupational hazards when his horse clipped the heels of another runner, cannoning the jockey into the ground so suddenly that the rest of the runners were unable to avoid him. Since I started riding there have been massive advances in racecourse safety, but riding remains a very dangerous and potentially lethal business, as the death of Steve Wood at Lingfield Park in 1994 attested.

Apart from disappointment in the Arc, the final phase of the season saw many bright moments, including winning the Cumberland Lodge Stakes at Ascot on the enigmatic Critique, owned by Sourien Vanian; the Middle Park Stakes on 20-1 shot Cajun; and the Prix Royal-Oak on Ardross, who decisively turned the tables on Arc winner Gold River and raised hopes of an even better year in 1982.

At the end of the season I had ridden 179 winners, 65 ahead of Willie and enough to make me champion again after a gap of nine years. I was particularly pleased with my strike rate of winners to runners, which was a shade over 25 per cent – tribute, were any needed, to the part played in my great year by the training and placing skills of Henry Cecil.

First port of call that winter was Florida, where I twice rode Blue Wind, then in training in the USA: but somehow she seemed to have lost her spark. Several British jockeys were then planning to ride in Barbados, but the Bajan Jockey Club took it into their heads to ban us as we had ridden in South Africa during the sporting boycott.

I had been asked by Pat Buckley, who had won the Grand National for my father in 1963, to ride in Bahrain in March 1982 for the Sultan of Oman, for whom Pat was training at the time. Bahrain was staging the Gulf Championship, an annual contest between Oman, Saudi Arabia, Bahrain and Iraq which had been won by Saudi Arabia the previous two years.

The meeting was held in the evening at the Sakhir racecourse, a grass track (unusual for the Middle East) of about a mile and three furlongs round, and the programme was a mixture of Arab and Thoroughbred races. In the four races of the Gulf Championship, each country was represented by two runners. Several of the horses had been imported from England, being allotted Arab names on arrival, and I was delighted to find that the handsome grey filly I rode to win the main race of the day was none other than Snow, on whom I had won the Sun Chariot Stakes at Newmarket in 1980 when she was trained in Ireland by Kevin Prendergast.

Saudi Arabia again won the overall competition. We – by which I mean Oman! – were not far behind in second place.

Although the 1982 season saw me win my eleventh – and last – jockeys' title with 188 winners, 43 ahead of Willie Carson with 145, it cannot be said to have provided me with the quality of rides I had enjoyed in 1981. And for the first time in twenty years – since the suspension over Ione at Lincoln in 1962 – I did not have a Derby ride: Henry's main hope Simply Great having bruised a heel soon after winning the Dante Stakes at York, he had nothing good enough to run, and since none of my other plans worked out I spent Derby day as a television pundit on ITV, discussing the runners with Brough Scott as they went to post.

On a brighter note, the season brought a memorable occasion on the charity day at Ascot in September when Long John Scotch Whisky staged a match race between me and Willie Shoemaker, the great American jockey whose career total of nearly 9,000 winners is a world record.

Two horses had been provided for the race – Spanish Pool and Princes Gate – and I had to make the choice. I picked Spanish Pool as I thought he would be more suited by the likely fast ground, but unfortunately it rained the night before and the going came up softer than I'd expected. Despite starting odds-on favourite I just couldn't get past Willie, who won by one and a half lengths.

I'd met Willie often during my travels over the years, and was second to none in my admiration for this wonderful little jockey: he looked far too small to have the strength to ride like he did, but – as with Gordon Richards before him – simply had the knack of getting horses to run. And his way of riding a race was noticeably distinct from most other American jockeys: instead of going flat out from the gate, he would sit still and give his mount a chance to find its legs, which I'm sure was a considerable help to the horses.

A month later Willie was back in England again, this time to take part in the UK–US Jockeys' Challenge at Sandown Park. He was joined in the US team by Steve Cauthen, Eddie Delahoussaye and Cash Asmussen, while the home team consisted of myself, Willie Carson, Pat Eddery and Paul Cook. We enjoyed a wonderful pre-competition dinner in London, at which I found myself seated next to Britt Ekland, who had joined the ranks of racehorse owners with a yearling bought for her by our mutual friend Billy McDonald.

But above all 1982 means one horse.

Ardross started off in fine style by winning the Jockey Club Stakes at Newmarket over one and a half miles, sprinting away from Glint of Gold and Amyndas, before getting stuck into the big staying races. He had to work quite hard to win the Yorkshire Cup and then used success in the Henry II Stakes at Sandown Park as the stepping stone to his main early-season target, a second Ascot Gold Cup. In both those races he had given weight away all round, and there was no doubt that he was the best stayer in Europe, so his Gold Cup starting price of 5–1 on to beat just four opponents was scarcely surprising. Nor was the manner of his victory: he was simply in a different class, taking the lead inside the final quarter of a mile and sauntering home by three lengths from the French challengers Tipperary Fixer and El Badr, in the process breaking the track record on ground which was firmer than he ideally would have liked.

This was Henry's fourth successive Gold Cup, and my eleventh in all: it was twenty-five years since Henry's stepfather Cecil Boyd-Rochfort had provided me with my first, Zarathustra.

Ardross next went for the Princess of Wales's Stakes at the Newmarket July Meeting. Sent off odds-on favourite, he soon found himself ten lengths adrift of the Queen's good filly Height Of Fashion (later dam of Nashwan), who set such a blistering pace over the mile and a half trip that Ardross could not get to her. Plans were revised, and instead of aiming Ardross at the King George at Ascot, Henry decided to concentrate him on longer-distance races before bringing him back to a mile and a half for his main target, the Arc.

He regained the winning thread in the Geoffrey Freer Stakes at Newbury in August, in the process giving me my 4,000th winner in Britain. It was marvellous to reach such a landmark, a moment made all the more special for me by being achieved on such a great horse owned by my long-time friend Charles St George, and Newbury gave me a memento to mark the occasion.

The only other British jockey ever to pass 4,000 was of course Sir Gordon Richards, and though I knew I could never get to his career total of 4,870, I thought I'd better make the effort, and within half an hour was on 4,001 after winning on Michael Stoute's colt Balanchine (not to be confused with Godolphin Racing's 1994 Oaks winner).

Ardross next went for the Doncaster Cup, needing only to be pushed out to beat Heighlin, and then faced his final racecourse appearance in the Prix de l'Arc de Triomphe.

The atmosphere on Arc day was as usual buzzing, but Ardross, by then a six-year-old and a battle-hardened professional, took it all in his stride. Understandably, he found the early pace of the Arc a little hectic, and quite early on I had to keep niggling at him to maintain his place. But as lesser horses started to fall back under the pressure of the pace he came into his element, and once we reached the straight he set about pegging back those in front of him. Responding with the greatest courage to what could not be considered one of my more tender rides, he started to eat up the ground. A hundred yards out only Awaasif, April Run and Akiyda were still ahead of him: he passed one, passed another, and was in full pursuit of Akiyda when the post came just too soon.

Ardross was beaten a head, and would certainly have won in another twenty-five yards.

This time there were no 'Did he come too late?' recriminations as there had been with my rides on Park Top and Nijinsky. The way Ardross ran that Arc was the only way he could possibly win it, and in being beaten so narrowly he ran the race of his life.

One characteristic above all stuck out with Ardross: his determination. More than any horse I've ridden, I could feel Ardross trying: come the moment for his maximum effort, he would lower himself towards the ground, put his head down, and stretch out as if his life depended on it. No jockey could ask more of a horse.

He did not run again after the Arc but was syndicated to stand at stud. Predictably, his great quality of stamina did not find much favour with breeders and he was not sent the quality of mares which might have made him more of a success as a stallion – though his offspring include the 1995 Champion Hurdle winner Alderbrook.

Ardross, a great horse, died in 1994.

In the spring of 1983 Henry's Classic hopes gradually evaporated. His 1982 Royal Lodge Stakes and William Hill Futurity winner Dunbeath had been sold during the winter to Sheikh Mohammed – who with his brothers Maktoum Al Maktoum and Hamdan Al-Maktoum had by then become a major force in world racing – for the staggering sum of $10 million, but on his three-year-old debut Dunbeath was beaten in the Heathorn Stakes at Newmarket. Despite this he remained co-favourite for the Derby with Dick Hern's Gorytus, whose notorious flop in the previous year's Dewhurst Stakes had been forgiven to the extent that he still remained on course for Epsom.

Lord Howard de Walden's Diesis, who in the autumn of 1982 had won that Dewhurst as the second leg of a rare double in Newmarket's biggest two-year-old races, having landed the Middle Park Stakes two weeks earlier, ran in the Two Thousand Guineas, but with his leg problems just couldn't cope with the firm ground and finished eighth.

Then Dunbeath was a disappointing third in the Dante Stakes at York, trailing in nearly twelve lengths behind the winner Hot Touch, and I was left with nothing definite for Epsom.

Luca Cumani approached me about riding Tolomeo, but that colt, useful as he was, had never struck me as a mile-and-a-half horse, and while I was deliberating – and wondering whether Brough would want my help again! – I was asked by Geoff Wragg whether I would be interested in riding Teenoso. This handsome colt by Youth had been partnered by Steve Cauthen when winning the Lingfield Derby Trial easily from Shearwalk, but Steve was being claimed for the Derby by Robert Sangster – with whom he had a retainer – to ride Robert's colt The Noble Player. So when Geoff asked me to ride Teenoso, I readily agreed.

Geoff Wragg is the son of the legendary Harry Wragg, nicknamed 'The Head Waiter' on account of his favoured riding tactics during a career in the saddle which brought him three Derby winners, and was then followed by a long and distinguished training career: when Psidium landed the 1961 Derby, Harry became the only person to have ridden and trained Derby winners. He retired at the end of 1982 and Geoff, who had been his assistant for thirty years, took over the licence.

Teenoso had the right credentials for the Derby. His pedigree left little doubt that he would get the trip, his relaxed style of running was ideal for Epsom (which is no place for a tearaway), and as the big day approached I knew he was in good order: a week before the race I rode him work at Newmarket and he gave me a wonderful feel. Finally, the weather played into our hands.

It had been a very wet spring, with several meetings abandoned on account of waterlogging and many of those which did take place providing very heavy ground. The few days before the Derby were so wet that at one time there was even speculation over whether the race could be run at all, and overnight storms on the eve of the race – half an inch of rain fell on the course in one hour – made the going heavy for the first time in over fifty years.

There is rarely much give in the ground at Epsom, but the soft conditions that year suited Teenoso very well, and we took full advantage. I had him out of the gates smartly and he settled easily in about third, which is where he remained all the way down to Tattenham Corner. As we entered the straight we were sharing second place, just behind the leader Mitilini, but once straightened up for home there was no point in waiting around, so off we went. In heavy ground you need a horse of exceptional acceleration to peg back a front-runner with a decent lead, and since I had no doubts about Teenoso's stamina, and I had been well aware at Tattenham Corner that most of the others were flat to the boards, kicking on once in the straight was the only tactic to use. It worked like a dream. Only the Irish challenger Carlingford Castle, a first Derby ride for Mick Kinane, mounted any sort of challenge, but Teenoso kept going without the slightest faltering to win by three lengths and give me my ninth Derby victory. He may not have been my most famous Derby winner, but he certainly felt like my easiest.

Susan and I, Geoff and Trish Wragg and Teenoso's owner Eric Moller were all invited up to the Royal Box, where the Queen offered us tea and showed us a re-run of the race.

The immediate reaction to Teenoso's Derby victory was that he was among the lesser lights of my nine winners of the race, but by the end of his career in 1984 he had shown what a rattling good horse he was. His immediate target after Epsom was the Irish Derby at The Curragh, but on this occasion the firmer ground was not in his favour, and he could finish only third behind Shareef Dancer. In the Great Voltigeur Stakes at York, his preparatory outing before a tilt at the St

Leger, he came third and sustained a stress fracture to his off foreleg (possibly caused by the hard ground at The Curragh) which ruled him out for the rest of the season. But he returned as a four-year-old and considerably enhanced his reputation. After running third in the John Porter Stakes at Newbury and winning the Ormonde Stakes at Chester, Teenoso faced his first major target of the season, the Grand Prix de Saint-Cloud.

Beforehand he looked in great form and on very good terms with himself: he was itching to get on with the job, and at the end of the pre-race parade, just as we were turning to go down to the start, he threw his head up and delivered an almighty clout to my right eye. The cuts above and below the eye were treated on the spot but there was still blood everywhere – adding a splash of red to the brown and yellow Moller colours! Despite being in considerable discomfort I insisted on going through with the ride, and was pleased that I did, as Teenoso ran his heart out on ground firmer than was ideal for him, and responded to my every urging to win narrowly.

Teenoso's next race in 1984 was the King George VI and Queen Elizabeth Diamond Stakes, in which he faced rivals of outstanding quality, including the previous year's winner Time Charter, Eclipse Stakes winner Sadler's Wells, 1983 Oaks and St Leger winner Sun Princess and the Prix du Jockey-Club winner Darshaan; seven of Teenoso's twelve rivals that day had won Group One races.

He started third favourite and ran the race of his life, making most of the running and maintaining his gallop all the way up the straight as the others tried vainly to get to him. Sadler's Wells – now the most influential stallion in the world – made the most effective effort and inside the final furlong came to about a length of us, but Teenoso that day was a quite magnificent racehorse, and at the line his challenger had been repelled by two and a half lengths.

Geoff Wragg gave his opinion that Teenoso was thirty pounds heavier – and therefore much stronger – than he had been the year before, and after Ascot the colt was installed as favourite for the Arc. But a few days before the race he broke down, and on the Friday it was announced that he would not take part, indeed would not run again. He was retired, initially to the Highclere Stud to replace the 1979 Derby winner Troy, who had died in 1983 at the tragically early age of seven.

If my ninth Derby was the high point of 1983, another bright spot was the flying visit I paid to Jersey at the invitation of Bunty Roberts, whose husband, a highly successful owner–breeder, was sponsoring one of the races that day. The evening meeting took place at the pretty little racecourse Les Landes, perched on top of the cliffs: although a mile round, it's a sharp track with a left-handed bend just after the winning post which required careful steering, and riding there was quite an experience. The usual crowd was around 800, but almost three times that number turned up, and I was glad that I could repay their support with a couple of winners.

My low point that year was probably the notorious incident in which Vacarme was disqualified in the Richmond Stakes at Goodwood.

Owned by Daniel Wildenstein and trained by Henry Cecil, Vacarme was a neat chestnut colt by Lyphard whose easy win in his debut race at Ascot in June had suggested that he could become one of the season's top juveniles. The Richmond Stakes was his next outing, and he started hot favourite at 3–1 on. All was going predictably enough until about a furlong out, when, just as I was wanting to start my run, I found a wall of horses in front of me, so had to switch to the inside to make my challenge. In making the switch I brushed against Pacific King, ridden by Tony Ives, who at that stage was rapidly dropping back, but once Vacarme got clear he won in a canter. It had felt like a harmless enough nudge, and neither Tony Ives nor Pacific King's trainer Bill O'Gorman was minded to object, so I was taken aback to hear the announcement of a stewards' enquiry – the stewards' deliberations made more complicated by the fact that Graham Sexton on the third-placed Godstone was objecting to Steve Cauthen on the runner-up Creag-an-Sgor.

The result of the stewards' ruminations was not made known until after two more races had been run, and when it came it was quite a shock: Vacarme was disqualified and placed last, and for good measure Godstone was placed above Creag-an-Sgor – so the horse which originally finished third was now the winner! I was judged guilty of careless riding and stood down for five days.

I thought the decision disgraceful, as any interference which did take place between Vacarme and Pacific King was minimal: indeed, I had done everything possible to avoid interference as I went through the gap, and had the other two horses kept straight there would have been no problem anyway.

But my disappointment at the outcome was as nothing to the reaction of the Wildenstein family. They were inveterate bad losers, and now saw fit to lay all the blame at my door by lambasting me in the popular press, which I did not find very amusing.

Nor was I the only jockey in trouble with the Goodwood stewards that week. Willie Carson had a good lead over me in the title race at the time, and I thought my five days off might put paid to any chance I had: then Willie got eight days for careless riding, a sentence which he found hard to believe.

There was more sourness on the approach to the 1983 Prix de l'Arc de Triomphe.

I had been approached by the French trainer Patrick-Louis Biancone to ride Daniel Wildenstein's good filly All Along, and also by John Dunlop to ride Sheikh Mohammed's filly Awaasif, on whom I had won the Yorkshire Oaks the year before. This was a very difficult choice as there was little between the fillies on form, but after due deliberation I decided to go with Awaasif. The fact of the matter is that, although Awaasif had had a few problems during the year, I was always going to ride her in the Arc if she ran, and my talking to the All Along connections was a fall-back position should the Dunlop filly not make it.

But it seems that either my French or Patrick-Louis Biancone's English was not good enough when we were discussing the possibility of my riding All Along, as there was a mix-up. He was convinced that I had agreed to ride his filly, and when it was announced that I would be on board Awaasif an almighty row broke out, with Daniel Wildenstein declaring: 'Piggott will never ride for me again.' This would make matters a trifle awkward for Henry Cecil, who trained several horses for Wildenstein and employed me as the stable jockey, but the owner stated that he would 'make my own arrangements with Mr Cecil, for whom Piggott is stable jockey, and my other trainers'.

Daniel Wildenstein was not renowned for being the easiest of owners, and both Yves Saint-Martin and Pat Eddery had felt his wrath in the past – which in the case of his disapproval of Pat's riding of Buckskin in the 1978 Ascot Gold Cup led to the owner's horses, rather than the stable jockey, leaving Peter Walwyn's yard – but that was little comfort to me at the time, and the first indication that Wildenstein was as good as his word came when I was replaced by Joe Mercer on Vacarme in the Middle Park Stakes. As it turned out, the colt (who started odds-on favourite) had no answer to shock 50–1 winner Creag-an-Sgor, and finished third.

If that result caused me some satisfaction, the feeling did not last long, as in the Arc the following Sunday the worst possible result – from my point of view – duly came about: All Along, ridden by Walter Swinburn, came scything through the field to beat Sun Princess, while Awaasif, who found the going at Longchamp that day too hard, finished way back in thirteenth.

As if that was not bad enough, the partnership of All Along and Walter Swinburn moved on to North America to scoop three major prizes: the Rothmans International at Woodbine, in Toronto; the Turf Classic at Aqueduct, New York; and the Washington International at Laurel Park. My decision not to ride All Along in the Arc had proved an expensive one, and although Awaasif brought a little compensation when winning the Gran Premio del Jockey Club, Italy's richest race, by six lengths, I was unhappy yet again to have been cast as the villain by Wildenstein in a situation I considered caused by a genuine mix-up.

Naturally enough my being barred from the Wildenstein horses would make a difference to my status as stable jockey at Warren Place, though I still held that position at the start of the 1984 season – which for me came after a highly enjoyable winter tour to Singapore and California for the fourth annual International Jockeys Competition at Bay Meadows, on the outskirts of San Francisco. Daniel Wildenstein was sticking to his guns, and I learned from Henry that the position of stable jockey had been offered to Steve Cauthen – though he could not take over until the following season as he was still under contract to Robert Sangster. But there was plenty of ammunition for me at Warren Place besides the Wildenstein horses, and enough demand for my services from other trainers to keep me busy.

In the Two Thousand Guineas I rode Lord Howard de Walden's Keen, trained by Henry – finishing unplaced behind the brilliant winner El Gran Senor, trained by Vincent – but I was able to make my own arrangements for the Epsom Classics. A cosy win in the Sir Charles Clore Memorial Stakes at Newbury on Sir Robin McAlpine's Circus Plume, trained by John Dunlop, sorted out my Oaks ride. The Derby, however, was proving a problem until Guy Harwood phoned to offer me the ride on his good colt Alphabatim – winner of the Classic Trial at Sandown and the Derby Trial at Lingfield: Guy's stable jockey Greville Starkey had had a bad fall some weeks earlier, and there were still worries about his fitness. At the time Alphabatim was second favourite for Epsom behind El

Gran Senor, so this was an offer I was not inclined to refuse.

On the morning that I received the approach to ride Alphabatim, a Sunday newspaper reported an imminent split between Henry Cecil and myself. After the disputes with Daniel Wildenstein over Vacarme and All Along in 1983, you wouldn't have to be the greatest investigative journalist in the world to work out that the riding arrangements at Warren Place were a cause for concern, and certainly a parting of the ways between me and Henry was on the cards. But it was not something we wanted to confirm at that stage, and in any case the nerve-wracking period leading up to the Derby was hardly the right moment for such a distraction. So we agreed to keep quiet for the time being.

The 1984 Derby was the first to be allowed commercial sponsorship – by the battery company Ever Ready – and the added support gave it a first prize of £227,680. That sum never looked destined for the pocket of Alphabatim's owner Khalid Abdullah, but the race produced a sensational and controversial finish when Pat Eddery and El Gran Senor, who were cruising through the final furlong and looked stone-cold certainties to win, were worried out of the race by Secreto, ridden by Christy Roche and trained by Vincent O'Brien's son David. Secreto never ran again and El Gran Senor went on to land the Irish Derby, though he did not truly get a mile and a half. Vincent told me later that El Gran Senor was the best horse he ever trained (and it is not true that I went up to Vincent and Robert Sangster after the race and asked if they were missing me!).

In the Oaks three days later Circus Plume took up the running a furlong from home and outstayed Media Luna by a neck to give me my twenty-seventh English Classic victory and thus equal the record of Frank Buckle, whose twenty-seven were achieved between 1792 and 1827. I began to wonder whether I could get one more and set a new record, though I little imagined that I would do so quite so soon.

At Royal Ascot I was in the money in fourteen of the twenty-four races – riding in the 1990s I was lucky to get even four rides there! – and rode all Vincent's runners at the meeting (including Magic Mirror, winner of the Norfolk Stakes), as Pat Eddery was suspended.

Ten days after Teenoso had won the King George I had yet another illustration of the ups and downs of racing. I finished third on a horse named Royal Octave in a race at Yarmouth, and as we were cantering back towards the paddock gate he ducked out and got rid of me. Unfortunately my foot was caught in the stirrup – every jockey's nightmare – and I was dragged along the ground until luckily my foot came out of the boot. I was taken off to the local hospital, dazed but able to sit up, and X-rays showed that the only damage I had sustained was that a small chip of bone had come dislodged from my hip.

At first I didn't feel too bad, and left hospital that evening fully intending to ride again within the week. In the event recovery took much longer than I'd anticipated, and I had to spend three and a half weeks getting myself back into shape. Luckily it was a very hot summer, and I was able to spend hours in the swimming pool at home under the supervision of a therapist who put me through exercises to bring back the strength in my leg. I also borrowed an exercise bicycle, and after a great deal of hard work eventually felt able to resume race-riding. By the time I returned early in September – winning the Solario Stakes at Sandown Park on a lovely two-year-old chestnut filly by the name of Oh So Sharp – Steve Cauthen was over thirty winners ahead of me, and it looked like I could forget any idea of winning the title.

Oh So Sharp caused a fair amount of drama before the Solario Stakes, getting so agitated while being saddled that she tried to bolt from the saddling box, in the process losing both her hind shoes and cracking her head on the door frame. But she settled down once she got onto the track and proved her toughness by running out such a convincing winner that her owner Sheikh Mohammed was already entertaining notions about the following year's Classics.

There was one Classic still remaining in 1984, however, and a week before the St Leger I was still without a definite ride. One real possibility was Commanche Run, who was owned by my old friend the Singapore trainer Ivan Allan and on whom I scored a runaway victory in the Gordon Stakes at Goodwood. The problem was that he was trained by Luca Cumani, and Luca was of the opinion that his stable jockey, the American rider Darrel McHargue, should be in the plate for the St Leger: Darrel had been under suspension when I rode the horse at Goodwood, but partnered him to follow up in the March Stakes on the same course. As was his prerogative, Ivan Allan asked me if I'd be available, and, when I indicated that I would be, insisted that I ride.

An announcement to that effect was made on the Tuesday evening before the big race on the Saturday and caused the usual complaints about Piggott jocking off a fellow rider, but a worse problem suddenly loomed three days before the race when Commanche Run stumbled and injured his knees. Cold water was hosed onto the affected joints to prevent the knees swelling or becoming stiff, and this simple treatment seemed to do the trick.

Doncaster was seething with people, as it always is on St Leger day, and I had high hopes of breaking the Classic riding record. Commanche Run was sent off favourite at 7–4, with Steve Cauthen's mount Baynoun second choice at 5–2 and Alphabatim 7–1.

Commanche Run was a late-developing sort, very genuine with few doubts about his stamina, and the impression I had got from him at Goodwood was that he would keep quickening, rather than produce one burst of speed. So I kept him close up during the first half of the race, when the pace was less than fierce, and once we had got into the straight took him into the lead. About three furlongs out I upped the tempo a little more and from then on just kept Commanche Run up to his work as a succession of challengers tried in vain to get past him. The most serious challenge came from Steve Cauthen and Baynoun, who got to within about a neck inside the final furlong but, despite running on as gamely as my fellow in the lead, just could not get the better of us. At the line Commanche Run was still a neck to the good, after what had to be one of the most exciting races of my life.

It was certainly one of the most significant, breaking the Classic record with my twenty-eighth victory, thirty years after my first way back on Never Say Die. For once I let my elation show, and we were granted a wonderful reception by the crowd as we returned to the winner's enclosure. I was reported as commenting, 'I didn't realize they cared so much,' and certainly the warmth of the reception was a genuine surprise.

On a less exalted but no less enjoyable level was the Dickins Invitation Handicap run at Newmarket in early November, a race in which leading lady amateur riders competed against professional men – in this case myself, Willie Carson, Walter Swinburn, Steve Cauthen and Tony Ives. We professionals nearly ended up with egg on our faces when Jennie Goulding on Ace Of Spies took the initiative and went six lengths clear with three furlongs to go. For a few moments it looked as if she had slipped her field, but I went charging after her on Jamesmead – a grand horse trained by David Elsworth who would go on to win the valuable Tote Gold Trophy over hurdles – and we just got there on the line, winning by a neck.

At the end of the season Henry Cecil and I, as predicted, went our separate ways. Steve Cauthen took my place, and in his first season as Henry's stable jockey would win four Classics! My last big-race winner for Warren Place was Lanfranco in the William Hill Futurity at Doncaster – in some ways a fitting finale, as Lanfranco's owner Charles St George had been instrumental in my moving to Warren Place.

I was sad to be leaving that great old yard again, but reflected that my three best rides of 1984 – Teenoso, Circus Plume and Commanche Run – had all been for outside stables, so started thinking about life as a freelance yet again in 1985 with a fair measure of confidence.

That winter's travels took me to California to ride Alleging in the Hollywood Derby and to Tokyo to partner the globe-trotting Australian horse Strawberry Road in the Japan Cup. It was almost fifteen years since we had been in Japan, and much had changed: women, for example, hardly in evidence on our first trip in 1969, were now holding responsible positions in the Japan Racing Association. The care of the horses and the standard of riding had improved significantly, but in Tokyo the smog and traffic had become far worse.

On the day we had to leave Japan we were able, on our way to Narita airport, to slip in a visit to the famous Symboli Stud, owned by Tomohiro Wada. We spent a couple of hours there and were introduced to their newest stallion acquisition – my 1976 Derby winner Empery. Small world!

Susan flew straight home to Newmarket, while I went off for a ten-day stint in Hong Kong which coincided with a dreadful tragedy. My old friend and weighing-room colleague Brian Taylor, who had won the Derby on Snow Knight in 1974 and was within a few months of retiring, was riding a horse called Silver Star in a race at Sha Tin. Silver Star already had the unfortunate claim to fame of having curtailed the career of the French jockey Philippe Paquet when he had fallen during a training gallop the previous season, and this time he was the unwitting cause of something far worse. Brian had not been feeling well for a few days, but earlier in the afternoon had ridden a winner, which must have made him feel fit enough to partner Silver Star. As they approached the winning post the horse stumbled and fell – for no apparent reason – and Brian was cannoned straight over his head into the ground. He was rushed

o hospital but never regained consciousness and died
a few hours later. He was only forty-five.

When the 1985 season started I knew that it would be
my last. I would be fifty in November, was ready to
start training, and was aware that without a big stable
behind me, rides would be harder to come by.

My old chum Peter O'Sullevan knew – as he usually
did – which way the wind was blowing, and announced
my forthcoming retirement in his *Daily Express* column,
but I was myself writing a regular piece in the *Daily Star*
at the time, so had to deny Peter's scoop until I was in a
position to make my own announcement. I was amazed
at the effect of the story breaking: at the time I was
riding in California in Bay Meadows, and was besieged
by reporters demanding information, while my agent in
England, Mike Watt, had to get me to issue a statement
in order to get the home reporters off his back.

We took our friend Lottie Dickson on that California
trip, and after she had returned to England I joined
Susan in Malibu, where she was staying with an old
family friend. On the night I got to Malibu one of the
guests at dinner was none other than Larry Hagman, of
Dallas fame, with his wife Mai. Larry does not smoke
and dislikes being in the company of those who do, so
that evening I had to forgo my usual cigar. But we got
along extremely well: not only did I become a loyal
Dallas fan, but I always enjoyed meeting him when
our paths crossed subsequently.

From California we went to Australia, where we were
able to spend time with Tommy Smith and with Bart
Cummings, both legendary Australian trainers and both
old friends. Small, talkative and excitable, Tommy was
the complete opposite of the heavily built, brooding
Bart Cummings, but both had long been masters of
their craft.

At the local Yacht Club, from where Bart was taking us
sailing, a lady directed us towards his boat, then looked
at me, paused and asked: 'Aren't you George Piggins?'

– presumably rolling the name of Lester Piggott up with those of two famous Australian riders, George Moore and Roy Higgins. At first I didn't quite hear what she had said, so thought it simplest to reply: 'Yes.' (The oddest case of mistaken identity I've encountered was when a little West Indian girl selling ice-cream on the Finchley Road in London once asked me if I was Wilson Pickett! The famous blues singer had recently been killed in a plane crash.)

Other old friends we encountered in Australia included Ron Mason, who had been a successful trainer in England and for whom I had ridden such horses as Track Spare, Smartie and Sovereign Path. We also saw our future son-in-law William Haggas, out there learning the training trade from another star in the Sydney galaxy, Brian Mayfield Smith.

It was then on to New Zealand for our final visit to Ellerslie in Auckland before returning to Australia to break new ground by riding in Tasmania at Launceston, a beautiful old racecourse on the coast where an occupational hazard is the presence of seagulls, who settle on the track waiting for the horses to come round and then play 'chicken' as they approach: once a seagull mistimed its take-off, collided with a horse's face and ended up lodged between the jockey's legs!

Back in the saddle in Europe, 1985 was a year to concentrate on quality, and a new connection with the Chantilly trainer André Fabre – destined to become the new Napoleon of French racing – promised a great deal in that direction. After training jumpers for a while he was building up his Flat string, and was just beginning to get such good horses that I found myself wishing I was ten years younger, and not in the twilight of my riding career.

My quest for quality naturally enough concentrated my mind on the Classics, and shortly after returning from my winter travels I rode work on two of Ben Hanbury's more likely candidates for top honours, both owned by Ravi Tikkoo – Kala Dancer, winner of the previous year's Dewhurst Stakes, and Kashi Lagoon, who was being aimed at the One Thousand Guineas and Oaks. Both went well enough, but I carried on casting around.

One live Two Thousand Guineas possibility was Sheikh Mohammed's Bairn, trained by Luca Cumani, on whom I won the Greenham Stakes at Newbury in April: Kala Dancer had hurt himself and was not able to run. Bairn looked like being my Guineas horse – but then, as so often, fate yet again intervened. Michael Stoute's stable jockey Walter Swinburn found himself landed with a suspension which ruled him out of the Guineas, and Michael asked me to take his place on Sheikh Maktoum Al Maktoum's Shadeed, who had slammed Damister in the Craven Stakes in such style that he became hot favourite for the Two Thousand Guineas. Sheikh Maktoum squared the riding arrangements with his younger brother Sheikh Mohammed, and although Luca Cumani was unhappy about the arrangement he could do nothing about it. I was on Shadeed, and Willie Carson rode Bairn.

In the event it was a very close-run thing. Shadeed, a son of Nijinsky, was a very highly strung horse, and got himself so worked up beforehand that Michael Stoute advised me to take him down before the parade was over – thereby incurring the wrath of the stewards and landing himself with a £550 fine. (The trouble with parades is that they put the highly strung horse at a disadvantage with regard to the quieter ones. In my view they belong in the past. If racegoers want to see the horses at close quarters they can do so in the paddock. It's no business of jockeys or trainers to bring a horse to racing pitch and then expect it to amble along calmly when all its instincts are telling it to get on with the job.)

In the Guineas itself Shadeed settled well, and, running along the far rail, took the lead going into the Dip. Inside the final furlong we were subjected to a fierce challenge from Willie Carson and Bairn, but I'd kept a little up my sleeve and was able to hold on, the winning distance being a head.

Shadeed, reunited with Walter Swinburn, then ran in the Derby, but failed to stay and was beaten a long way out. In that race I rode Dermot Weld-trained Theatrical for Bertram Firestone, but none of us had any chance against the runaway winner Slip Anchor, ridden by Steve Cauthen for . . . Henry Cecil.

The Classic-winning quality was not confined to home shores, and I landed the Prix de Diane (French Oaks) on Lypharita, my first big winner for André Fabre: though unfashionably bred, she was a real tough nut, and stuck her nose out that day to win narrowly from the favourite Fitnah.

An enjoyable distraction from the big-race round that summer came on a damp and miserable evening in mid-May at Warwick, where 7,000 fans came to see a match race between myself and the best National Hunt jockey of the day, John Francome, who had recently retired from race-riding. The Walton Hall Duel of Champions was held during a Warwick jump meeting, and although my journey from Ireland, where I had been riding in the afternoon, was rather hairy on account of nobody turning up to check us for customs when we landed for that purpose in Coventry, the race itself went smoothly enough: my mount The Liquidator beat John on Shangoseer by three-quarters of a length. John immediately requested a rematch over hurdles!

What I thought at the time would be my final Royal Ascot produced three good winners: Bairn in the St James's Palace Stakes; the Marquess of Tavistock's grand old campaigner Jupiter Island in the Hardwicke Stakes; and that fine sprinter Never So Bold in the King's Stand Stakes. Another of Susan's purchases trained by her brother, Never So Bold was all but unbeatable in 1985, despite having a problem in one of his knees which caused him to hobble back to the unsaddling enclosure temporarily hopping lame.

The following week I had my first ride in the Swiss Derby at Zurich, and managed to finish second despite my horse Tacaro being rather slowly away and finding it difficult to make up ground on a very tight track. It was not a happy experience, and was made worse by my being paid in French francs rather than the Swiss francs I was expecting.

But apart from Shadeed, the highlight of what I thought was my final season in the saddle in Britain was my partnership with Commanche Run. On his reappearance in late May he won the Brigadier Gerard Stakes at Sandown Park by the vast margin of twelve lengths, was surprisingly beaten by Bob Back and the great filly Pebbles in the Prince of Wales's Stakes at Ascot, and then was withdrawn lame at the start before the Eclipse Stakes. His next outing was in the Benson and Hedges Gold Cup at York, where he was opposed by Oh So Sharp, who already in 1985 had won the One Thousand Guineas and Oaks and been narrowly beaten by Petoski in the King George. Oh So Sharp was hot favourite, but people should have known better than to underestimate Commanche Run. Luca Cumani wanted me to come from behind on the horse, yet I thought we'd have a better chance if I tried to make all – which is just what I did. Gradually picking up the pace up the long York straight, we soon had Oh So Sharp stretched to the limit, and try as she might she could not get by us. At the post we were three-quarters of a length to the good, but it could have been much more.

There was a million-dollar bonus for any horse which could win the Benson and Hedges, the Irish Champion Stakes and the Champion Stakes at Newmarket, and having notched up the first leg Commanche Run went for the second at Phoenix Park. He again made all, and had his rivals beaten a long way out. Sadly, the bonus was denied him – he ran disappointingly in the Champion Stakes behind the brilliant winner Pebbles – but Commanche Run was a wonderful horse, certainly among the best I'd ridden, and to have had such success for my old friend Ivan Allan was very satisfying.

But as the 1985 season drew to a close there were fewer and fewer horses left to be ridden. Back in the summer, after the formal announcement of my retirement had been made, I had been approached by the executive of Nottingham racecourse asking whether I could make their fixture on Tuesday 29 October my final riding day in Britain. Since there was little racing of note in this country after that I had agreed – and thereafter found myself putting my name to all sorts of memorabilia being prepared to mark my retirement that day.

Come the afternoon itself, I had no regrets or second thoughts about hanging up my saddle. A new career beckoned, one that I had been planning for a long time, and I was ready to make the transition. The difficult part had been finally making the decision; once that had been done the rest was straightforward.

There was a huge crowd at the track, and hundreds of people formed a queue to get their racecards signed. But what they really wanted from me, of course, was not just a signature but a winner. My first ride, Gold Derivative, was unplaced. My second, Full Choke, won by a length, giving the crowd the excuse to give me a wonderful reception. My third, Ice Breaker, was second, my fourth, Among The Stars, unplaced.

One more ride to go: Wind From The West for Patrick Haslam in the appropriately named Final Handicap. Wind From The West ran well, but not well enough to give the crowd the result they most of all wanted, and was beaten four lengths into second place.

My next ride in Britain would be nearly five years later.

12

Training and the taxman

The months leading up to my retirement from the saddle had seen a succession of farewell presentations from courses at which I had ridden around the world – the Ascot Authority, for example, and Phoenix Park in Dublin, whose beautiful glass bowl inscribed 'Lester: Happy Memories' was presented in September 1985 and is now a permanent fixture on the dining table at Florizel. There were even presentations from some of the authorities with which, over the decades, I had had my brushes – the Jockey Club, the Société d'Encouragement in France, and others – and my weighing-room colleagues gave me a Long Tom (hunting whip) mounted with a silver plaque inscribed: 'Lester Piggott on retirement from his fellow jockeys'.

The presentations continued that October afternoon at Nottingham, but the British finale was by no means the end of the matter, as there were other places where I had to say my goodbyes.

My last winner in Europe was Old Country, trained by Luca Cumani, in the Premio Roma in Rome on 10 November. On Sonny Barich at Bay Meadows in January 1986 I bade farewell to the US racing scene, and my last winner (as I then thought) was Longest March – appropriate name – in Penang, Malaysia, on 22 February.

The last port of call on a farewell tour which took me to France, Italy, the USA, Germany, Malaysia, Australia and Hong Kong was Sha Tin on 1 March. It was a wet and dull afternoon, and my final ride was in what was known as a Griffin race, in which horses who had not run at the track before were given experience. My horse Consistent Rise did not feel right going to the start, and having reached the stalls had to be withdrawn.

It was a downbeat ending, but in any case it was time to get back to England and begin my new way of life.

Having known for so long that training would be the natural successor to my riding career, I had been quietly picking up hints and ways of doing things from the various great trainers for whom I had been riding over the years. Everybody trains horses a little differently from everybody else, but I knew that any clues I had gleaned from having ridden for the likes of Noel Murless, Vincent O'Brien, Jeremy Tree, Henry Cecil and François Boutin would stand me in good stead.

By the time I returned home, the yard was in full swing. We had rented out Eve Lodge to various trainers over the years – most recently to my ex-chauffeur Mick Hinchcliffe, who had moved out in 1984. Mick's head man had been Joe Oliver, who lived in one of the yard's bungalows and agreed to continue as head man for me. An Ulsterman in his early forties, Joe had been in racing since leaving home at the age of thirteen: he had ridden as an apprentice for a few years until increasing weight forced him to hang up his boots, and had then worked for several top trainers (including Noel Murless, Paddy Prendergast and Mick Easterby) before joining us from Robert Williams's yard, where he had been travelling head lad. Still a capable work rider, and with a deeply grounded all-round knowledge of looking after horses both at home and at the racecourse, Joe was everything a trainer could want in a head man.

The previous year I had taken time off from race-riding in July to go with Susan to the yearling sales at Keeneland, and the following month we attended the sales at Deauville while I was riding at the meeting: although we did not make any purchases there, we had several promises of horses to train, and the important thing was to be seen about the sales looking as if we meant business! Susan went back to Kentucky in

September, this time buying the first horse for Eve Lodge, and through the autumn the yard had gradually filled up.

Although we had hopes of plenty of yearlings, we needed older horses as well, and at the one-day Tattersalls sale at Newmarket in September 1985 Tracy and I had been taken by a three-year-old gelding named Vague Melody, which we bought for 15,000 guineas: formerly trained by Toby Balding, he had been owned by the guitarist Eric Clapton.

By the spring of 1986 the yard was up and running, with seventy-four horses in residence, of which sixty-three were two-year-olds. Sheikh Mohammed sent us four three-year-olds from the stable of his private trainer John Ciechanowski, which was a great boost. The most expensive youngster was the Master Willie colt Deputy Governor (owned by Prince Ahmed Salman) who had been bought for 120,000 guineas at the previous year's Highflyer Yearling Sales at Newmarket, but all in all we had a nice balanced team, with good owners, and although the news that I was being investigated by the tax authorities was a dark cloud on the horizon, on the training front everything seemed set fair as we sent out our first three runners on Easter Monday, to come home with a second and two thirds.

With Susan enjoying her role as assistant trainer, I rode as many of the horses in their gallops as was practical, supported by our lightweight jockey Bryn Crossley, with Tony Ives coming in to ride work two mornings a week.

Towards the end of April 1986 my own retirement from the saddle nearly came to a temporary halt when Vincent O'Brien phoned: Pat Eddery had incurred a suspension and would be unable to ride Tate Gallery in the Two Thousand Guineas, so would I consider taking over? I was only too pleased to help Vincent out, and went across to Ballydoyle to give Tate Gallery a gallop. He went very well, and I agreed to ride him in the Guineas. When this news was reported in the press my phone instantly became red hot with indignant calls from people who had produced 'Lester Piggott Retirement' memorabilia the previous autumn. They threatened all sorts of dire consequences if I broke those contracts by returning to the saddle, so I had to drop the idea.

Tony Ives rode Tate Gallery in the Two Thousand Guineas, and they finished last behind Dancing Brave.

But Tony had a happier experience when bringing home my first winner as a trainer, Sheikh Mohammed's Geordie's Delight in the Banstead Maiden Stakes at Epsom on 23 April 1986. It was good to get that first one under our belt, but the highlight of the summer came in June at Royal Ascot, when Cutting Blade, a Sharpo colt owned by Mahmoud Fustok and ridden by Cash Asmussen, won the Coventry Stakes in a finish of two short heads. The first three were so close as they passed the post that I genuinely did not know whether we'd won or not, but Sheikh Mohammed, in whose box I was watching the race, had no doubts: 'You've won – come on, you've got to lead him in!' He was right.

I've always had the greatest affection for the Royal meeting, and fully approve of its traditions – I have to say that in 1986 I looked much more dapper in my morning suit than I ever did in riding silks! – so to have trained a winner with my first ever runner there was a real thrill.

The following month the stable landed its first treble, at Ostend, and hopes for the future were kindled when a very nice filly named Lady Bentley won the Chesterton Maiden Stakes at Newmarket at 33–1 on her racecourse debut in October: that year Newmarket's autumn fixtures were held on the July Course, as the Rowley Mile stands were being developed.

At the end of the season I was well satisfied with our total of thirty winners at home plus the three at Ostend. We'd had a few near misses in good races, and there was plenty to which to look forward.

Then that cloud on the horizon darkened.

The first warning signal had come in February 1985. I was sitting in a hotel on Manley Beach in Sydney when *The People* newspaper from London phoned to alert me to the fact that they were publishing a letter concerning myself and Henry Cecil which had been sent to them by a man named Melvyn Walters, who had long been on the fringe of the racing world and was a former owner at Warren Place.

Walters had had a disagreement with Henry following a mix-up concerning the sale of a yearling which belonged to the bloodstock company Alchemy, of which Walters was a director. Back in September 1983, Alchemy had sent to the Highflyer Sales at Newmarket a Riverman colt who had been prepared by Henry's brother David. The trade was very strong at the time and the colt fetched a final bid of 430,000 guineas – only for the purchaser to disappear. Tattersalls approached the underbidder about buying the colt but he declined, reportedly suspecting that he had been 'run up' in the sale. So there was no alternative but to resubmit the colt: two days later he entered the ring again, but this time realized only 200,000 guineas. Alchemy decided that Tattersalls had been negligent in the way they sold the colt, and proposed to sue the auctioneers for the 230,000 guineas shortfall between the original selling price and the later price.

Months later, when Alchemy were trying to resolve this difficult situation, Walters tried to enlist Henry's help. Henry wanted nothing to do with the matter, thereby incurring Walters' wrath to such an extent that the disgruntled owner decided to blow the whistle by publishing the letter which he, along with Henry's other owners, had been sent at the start of the 1982 season.

The letter contained details about the retainer between Henry and me, and asked each owner for a proportion of the money we had agreed I should receive above the amount formally declared to Weatherbys under the Rules of Racing. A separate note suggested that the bearer should destroy the letter, but Walters had not done so, and now, in his pique, was hawking it around Fleet Street in order to hit back at Henry. The newspapers refused to touch it – all except *The People*, whose publication of the document encouraged the tax authorities to take a close look at how racing's finances operated, and the can of worms was opened.

I had been investigated by the taxman twice before – in the early 1970s and early 1980s – and on both occasions had come to a settlement. This time the first to move in were officers not of the Inland Revenue but of Customs and Excise, investigating VAT irregularities.

Early one morning in January 1986 I was in London, having attended a dinner the night before, when Susan phoned to say that three men and a woman had arrived at the house unannounced: could I get back as soon as possible? What I was not aware of as I tore back to Newmarket was that Customs and Excise were making simultaneous dawn raids on a number of people in racing, and having reached home I spent most of the day answering questions, mainly about the stallion shares I had acquired – though they obviously knew the answers already as they had been through the books of several well-known owners.

The issue of jockeys receiving shares in the stallion careers of horses they had ridden to big-race victories grew up in the 1980s as bloodstock values went through the roof. Individual arrangements varied from owner to owner, and usually applied only to an owner for whom a jockey was riding regularly, but a typical arrangement would be that if you won a Classic or other Group One race on a colt, you would get an annual nomination to that horse (which you could use or sell on) once it had become a stallion. So when bloodstock values went berserk, the paper values of such transactions became huge – and the jockeys in question ended up paying tax on inflated stallion values.

Before they left Florizel, the Customs and Excise team searched the house, in the process finding a couple of old guns that had lain in a drawer for a number of years and which – as my rapidly diminishing luck would have it – were not licensed. I was subsequently fined £1,000 for that omission. When the C&E people left, they took with them all my accounts books, along with various old letters and documents which they considered might be relevant.

Things did not look good, but I tried to get my head down and concentrate on the start of my training career.

Matters next came to a head in December 1986. On the Friday before Christmas there was a knock on the door – not carol singers but three policemen with a warrant for my arrest. They took me off to Newmarket police station, where I was joined by my solicitor Jeremy Richardson, who spent the rest of the day trying to raise the bail – no less than £1 million – which had been set. The last working day before Christmas is not the ideal time to be sorting out that amount of security, but Jeremy worked away tirelessly, and eventually the police agreed to settle for the deeds to my property, plus hefty sums put up by Henry Cecil and Charles St George. At such times you find out who your true friends are.

Christmas that year was not a particularly joyous one.

In the New Year Jeremy applied successfully for the bail to be reduced by 50 per cent, for my reporting period to be extended from once every two weeks to once a month, and for my confiscated passport to be returned. The High Court granted these requests, which was a particular relief in the case of the passport, as I was hankering to leave the whole mess behind, if only temporarily.

We had a few runners at Cagnes-sur-Mer, and notched up three wins and six places, before Susan and I, along with Cormac McCormack, went to Singapore for a few days to visit one of our main owners, Danny Jananto: he wanted to discuss the progress of his horses, and this short break in the sun, well away from the February gloom of Newmarket, proved highly beneficial. The trip home was broken in Dubai, where several of my owners (notably, of course, Sheikh Mohammed) lived.

Our first winner of the 1987 season was again Geordie's Delight, but the two best prospects we had in the yard were Genghiz and Deputy Governor. Genghiz was a chestnut colt by Sir Ivor of whom we had very high hopes, but these were somewhat dented when he ran so badly in the Craven Stakes that we had to forget about the Two Thousand Guineas. Instead he went for the Newmarket Stakes, which he won, but we felt that a mile was his ideal distance and so shelved earlier plans to run him in the Derby.

Deputy Governor, on the other hand, ran second to Risk Me in the Greenham Stakes, a good fifth to Don't Forget Me in the Two Thousand Guineas, second to Lauries Warrior in the Diomed Stakes at Epsom and third to Midyan in the Jersey Stakes at Royal Ascot, and was then sent off to race in the USA, where he continued to do well before going to stud in New Zealand. Genghiz went to stud in Australia, where sadly he died.

Lady Bentley, who had been so promising on her only outing as a juvenile, brought us our first Classic victory when landing the Italian Oaks in Milan in May, a week after Our Eliaso and Brother Patrick had finished third and fourth in the Italian Derby in Rome. The following month Sunset Boulevard won the Grand Prix de Bruxelles at Groenendael in Belgium.

My own troubles were not the only distraction from training. I was very saddened by the death in 1987 of Noel Murless. He had always had a bad chest – not helped by heavy smoking, cigarettes at home and a pipe while riding out – and passed away peacefully in his sleep. He had played such a large part in my life, and after his retirement I often used to go and visit him at his bungalow, just outside Newmarket at Woodditton.

Our stable apprentice was Philip Barnard, who had come to us from Mick Ryan, with whom he had spent three years. He was a very promising young jockey, but his frame was on the large side and his weight started to go up, not helped by being out of action for a while after a fall at Folkestone. Eventually he left us to try his hand at the jumping game; tragically, he was killed in a fall at Wincanton on Boxing Day 1991. (Another of our apprentices who went on to make a name for himself over jumps was David Bridgwater, who was at Eve Lodge at the same time.)

Throughout 1987 I had been attending meetings with lawyers and accountants as we tried to make sense of the mess I had allowed my finances to become. I was spending so much time away from the horses that I found the whole process extremely wearing, and in a way it was a relief when the date for the trial was set: 23 October, at Ipswich Crown Court.

The case – most of it tedious for me, since I had heard all the details over and over *ad nauseam* during court appearances earlier in the year – lasted almost all day. There were ten charges, one relating to VAT and the other nine regarding failure to make complete disclosure of my income to the Inland Revenue.

All the advice I had received made it clear that the sensible course was to plead guilty, and I did so; and, although my defence put up a sturdy case in mitigation, I had a pretty good idea that a jail sentence would be the upshot. I none the less felt gutted when the judge pronounced the sentence – three years – and my next reaction was that I just had to get on with it. The only consolation – if it could be called a consolation – was that I was aware that a three-year sentence could mean only one year locked away, assuming I might get parole after a year and formal release a further year after that.

I was taken down to the cells, where Susan, who had been in the courtroom all day, was allowed to have a few words with me before I was taken away, handcuffed to another prisoner, and put on the prison bus for the trip to Norwich, where I would spend my first night behind bars. Hordes of pressmen pursued the bus, and this was one time when I really could have done without them

– though I was amused to see one show some initiative by hijacking a child's bicycle and pedalling as fast as his legs would let him to get one final photo of me.

I spent that first night in prison in a cell by myself. It was cold and I felt very alone, my thoughts simply of the year ahead of me that held no promise, just a massive waste of time with absolutely nothing constructive to show for it at the end. I managed a decent night's sleep, then the following day was moved into a dormitory in the hospital wing with about twenty other prisoners, which I found much more congenial than being locked away on my own.

Shortly afterwards I was transferred to Highpoint, a prison near Haverhill, about ten miles from Newmarket, where for the first two months I shared a room on the ground floor with one other prisoner.

Naturally it was immensely difficult adjusting to time in prison after such an active and outdoor life beforehand, but I was hugely cheered by the messages of support I received, both from friends and from thousands of complete strangers, whose cards and letters had my postbag brimming for the first few weeks of my imprisonment. Brough Scott kindly arranged for me to be sent the *Racing Post* every day, which kept me closely in touch with the sport.

I was given duties in the storeroom along with other odd jobs such as loading and unloading lorries, and during periods off prisoners could use the gym to keep fit by playing badminton and other games. The rest of my time I spent reading.

In January 1988 I was moved to the more open part of Highpoint, where the regime was much more relaxed and gave me the feeling that if I had to be in this situation at all, this was as good a place as any. My room, which I shared with three others, was on the first floor overlooking fields, and although we still had our jobs to do during the day, we were allowed a great deal more freedom than in the other part of the prison: I spent much of my time walking and playing cricket or golf. Every now and again there would be a change of room-mates as one was released and another came in to take his place, and there was one in particular who had a passion for racing and with whom I spent hours perusing the *Racing Post*. On the whole I found the other prisoners – most of whom seemed to be there on account of some involvement in the drugs business – easy enough to mix with, but my greatest problem was with the press: they would offer my fellow inmates money and a camera with which to get a photograph of me inside, and once I realized that this was happening it put me on my guard, making it very difficult for me to relax in the presence of others.

The day would start with breakfast at eight-thirty, followed by work, with a break for lunch, until four in the afternoon. The only change to this routine was for visitors: once every three weeks, and no more than three per visit. The prospect of visitors gave me something to look forward to, but we prisoners were always brought back to earth with a bump when being searched after each visit.

One of my major problems while inside was the food. I had eaten frugally but well all my life, and now suddenly found myself faced with sloppy and stodgy food designed to fill you up. Meals were prepared by the prison chef, ably assisted by several inmates – a duty I was pleased to have missed!

The time dragged on and on. Kahyasi and Ray Cochrane won the Derby, and the racing world seemed to be getting on fine without me. Five days after the Derby came the news that the OBE I had been awarded in the 1975 New Year's Honours List was being stripped from me. Why an honour which had been awarded for my services to horse racing should have been removed on account of my misdemeanours in a different area altogether was beyond me, and I felt saddened at the pettiness. I know now that I wouldn't take it back if they came and offered it to me!

That slight sank into insignificance with a family crisis in August. Susan, who had been granted a licence to train from Eve Lodge immediately after I had been convicted, was out on the gallops riding a horse named Versailles Road – who, incidentally, was responsible for Frankie Dettori losing his three-pound apprentices' allowance. They were nearing the end of their canter when Versailles Road slipped up and fell on top of Susan, leaving her with a broken collarbone, ten broken ribs and head injuries so severe that they put her in a coma.

The press, ever alert to a juicy story even in the midst of a domestic catastrophe, had staked out Addenbrooke's Hospital in Cambridge, where Susan had been taken, and the only way I could pay a visit – once it had been decided that I should be allowed to make the trip from Highpoint – was to go there a few days after the accident late at night in the hope that the press would have lost interest. They hadn't: as I was being taken up the hospital corridor to where Susan was lying in intensive care, they were still there, cameras at the ready, waiting for me to appear so they could get their story and pictures.

Susan was in an oxygen tent and clearly in a very bad way, but the doctors assured me that they were hopeful of a full recovery, so I left in better spirits than I had arrived.

When the news about Susan's fall got out, two 'facts' were spread around which reflected the standards of accuracy of some journalism and by which Susan, once she was fit enough, was highly incensed – that the horse from which she fell was her faithful Appaloosa pony Peppy Snowman, which it was not (the horse was the racehorse Versailles Road); and that the helmet she had been wearing at the time was dented from a previous fall, which it was not. Even now, you debate these points with Susan at your peril!

My daughter Maureen was granted a temporary licence to train. She had been helping Susan closely over the period I had been in prison and took up the reins with great determination and efficiency during what was a very stressful time for her. She sent out six winners before the end of the 1988 season, the first being Cielamour – owned by our most loyal owner, Henryk de Kwiatkowski – at Yarmouth on 15 September. I wanted to give her as much support as I could, and used my weekly allocation of £2.50 to buy phonecards so that I could telephone her each evening. Between them, Joe Oliver – as head lad, long used to being one of the unsung heroes of racing – and Maureen kept the show on the road.

Susan made a gradual recovery, and a month after her accident was back home. Her delivery from death's door – no-one in the hospital had disguised how close she had come to being killed – was taken as an omen of better days to come, and as the date for my release on parole came ever nearer I was beginning to feel that I would soon be home, with the nightmare of trial and prison behind me.

There were other good signs, too. Tracy, by then working for Tommy Stack in Ireland, rode her first winner in a ladies' race at Leopardstown – to date her one and only ride in public. About a month before my release I was allowed the four-day home visit which all prisoners are granted to readjust to outside life, and then, on 24 October 1988, a year and a day after my trial and conviction, it was all over. I emerged from Highpoint to find Maureen waiting to drive me home and rebuild my life.

Many people who didn't know me well enough were of the opinion that I would find it difficult – if not impossible – to cope with prison life, but I felt I had managed pretty well. Mindful that all I wanted to do was get out of there, I kept my nose clean and stayed out of trouble. Before I was convicted, somebody told me that going to prison would be like going back to school, with all the restrictions and discipline. In the event it was not that bad.

The hardest part of the whole experience is that it was simply – as I knew when I heard the judge's sentence it would be – a waste of time.

13

The comeback

My strongest feeling on being released from prison was the obvious one – sheer relief, and relishing the freedom simply to be able to wander around the yard and ride out again. It was only then that I realized how acutely I had missed the horses themselves. Never before in my whole life had I been forced to spend more than a few days away from horses, and to be forcibly removed from them was a severe deprivation.

That winter we had a holiday in Africa, and on our return I started to bring some sort of normality back to everyday life by fitting myself into the routine of the yard.

During 1989 we had about thirty horses at Eve Lodge. I would ride out regularly, and when not doing so would be up at about 6.30 a.m. to help around the yard and go and watch each lot work on the Heath, finishing mid-morning after the second lot had returned. In addition to the horses themselves there was the never-ending round of paperwork – entries and so on – which is a necessary chore of any trainer's life.

Susan – who had by now made a full recovery from her fall – still held the licence and was clearly enjoying herself, so I was content to help out in any area where I could be useful. My problems with the Inland Revenue were not finally sorted out until late in 1989, and I knew that I could not apply for my own licence back until they were well and truly behind me.

This was a period of readjustment after the difficulties of the previous two years, but one occasion when all those troubles were forgotten came in March when

Maureen married William Haggas. William was by then training a string of some fifty horses from Somerville Lodge in Newmarket, and the wedding took place at the church in Exning: the proud father leading his daughter up the aisle was more nervous that day than before any Derby or Arc!

At this time thoughts of a return to the saddle were far from my mind, and had I had any such notion it would have been dented one spring morning when, as I went to shorten my leathers while riding out, I felt something go in my right thumb – the same thumb which had been damaged in a starting stalls accident at Lingfield some years before and had never been quite as strong since. It appeared that I had snapped the tendon, and although it was not painful I was quite unable to flex my thumb at all. I decided to keep on riding out each morning in the hope that the problem would go away of its own accord, but when by June it had still not healed I decided to consult a specialist in Cambridge. After an operation I was advised not to ride again for two months, but the specialist did not warn me quite how painful the thumb would now be! I spent the next couple of weeks with my hand stuck up in the air at the angle at which it throbbed least.

I started riding again in September, but with few horses in the yard and no immediate prospect of being able to build up our establishment, I was becoming rather bored with life. Then, towards the end of the year, two conversations took place which set in motion a chain of events which were to bring about a momentous change.

The first came at the December Sales at Newmarket. I was chatting to Alan Lillingston, the owner of a successful stud in Limerick whom I had known for many years – ever since he was a pupil of that great trainer of jumpers Fulke Walwyn. (Alan was no mean jump jockey himself, winning the Champion Hurdle on the one-eyed Winning Fair in 1963.) He was looking for veteran jockeys to ride in a race to be run at The

Curragh the following July as part of the celebrations commemorating two hundred years of the Turf Club (the Irish equivalent of the Jockey Club): would I be interested?

I had not gone short of similar offers in the years since I had retired at Nottingham, but had always declined. This time, however, I felt keen to participate, as Alan explained that the idea was to bring together veteran jockeys from all over Europe, and that he would make sure the horses in the race were of a decent quality (which was not always the case in such events).

The next invitation gave rather shorter notice.

A few days after my talk with Alan Lillingston, I was having a chat with Charles St George over a cup a coffee at his house in Newmarket when he mentioned that a friend of his who owned racehorses in Peru had invited Walter Swinburn to go to Lima to ride at a meeting there in ten days' time. After initially accepting, Walter was now having to withdraw, and Charles had been asked to try to find a replacement. Half jokingly, I volunteered – 'I'll go!' – and to my horror found that I'd landed my first ride for nearly four years!

Horror soon gave way to excitement about making the trip, coupled with satisfaction that I would have something – however temporary – on which to concentrate my energies, and it was with a sense of anticipation which I had not experienced for years that I fished out my riding bag and started to check over my saddles and girths.

My own fitness was not too much of a problem. I had been riding out for most of the year and felt in good trim, and although the acid test is actually riding in a race – which is a great deal more physically demanding than many riders in the stands appreciate – I was confident of being able to acquit myself well enough in any race at a distance up to a mile. After that I would be going into unknown territory.

Nor was there much of a problem with my weight. By the time I came out of Highpoint I had ballooned to a gross 9 stone 7 pounds, but once I was back at home and able to monitor my diet more strictly I soon had matters under control. For the first couple of months I had eaten plenty of good food, then after Christmas started to consume less and less, and without too much difficulty was able to get down to the weight I had been before my time in prison.

It was all systems go for Peru.

Charles St George's enquiries had confirmed that I would have no problems getting a licence to ride once I had arrived over there, but there was real difficulty on the travel front. We discovered that Lufthansa ran a direct flight from Frankfurt to Lima and I was booked on that, along with Charles's son (and my godson) David. But fog delayed the Heathrow to Frankfurt leg of the journey, and on our arrival in Frankfurt we had to race through the terminal to the Lima plane – only to discover that the flight had closed and they would not let us on! This hiccough entailed a journey via Paris, Caracas and Bogota – a trip which took over twenty hours, and proved a rather exhausting start to my new career.

The racecourse at Monterrico, which featured both turf and sand tracks, had superb stands and facilities and the horses themselves showed a great deal of quality, but the tack used on them left much to be desired, with saddles and bridles apparently held together by bits of string. My substitution for Walter Swinburn had occurred so late in the day that word had hardly filtered through to the course before I got there, which suited me well enough as the whole affair was rather low-key: too low-key in one way, as several of the local owners and trainers turned out to be apprehensive about giving rides to someone who had not competed in a race for so long. I ended up with just three mounts, none of which managed to win.

There was no huge interest in my excursion in the British press as information from Peru seemed to take its time to reach the outside world, but one wonderful piece of news which came the other way was that I had become a grandfather: Maureen had produced a bouncing healthy baby girl who was christened Mary-Anne after the wife of my brother-in-law Robert, who had tragically died of cancer in her late forties not long before.

On the trip back – which mercifully was much more straightforward than the journey out – I was able to reflect on how it felt to be back in the saddle again. I had not managed to ride a winner, but I had hugely enjoyed that feeling of getting the adrenalin flowing. Not that I harboured any thoughts taking the race-riding further – or at least, not any further than the veterans' race at The Curragh, still many months away; for one thing, I was bothered that my damaged thumb had not stood up to the rigours of race-riding as well as I had thought it would, and in the Peru races I was able to make only limited use of it. There was no point in even contemplating a return unless my body was in proper working order.

By July 1990 my hand had greatly improved, so I resolved to keep my commitment to Alan Lillingston, and when it was announced that I would be riding in the veterans' race I was contacted by the executive at Tipperary to ask whether I could take part in a similar event two days before the Curragh race. I agreed, and before I knew it found myself lining up at the mile-and-a-half start against just four other riders: Captain Donald Swan (father of the brilliant Irish jump jockey Charlie), Jonjo O'Neill, Tommy Murphy (former Irish Flat champion) and Peter Ng from Hong Kong.

Our mounts were all old jumpers with mouths like iron, and the Captain set off like a bat out of hell, leaving the rest of us to scrub along after six furlongs just to keep in touch. But the Captain could not maintain the pace, and as he dropped away Jonjo took up the running, with me on his heels. Halfway up the straight I was almost upsides, but he drew away in the closing stages and beat me by about a length.

Still no winner, but the adrenalin was certainly flowing, and it flowed again at The Curragh two days later.

Earlier that year I had visited Vincent O'Brien at Ballydoyle and – mainly for old times' sake – had ridden work for him. Realizing that the veterans' race was not far off, I'd asked Vincent if he could find a decent runner for me, and he had come up with Legal Legend, whom I had put through his paces on that visit to Ballydoyle. Legal Legend was a decent handicapper, but in the race itself wasn't quite good enough, finishing third behind Yves Saint-Martin (riding the Aga Khan's Chirkpar, later a good hurdler) and Willie Robinson – one of the few jockeys to have won the Grand National, Gold Cup and Champion Hurdle.

About three weeks after that race I was speaking on the phone to Vincent, and during the conversation he asked outright: 'Why don't you make a comeback?' I said I'd think about it, but gave it very little serious thought – unlike Vincent himself, who rang again a few weeks later and invited me to lunch with him in a private room he'd booked in the Berkeley Court Hotel in Dublin.

At that lunch in September 1990 Vincent pointed out that if I was going to ride that season I'd better get things moving, and promised that if I did return he would give me first choice of mounts on his horses in 1991. His retained jockey at the time was John Reid, but the arrangement was not due to run beyond the end of the year, and the chance for me to ride the O'Brien horses – even if he was training a much smaller string than in his heyday – put a wholly different complexion on the matter. And with my injured hand now back to normal, there was no obvious physical barrier to my making a comeback.

There were other considerations to take into account, though, first of which was to assess the alternatives. When I had taken out a trainer's licence we'd had a full yard, including some very promising performers, and in those early days I'd really enjoyed my new way of life. But while I was in prison and the future of the yard was uncertain, some of the owners had sadly not sent us their yearlings, and with the older horses not being replaced as they came to the end of their careers on the track the number of horses at Eve Lodge had so dwindled that I did not really have enough to occupy me. The more I thought about it, the more attractive a return to the saddle – however bizarre it might have been to contemplate at the age of 54 – became.

But my own view was only one side of the equation, and the other side was less easy to predict: would I get enough rides to make the comeback worthwhile, and would I be taken seriously? The history of sport is peppered with instances of leading players staying on too long or trying to make comebacks when their skills have departed, and I was only interested in a return to the saddle if I could achieve it at the highest level.

Since I had retired in 1985 there had been significant changes in the nature of jockeys' arrangements at the top tier of racing, and many of the biggest names had retainers not with one particular stable but with one major owner: by the middle of 1990, for example, Willie Carson was contracted to ride Hamdan Al-Maktoum's horses, Steve Cauthen had a retainer to ride for Sheikh Mohammed, Pat Eddery for Khalid Abdullah. With such arrangements in place I was unlikely to be coming in for the plum rides in the top races, and I could not be sure that there would be enough spare rides around to keep me busy enough.

An additional factor as I pondered that autumn was that October was not going to be an easy time to return: it is so late in the season the fields tend to be big, as owners and trainers try to notch up a few more winners before the end of the season or to get a race into their late-developing two-year-olds, and this makes it harder to ride winners. (On the other hand, it means that more jockeys are needed for each race!)

Eventually I decided to give it a go, secure in the knowledge that if it did not work out I could always stop again at the end of the season and rebuild my working life in another way without any harm done.

Once I had made my own decision there came the practical necessity of obtaining a licence from the Jockey Club, and since I did not want the whole business proclaimed in the press I had to make discreet enquiries. On the evening of 9 October 1990 I telephoned Michael Allen, then the Jockey Club medical officer, and explained what I was contemplating. As chance would have it, his duties were taking him close to Newmarket the following day, and he kindly agreed to make a detour to check me over. I was passed one hundred per cent fit.

The next step was to present myself at the Jockey Club headquarters in Portman Square before the Licensing Committee, which sat each Thursday. After an interview lasting a few minutes (during which the committee satisfied itself that I knew what I was doing, and that I would have sufficient horses to ride) the licence was granted, at which point David Pipe, public relations chief at the Jockey Club, issued the news to the press – whose reaction, for the most part, was one of pleasure. That was certainly the response of the general racing public, and over the next few days I was bombarded with messages of good will. I began to feel really optimistic about the future for the first time in years.

More immediately there was the matter of when and where I should have my first ride in Britain. My brother-in-law Robert Armstrong asked me to ride his runner in the Cartier Million, a valuable two-year-old race run that Sunday at Phoenix Park in Dublin, but I decided that I would rather make my reappearance on home territory, so waited until the Monday – 15 October – and the meeting at Leicester, where Henry Cecil was running a couple of unraced two-year-olds owned by Charles St George. These seemed to provide just the sort of opportunity I was looking for.

It was bedlam when I arrived at the track – not the usual mood at all on an October Monday at Leicester with a large crowd to welcome me back and the press everywhere, cameras flashing and microphones being thrust under my nose at every opportunity: when asked if my technique had changed, I could only think to reply, 'No – still one leg each side.'

My first ride of the afternoon was on one of Charles's juveniles, a nice filly named Lupescu. She ran well but a little green, and after taking the lead a furlong out just got touched off in the last strides by the 5–2 on favourite Sumonda, ridden by Gary Carter. The fairytale return had not quite come off, but I was not complaining.

My second ride was on John Jenkins's Balasani – later a top-notch staying hurdler – who started favourite (the punters couldn't have lost too much faith in me, anyway) but finished down the field, and my third came on the other Charles St George youngster Patricia, who ran disappointingly.

One day, three rides, no winners. But it was a wonderful feeling to get back into race-riding, and an even better one the following day at Chepstow when I rode my first winner in Britain since Full Choke at Nottingham on 29 October 1985.

This was Nicholas, a lovely four-year-old sprinter trained by Susan and owned by Henryk de Kwiatkowski, who had been with us since I started training: a mark of his place in our affections, as the most loyal owner in the yard, is that a hitching post in the form of a jockey in his red and white colours stands outside Florizel opposite the one bearing the colours of Sir Victor Sassoon. Nicholas, who had done well in the USA before coming to us, was one of the star turns of Eve Lodge, and success on him that day – a hard-fought victory by half a length from Amigo Menor – was the perfect way to pick up the winning habit again.

The first winner since my comeback turned out to be also the opening leg of my first double, as in the very next race Shining Jewel, trained by my old friend and weighing-room comrade Eric Eldin, hacked up; an three days later at Newmarket came my third winne on Sheikh Mohammed's Chimayo for Barry Hills. Th same day saw my return to Group One races when rode Surrealist into third place behind 50–1 winne Generous in the Dewhurst Stakes, and on the Saturda I partnered Sikeston for Clive Brittain in the Champio Stakes won by In The Groove.

All in all, a very satisfactory week.

The following Tuesday it was time to take up Vincen on his offer, somewhat sooner than I had anticipated John Reid had been injured in a fall from Whippe before the Prix de l'Abbaye at Longchamp a coupl of weeks earlier, and Vincent asked me to go to The Curragh to ride four of his – three juveniles and a three-year-old. All four – Legal Profession, Fairy Folk, Classic Minstrel and Passer By – won.

At the end of that week the Breeders' Cup was to take place at Belmont Park, New York. Here, in the Mile (with prize money of $1 million), Vincent was running the July Cup winner Royal Academy, owned by Classic Thoroughbreds, the top-of-the-range syndicate masterminded by Robert Sangster and himself. I had mentioned to Vincent that, with John Reid sidelined, I would be happy to ride the colt in America, and his confirmation that he wanted me to partner Royal Academy put me in for one of the most remarkable rides of my life.

The trip was not without its problems, however, and – not for the last time – I was to discover how you can never put a prison sentence behind you: on account of my conviction, I was no longer able simply to have a normal visa for entry to the USA, but had to have one which, at that time, allowed me just one visit per year. (Even that was better than the situation with regard to Japan. I was delighted when in 1995 I was asked to ride in Tokyo, then taken aback to learn that I could not do so, as according to the rules there I had to wait ten years from the time of my release before I could ride in the country.) In the event my visa for the Breeders' Cup trip came through just two days before I was due to leave.

The race was on Saturday 27 October. On the Thursday I rode at Newbury, then immediately after finishing unplaced on Luca Cumani's Arabat in the last hared off to Heathrow to catch Concorde for New York, where I checked into the Waldorf Astoria. One irritant was that I could tell I was getting a cold, which tends to make me two or three pounds heavier than normal. Royal Academy was due to carry 8 stone 10 pounds in the Breeders' Cup Mile, and since Vincent liked to have his horses equipped with various bits and pieces such as his own special rubber pad under the saddle, and heavier girths than was common, I realized I was sailing very close to the wind, and during the two days before the race was very careful about what I ate.

Sadly Vincent was suffering from a bout of flu which confined him to bed, so he could not make the trip to New York: representing him were his wife Jacqueline and younger son Charles. On the Friday morning we went out to the Belmont Park track, where I cantered Royal Academy, all by himself, round the training area allocated to us, a two-furlong track near the stables. This was the first time I'd sat on him, and he gave me such a good feel that our confidence was high as we went off to spend the rest of the day dealing with the essential paperwork which seems to go with any racing trip to the USA: I had to pass a medical and obtain a jockey's licence – which cost $300 for the one day – and Jacqueline even had to get a trainer's licence to allow her to supervise Royal Academy during his stay.

The following morning – brilliantly sunny but cold – the O'Briens and I set off from the Waldorf Astoria in a stretch limousine and arrived in good time to see the early races, which gave a sensational start to the Breeders' Cup programme. First the top English sprinter Dayjur was beaten in the Sprint because he jumped a shadow thrown across the track by the time-keeper's box on top of the grandstand, and then a wonderful head-to-head duel between the top American fillies Go For Wand and Bayakoa in the Distaff ended tragically when Go For Wand broke a leg close home and had to be destroyed on the spot.

The confidence we felt about Royal Academy was shared by the punters, and he went off a warm favourite at nearly 3–1. A son of Nijinsky, Royal Academy shared some of his sire's temperament, but he took the saddling-up process in the small crowded paddock well enough, and gave no sign of edginess apart from putting in one almighty buck which shot me up into the air as we paraded in front of the stands alongside an outrider on a pony: luckily I came down in the saddle, but I thought it wise to abandon the outrider and canter slowly to the start in the European fashion, which seemed to settle him.

Royal Academy had had trouble with his feet, which tended to break up if shod in the conventional way with nails, and Vincent arranged for him to be fitted with stick-on shoes made of steel embedded in a plastic which was then glued to the hoof. These could last up to a month; the only problem was that they were heavier than orthodox racing plates.

A more immediate problem was that Royal Academy was a long horse, and therefore somewhat reluctant to enter the stalls. For this race runners were put in according to post position, so we had to go in first, which meant that Royal Academy was in the stalls longer than any other runner; but rather than causing him to fret this seemed to make him relax, so that when the stalls opened he seemed half asleep and came out all in a heap.

The start of the Breeders' Cup Mile was on a spur at the beginning of the long Belmont back stretch, so he had plenty of time to take up a position, and in any case we had planned to ride him from behind as he had not run over a mile since the Irish Two Thousand Guineas and had become basically a sprinter: we knew that the pace in the Mile would be furious in the opening half mile, and to ensure that Royal Academy got the distance we had to bring him from off the pace.

For most of the back stretch I had just three behind me and was content enough. Then, coming to the long sweeping turn into the straight, I started to make a forward move. As we began to straighten out for home Royal Academy was going very easily when suddenly, for some reason I never fathomed, he lost his action completely – and along with it, it seemed, any chance he had. He had probably put his foot in a hole, but there was no time to mount an investigation. I gave him a moment to get balanced and then started to ride him hard for the winning post, with some five lengths to make up in about two furlongs.

A grey horse named Itsallgreektome, ridden by Corey Nakatani, was powering towards the wire, but once Royal Academy had found his stride again he just flew, charging up the centre of the track. We caught Itsallgreektome a few yards from the line and won cosily enough for me to be able to take a good look across at Nakatani as we passed him.

Royal Academy had proved himself a very brave horse in what was his final race before retiring to the Coolmore Stud, and I – at the end of the week following my return to the saddle – had netted the biggest prize of my career. We got a wonderful reception from the crowd – especially from the English and Irish contingents, who were there in droves that afternoon – and as Jacqueline led Royal Academy in it was truly like a fairy tale: the old times had returned, with the Piggott–O'Brien team winning one of the biggest races in the world. For once I could not disguise my feelings during the post-race interview with Brough Scott for Channel 4 Racing: this was a very special moment indeed, and I was genuinely ecstatic.

Unfortunately I could not indulge this mood as I had only a short time in which to get to the airport for the plane back to London, but as I sipped a glass of champagne soon after take-off I was able to reflect on

the events of an amazing day, and give thanks to Vincent
– not only for encouraging me to make the comeback
at all, but for backing his judgement to the extent of
putting me up on his horse in such a hugely important
race. If M. V. O'Brien thought I could still deliver the
goods, who was I to dispute it?

On the Monday I was back riding for Ballydoyle,
this time at Leopardstown, where Judicial Wit gave me
another winner.

I was then asked by Lady Tavistock to go and ride
her colt Phountzi in the Prix Perth at Saint-Cloud,
and up popped another obstacle, this time not my
prison record but my extreme old age: the French
Jockey Club informed me that they had a rule which
prohibited jockeys from riding in that country after
the age of 50. Mindful of the rich pickings to be
had from riding in France, I was not prepared to take
this lying down, and after much discussion they agreed
that I could ride if passed fit by a French doctor. I
took a private plane to Maisons-Laffitte, where after
a thorough going-over from the official doctor and
various blood tests – I have no idea what for – they
finally saw fit to grant me a licence.

Between 15 October 1990 and the end of the year I
had ridden in Britain, Ireland, France, Germany, Italy,
Spain and the USA. I had won sixteen races (three of
them in England), and brought the owners of my mounts
prize money worth over £400,000. In the short term the
comeback – highlighted by Royal Academy's victory in
the Breeders' Cup Mile – had been a huge success, and
a complete vindication of my decision to return. My
riding skills were still intact, and as long as people
wanted to put me up, I wanted to continue racing. Yet
there remained the nagging doubt that some countries
wanted me more for the novelty – or celebrity – value
of my presence than simply for my riding ability, and
in the knowledge that getting on the good horses would
be no easy matter in 1991, I started to prepare myself
for my first full season back.

14

'Oh no – it's bloody Lester again!'

My suspicion that by the start of the 1991 season
the novelty of my comeback would have worn off
turned out to be fairly accurate. As far as my fellow
jockeys were concerned, they accepted my return to the
weighing room without turning a hair, and the racing
public seemed pleased to see me back. As for the major
owners and trainers, I just had to wait and see: naturally
it would not be easy to get rides on the best horses for
the top owners, who had their own jockeys firmly in
place, and any owner looking for a regular jockey for
a promising two-year-old might pause before putting
up a man of 55, thinking: he's old, is he going to be
around next year to ride my horse in the Classics?

After a winter keeping in trim in Singapore, India
and Hong Kong, my season in the UK began in March
with an afternoon on the all-weather surface at Lingfield
Park (all-weather racing had been merely a gleam in
the Jockey Club's eye when I retired in 1985) which
delivered me a double. My first ride of the season on turf
brought a win on Rare Detail for Susan at Folkestone.

The following month a winning ride on a horse named
Golan Heights at the Newmarket Craven meeting caused
great satisfaction, as he was the first winner sent out
by first-season Newmarket trainer Julie Cecil. Julie
had been a friend for so long – as Noel Murless's
daughter when I first went to Warren Place, then
as Henry's wife in a much later phase of my riding
life – that to ride her first winner as a trainer in
her own right was a particular thrill. Since she had
set up her own yard I had often gone to ride work

for her, and was delighted that she was making such a great start.

This all made for a very good opening to the 1991 season. Then, at the beginning of May, came my first ride in an English Classic since Lanfranco in the 1985 St Leger. Kooyonga, trained by County Meath-based trainer Michael Kauntze – who had been assistant to Vincent O'Brien at Ballydoyle in the glory days of Nijinsky and Roberto – seemed to have only a fair chance in the One Thousand Guineas, the first Classic of the season, and started a 14–1 shot, but ran a blinder to finish runner-up, beaten two lengths by odds-on favourite Shadayid: a tremendous performance from a filly who went on to prove herself top-class, winning the Irish One Thousand Guineas later that year (ridden by Michael's star young jockey Warren O'Connor, as I had chosen in that race to ride Rua d'Oro for Vincent) and the Eclipse in 1992.

On paper I seemed to have a better chance in the Two Thousand, where my ride on Bog Trotter was loaded with family significance. A chestnut colt by Irish River, Bog Trotter was trained by Maureen's husband William and owned by his father Brian. I rode Bog Trotter in his Guineas prep race, the Greenham Stakes at Newbury, where he battled on with such gusto to beat Mukaddamah that I gave him a good chance in the Guineas itself. But at Newmarket he failed to stay and weakened three furlongs out to finish twelfth behind Mystiko.

After the Guineas, attention switched to the Derby, and trying to find an answer to that traditional old question 'What does Lester ride?' was far from straightforward. Naturally all the major candidates were tied to existing jockey arrangements, but eventually, a few days before the race, Henry Cecil offered me the ride on Charles St George's Hokusai. I rode my usual Derby on the colt and had him handy at the turn into the straight, but although for a moment he looked like getting a place, he faded to finish seventh behind

Generous. Alan Munro, who partnered Generous to that brilliant victory, often rode for Susan, and I could claim some part in his achievement as a few days before the Derby he had spent time with my father going over films of my nine wins in the race.

Royal Ascot brought me better fortune in the shape of Michael Stoute's Saddlers' Hall, who made most of the running and then stormed clear of his rivals in the straight to win the King Edward VII Stakes by six lengths. It also brought me one of the more unusual bookings of my riding career – 1990 Cheltenham Gold Cup winner Norton's Coin for Sirrell Griffiths in the two-and-three-quarter-mile Queen Alexandra Stakes. Norton's Coin never made a show, and gave me the feeling that he was not at his best.

I did manage to win another Derby in 1991 – the Swedish version, on the German-trained Tao – but in many ways the highlight of that summer was my trip to ride at the wonderfully scenic racecourse in Killarney, in County Kerry, where the racecourse manager at that time was the irrepressible Finbarr Slattery. I had known Finbarr for many years, and even after I stopped riding we had kept in touch: he was among my most regular correspondents while I was in Highpoint, and I was grateful to him for his consistent kindness and support. For almost as long as I could remember he had been trying to arrange for me to ride at Killarney, and with the easier schedule that I was enjoying after my comeback I found that I could get there for the meeting in July 1991.

The intention was to fly to the local airport, but low cloud cover in the area scuppered that plan, and we had to land in Cork, some 60 miles away. Finbarr, ever resourceful, arranged for a couple of policemen on motorbikes to drive out from Killarney, meet us halfway and escort us to the track, and his plan worked beautifully. I arrived at the course to be greeted by a wonderful reception from the huge crowd, but the cloud cover was still a problem: then, half an hour before the first race, the sun came out and the cloud disappeared. I had a great day, and not only because from five rides I managed three winners – all for Vincent – and two places. It was Finbarr Slattery's final year as manager at Killarney, and I was delighted that I was able to help him bow out in such style.

Back in England, the Goodwood July Meeting yielded one winner (20–1 chance Itsagame for Epsom trainer Simon Dow) and the York August Meeting likewise a single victory, Micheletti for Charles St George and Henry Cecil in the Melrose Handicap.

Micheletti was a son of Critique, whom I had ridden often for Sourien Vanian, and a half-brother to 1989 St Leger winner Michelozzo, and himself seemed to have a decent chance in the final Classic of the season. He started third favourite at Doncaster – and third is where he finished, well beaten behind Toulon and Saddlers' Hall.

There were, however, three great moments for me during the St Leger meeting. The first was when Bog Trotter returned to form in the Kiveton Park Stakes on the Thursday: I was able to dictate the pace from the front, and inside the final furlong William's colt ran on stoutly to hold off Steve Cauthen and Satin Flower.

There was a strong family connection with my ride in the next race, too: Mudaffar for my brother-in-law Robert Armstrong. Halfway up the straight there didn't seem much prospect of a joint celebration that evening, though: Mudaffar was struggling to go the pace, and as Pat Eddery on Troupe took it up with a furlong to go it seemed the best I could hope for was a place. Then Mudaffar suddenly got into gear and started making up ground at a phenomenal rate, flying past horse after horse and collaring Troupe in the shadow of the post to win by a neck.

And the third magic moment came in the Reference Point Sceptre Stakes on St Leger day, when You Know The Rules, trained by Mick Channon, went from last to first to beat Willie Carson and Silver Braid by a short head.

Other highlights of a busy year were a memorable and highly successful trip to the big meeting at Baden-Baden in Germany (where I ended up leading jockey with six winners, including a Group Two winner from Eve Lodge – Nicholas in the Jacobs Goldene Peitsche); a chance to renew my acquaintance with Red Rum: the old boy came to Newmarket to open a betting shop, and stayed overnight with us; and partnering a really good grey two-year-old of Vincent's named El Prado, who won the National Stakes and Beresford Stakes at The Curragh.

I marked the first anniversary of my return to the saddle by winning on Dick Hern's Claret at Leicester – my 102nd winner at home and abroad since the comeback began – and in early November went to Churchill Downs, Kentucky, for another Breeders' Cup. Churchill Downs is famed as the home of the Kentucky Derby, but this was the first time I had ever visited the track, and it was not a particularly happy experience. My only ride was on Richard Hannon's good two-year-old Showbrook in the Juvenile, and his starting price of 25–1 just about reflected his chance in a field which included the brilliant French colt Arazi. All the same, Showbrook never had the chance to prove himself properly. To protect him against the flying dirt on the track, Richard fitted Showbrook with transparent plastic eyeshields, but these got covered in wet sand once the dirt started flying, and the poor horse could not see where he was going: I had to ease him right down and practically pull him up as Arazi scorched round to pull off his famous victory.

By the end of the season in Britain I had ridden forty-eight domestic winners, which put me twenty-fifth in the jockeys' table – not that such considerations bothered me any more! – and was ready for a trip to South Africa (where I rode one day at Durban) before fitting in a quick visit to Mauritius on the way home.

My return to the saddle afforded me the opportunity of filling in some of the gaps in my riding career, and at the start of the 1992 season there remained two holes in my big-race record in Britain which I was keen to plug, the Lincoln Handicap at Doncaster and the Cambridgeshire at Newmarket. As chance would have it, I was to finish runner-up in both that year.

In the Lincoln my ride was Mudaffar, on whom I had so enjoyed myself at Doncaster the previous September and to whom I gave a good chance. In the event he never looked like winning, though running on well inside the final furlong to finish second – but it could have been worse, since the winner was High Low, trained by my son-in-law William and owned by his father. (Anyone wondering why I was not riding High Low should note that the weight he carried was 8 stone – several pounds below what I could possibly get down to.)

That was an encouraging start, but winners that spring proved hard to come by, and by the time of the Two Thousand Guineas I had ridden only one winner in Britain – Fylde Flyer for Jack Berry in the Abernant Stakes at the Newmarket Craven Meeting. I had no idea what I might ride in the Guineas itself until, quite out of the blue, there came a call from Peter Chapple-Hyam, then in just his second year as trainer at the famous Manton estate near Marlborough, where he had been established by Robert Sangster after Barry Hills, the previous incumbent there, had decided to return to Lambourn. Peter had spent several years learning his skills under Barry and had made a marvellous start in his first season as a trainer in his own right, winning the Middle Park Stakes with Robert's El Gran Senor colt Rodrigo de Triano and the Dewhurst with Dr Devious. Now Peter asked me whether I could ride Rodrigo de Triano in the Guineas – and I said I could.

Rodrigo de Triano had good form as a two-year-old, including victories in the Champagne Stakes at Doncaster as well as the Middle Park, but had been disappointing on his first outing at three when fourth in the Greenham Stakes at Newbury. His rider that day was his regular partner Willie Carson, but for the Guineas Willie had been claimed to ride Muhtarram for his boss Hamdan Al-Maktoum, which left Rodrigo without a jockey.

I went down to Manton to ride the colt and he gave me a very good feel. A free-going horse, he was genuine and willing, and since Peter assured me that he had been far from fully wound up before his Newbury defeat I felt that he had a reasonable chance at Newmarket.

On the day he started third favourite behind Alnasr Alwasheek and Pursuit of Love. I kept him well covered up in the early stages before asking him to take closer order with about three furlongs to run, and the ease with which he picked up for me was such that I knew then that he was going to win. A furlong out I pushed him into the lead past Pursuit Of Love and he kept on wonderfully well up the final hill as Lucky Lindy tried in vain to mount a challenge. Rodrigo won by a length and a half, and I had landed my thirtieth English Classic.

There was bedlam as we returned to the winner's enclosure, and although attention understandably focused on the 56-year-old grandfather in the saddle, I felt then – and subsequently – that Rodrigo de Triano did not really get the credit he deserved. For he was, over the right distance and in the right conditions, a very good horse indeed, as his exploits later in the season proved.

From Newmarket he went over to The Curragh for the Irish Two Thousand Guineas, and easily brought me my sixteenth Irish Classic. It was then decided to run him in what looked like a very open Derby, and although there were doubts both about his stamina and about his ability to act on the course, he went off favourite at 13–2. I came in for some criticism afterwards from people who said I never put him in the race with any chance, but the fact was that he simply did not act on the track at all, and I was not prepared to risk ruining him for the future by subjecting him to too hard a contest at Epsom.

Less than two weeks later he ran in the one-mile St James's Palace Stakes at Royal Ascot, but he did not seem in form, and finished fourth behind Brief Truce, a short head in front of Arazi.

Rodrigo was then given a break before having his first race over a mile and a quarter in the Juddmonte International Stakes (the race which started life as the Benson and Hedges Gold Cup) at York, where he regained the winning thread with a vengeance, taking up the running a furlong out and only needing to be pushed out to beat Oaks runner-up All At Sea by a length, with Derby winner Dr Devious (also trained by Peter Chapple-Hyam) back in fourth.

That was a great moment, but the day of triumph was very nearly followed by one of catastrophe.

York is a fairly easy journey from Newmarket in a light plane, and rather than stay up there during the Ebor meeting I returned home after racing each evening. On the Wednesday morning, the middle day of the meeting, a group of four jockeys – George Duffield (who had an important date in the Yorkshire Oaks that day on his Oaks winner User Friendly), Michael Hills, Philip Robinson and myself – were flying back up to York in a Piper Seneca piloted by David Smith. As we flew over Lincolnshire all was going smoothly – which means that I as usual was reading the paper – when suddenly a dark shadow came over the plane, we flipped over and plummeted for what felt like ages, and I ended up on the ceiling. In a moment David Smith had managed to right the plane, but it was very frightening indeed, and I was not proposing to argue with him when he pronounced that we had to land to check that there had been no damage. Luckily there was an airfield handy, so we made a hasty descent – to discover that the plane had escaped its ordeal unharmed, and that the passengers would live to fight another day: George Duffield managed to put the scare behind him that afternoon in the best possible way, with victory on User Friendly.

It transpired that our plane had been somersaulted by the airstream from an RAF Tornado which had been on exercises in the area and had been assured that there were no light planes around. An investigation was mounted, and when the report was published the following spring it declared that the Tornado pilot had thought he had hit us: in fact he had missed by a mere ten feet!

But for those ten feet Rodrigo de Triano would have been my last winner, and the International Stakes certainly saw him at the peak of his form. He did not run again for two months, reappearing in the Champion Stakes at Newmarket, where his only serious rival in a ten-runner field appeared to be the Queen Elizabeth II Stakes winner Lahib, ridden by Willie Carson. Rodrigo had been suffering from foot trouble and we had been able to get very little work into him at Manton – indeed, it was touch and go whether he would be able to run at all – and when Lahib took up the running a furlong out, looking all over the winner, it was time for my colt to dig deep. But once shaken up Rodrigo de Triano accelerated brilliantly, and collared Lahib close home to win by a neck. Willie later told the press that as we passed his reaction had been 'Oh no – it's bloody Lester again!', but in truth few horses could have lived with Rodrigo de Triano when he was in that sort of form. In essence he was a miler, but he had the class to prove himself top of the tree at ten furlongs, and if he had not run in the Derby he might, with a bit of luck, have gone through the rest of 1992 unbeaten.

Rodrigo de Triano's last race before going off to stand as a stallion in Japan was in the Breeders' Cup Classic in the fierce heat of Gulfstream Park, Florida, on 31 October: partnered by Walter Swinburn as I had suffered a fall earlier in the afternoon, he finished last.

The fall which had kept me off Rodrigo in the Classic came in the first race of the Breeders' Cup programme, the Sprint, where I was riding the other top-notch

horse with whom I was associated in 1992, Richard
Hannon's sprinter Mr Brooks.

In 1992 Mr Brooks was a five-year-old. At three
trained in Ireland by Kevin Connolly, he had run behind
Quest For Fame in the Derby, but it soon became clear
that his real strength was sprinting, and after he had
moved to Jim Bolger he became one of the better
sprinters in Ireland. I first rode Mr Brooks in the Duke
of York Stakes at York, his last race for Jim Bolger, when
he was second. Between then and his brilliant victory in
the Prix de l'Abbaye he had finished runner-up in the
King's Stand Stakes at Royal Ascot (his first race for
Richard Hannon), won the July Cup and the Grosser
Preis von Berlin at Hoppegarten and finished second to
Lyric Fantasy in the Nunthorpe at York and to Sheikh
Albadou in the Haydock Park Sprint Cup.

Sheikh Albadou had landed a sensational victory in
the previous year's Breeders' Cup Sprint at Churchill
Downs and Mr Brooks had a live chance of emulating
that feat. The fact that at Gulfstream Park he did not
move particularly well to post, and did not walk well
when he got there, did not at the time trouble me greatly,
since he never moved fluidly in his slower paces.

In the early stages of the race, a six-furlong sprint run
at a manic pace, he was travelling well enough towards
the rear of the field. Then, as soon as he started to
move into the long left-handed turn, I could sense that
he was in trouble. His off-foreleg had snapped: but he
kept going for several yards before he turned over,
throwing me clear but then skidding along the ground
and catching me round the face with one of his hooves
– knocking me out – before rolling on top of me.

Mr Brooks was put down instantly, a tragic loss of
a fine horse.

I came round in the jockeys' hospital room, where
I was taken before going to the Hollywood Memorial
Hospital. Although the fall had looked horrendous,
my injuries were mercifully light: a broken collarbone,
two broken ribs and a gashed head where Mr Brooks

had caught me with his hoof. One of my lungs had temporarily collapsed, but the brain-scan I underwent was only precautionary, and before long I was able to sit up in bed eating ice-cream and jelly – much to the astonishment of Tracy and my assistant Anna Ludlow, who were both with me in Florida and had rushed off to the hospital once Anna had collected my gear from the jockeys' room.

While I was lying in hospital I received a visit from the British Consul bearing a message which had been faxed from the Queen: 'I am terribly sorry to hear about your accident and hope you make a quick recovery.' Less welcome was the attention of some elements of the British press, who staked out the ward and went to extraordinary lengths to get an embellishment for their story. On one occasion I had been taken out of my room for an X-ray, and while Anna waited for my return she was joined in the room by a man in a white doctor's coat who proceeded to try to interview her about my condition. He was, she quickly realized from his accent, an English tabloid journalist.

Things became so bad that when, after my discharge from hospital, we all moved down to Miami to allow me to recuperate out of the limelight, I checked into our hotel under an assumed name. One day Tracy and Anna went out shopping, leaving me by the poolside, and when I went to the reception desk to get the key to my room, not only could I not remember its number, nor could I remember the name under which I had booked in!

Eventually press interest in my condition died down and I was allowed to recover in peace, though it was not until some three months later that I returned to the saddle.

At this time – as throughout my career, especially during times of great triumph or great crisis – I was very buoyed up by the hundreds of messages of support which I received from racing fans all over the world. Whenever I rode a big winner the postbag would be full, as it was too if there was some well-publicized problem in my life – notably, of course, the difficulties with the taxman. Whatever the circumstances, there are always a few correspondents who write to offer abuse (all top jockeys suffer from this), but the vast majority of letters I have received throughout my riding life have been a tremendous support at times of difficulty and an extra cause for celebration when things have been going well. As far as we could, Susan and I have sought to answer letters we have received from fans, and we have always been grateful to them for their support.

If the thirtieth Classic on Rodrigo de Triano was the high point of 1992 and the fall from Mr Brooks the low point, it was in many other ways a busy and memorable year.

A special joy was the birth in September of Maureen and William's second child and our second grandchild – Sam Haggas.

And a particular sadness was the sudden death in May of Charles St George. I had been closely involved with Charles and his family for so long and ridden so many fine horses for him – including Bruni, Giacometti and my particular favourite, Ardross – that I felt his death, at the age of 66, deeply.

Charles's funeral sadly coincided with that of Peter Smith, founder back in 1969 of the Jockeys Association of Great Britain. The JAGB had done wonders for jockeys over the years, and in 1991 had inaugurated its annual dinner and awards ceremony, held each spring, where jockeys are voted for by their fellow riders in different categories and each winner is presented with a statuette of a jockey. These awards were soon dubbed 'the Lesters', and I was honoured to be voted Personality of the Year in both 1991 and 1992.

Another old friend who passed away in 1992 was Nijinsky, put down in April at the age of 25.

For the second successive year I was among the winners at Royal Ascot, in 1992 landing the Norfolk

Stakes with the lovely filly Niche – on whom I followed up by winning the Lowther Stakes the day after the near-miss in the plane to York. Lord Carnarvon, owner of Niche, is the Queen's racing manager, and I had my first winner in the Royal colours since my comeback when partnering the Queen's Sharp Prod to win the valuable Moet & Chandon Rennen at Baden-Baden.

A less prestigious race at Doncaster in October brought its own reward when a horse named Thamestar, trained by John Dunlop, got into all sorts of trouble when stumbling over that little hill on the far side of the track and throwing me up into the air. He completely lost his action and, it appeared, any chance in the race, slipping from a prominent position to the rear of the field as I gave him time to recover. Once in the straight, however, he started to motor to such effect that by the final furlong he was absolutely flying, and just before the line got up to beat Pat Eddery and Simonov by a head. Channel 4 Racing viewers, who voted me their Personality of the Year, nominated that as my ride of the season, and I was not inclined to dispute their decision.

Alongside my revived riding career I was still closely involved with the training operation at Eve Lodge, and one memorable moment for the yard came in June when the great event rider Ginny Leng – now Ginny Elliott – won a charity race at Kempton on Shining Jewel, now trained by Susan. This helped eradicate the memory of the same race in 1988, when Maureen was riding Nero (also trained by Susan) to an easy victory when she dropped her hands and was caught on the line by Ian Balding's grand old campaigner Mailman. Maureen was fined £250, and never repeated the error!

My total at the end of the 1992 season was just thirty-five winners from 329 domestic rides, though my total prize money won at home and abroad was over £1 million: it had been a year for quality, not quantity.

After returning home following the Gulfstream Park fall I concentrated on getting fit by putting in a great deal of time swimming and walking, and in February 1993 made my return to the saddle at the Jebel Ali racecourse in Dubai, winning a couple of races on my second day back. From there I went to Hong Kong, where an eye injury sustained when one of my horses flung his head back and walloped me in the face – an occupational hazard for jockeys, as my experience with Teenoso at Saint-Cloud back in 1984 had shown – required two stitches.

The ride I was really looking forward to early in the season was on Niche in the One Thousand Guineas, and after she had beaten Sayyedati in the Nell Gwyn Stakes I felt that I had a great chance of taking my Classic tally to thirty-one. In the Guineas she ran a wonderful race, rallying gamely after being headed by Sayyedati but failing by just half a length to pin her back. Niche then went on to score a handsome victory in the Falmouth Stakes at the Newmarket July Meeting, but the following month was tragically killed in an accident: she was hit by a van after getting loose on the gallops.

At the same July Meeting where Niche showed her worth, another filly whom I rode in Lord Carnarvon's colours offered high hopes for the 1994 Classics. This was Lemon Souffle, a daughter of Salse who had won two minor races at Windsor and Newbury before landing the Cherry Hinton Stakes at the July Meeting. From there she went on to be such an impressive winner of the Moyglare Stud Stakes at The Curragh that she became ante-post favourite for the One Thousand Guineas, but a badly gashed leg in the Cheveley Park Stakes in October not only ended her season on a downbeat note, but seemed to have ended her racing career. (In the event she ran just three times as a three-year-old in 1994, missing the Guineas but emulating Niche by winning the Falmouth Stakes.)

At the 1993 May Bank Holiday meeting at Kempton Park I scored my first treble since my return – on Brockton Dancer, Pay Homage and Dramanice – and less than two weeks later failed by only a head to and the Irish Two Thousand Guineas on Fatherland, who ran on stoutly in pursuit of Barathea (runner-up to Zafonic in the Two Thousand at Newmarket). Fatherland had been a good two-year-old, numbering the National Stakes at The Curragh among his four straight victories before running fifth behind Zafonic in the Dewhurst, and on the strength of his Irish Guineas run looked set for a good season.

In particular, the result at The Curragh opened up an intriguing possibility for the 1993 Derby. Fatherland was trained by Vincent O'Brien and ran in the colours of his wife Jacqueline, and on the form of the Irish Two Thousand Guineas would go to Epsom with a real chance, though on the evidence of that race it was impossible to know whether he would stay the Derby distance or not. Fatherland always tended to hang to the left a little so we thought that Epsom might suit him, and we were not alone. His price at the off was 8–1, third market choice behind odds-on chance Tenby – an unbeaten colt who had won the Newmarket Stakes and Dante Stakes en route to Epsom – and his stable companion Commander In Chief. The latter won well under Mick Kinane while Fatherland, whom I had moved up early in the straight to try to get into a challenging position, simply failed to stay. To have won my tenth Derby on a horse trained by Vincent, whose retirement was certain to come in the foreseeable future, would have been a fairy tale even by my standards, but it was not to be. Fatherland ran only once more in Europe – fourth in the Prix Eugene Adam at Saint-Cloud – before being moved to the USA, where he sadly had to be destroyed after breaking a pastern in the Hollywood Derby.

A happier association with one of the small number of horses still being trained at Ballydoyle came with the three-year-old College Chapel, who enabled me to score at Royal Ascot for the third successive year when winning the Cork and Orrery Stakes on Gold Cup day. College Chapel had not run at two, but prior to Ascot

had won two good races in Ireland in such style that h[e]
started favourite for the Cork and Orrery: he justifie[d]
that market position by quickening nicely when I aske[d]
him and beating Keen Hunter without too much ado. [I]
was an emotional moment after the race when Vincen[t]
was persuaded to lead in the horse himself, to a gloriou[s]
reception from the Ladies' Day crowd. Royal Ascot ha[s]
always been my favourite race meeting, but I've rarel[y]
enjoyed it as much as I did that day.

Two days later there was more cause for family
celebration when Maureen rode her first winner – Let's
Get Lost (trained by William) in a ladies' race at Redcar.

But there was also sadness in June 1993 with the
death at the age of 89 of my father, to whom I owed
so much. He and my mother (who had died in January
1987) had spent their last years in the house we had had
built for them next to the yard, and his presence about
the place had been an invaluable support.

On 18 July 1993 I achieved what must be the unusual
distinction of winning the Derby in the afternoon and
the Oaks the same evening: that is, the Slovenske Derby
in Bratislava on Zimzalabim, and the Austrian Oaks in
Vienna on Soft Call. That was quite a day, as I rode a
treble at Bratislava and a double in Vienna: five winners
on the one day in two different countries!

The same month the Jockey Club introduced new
guidelines on the use of the whip, which had long been
a contentious issue in racing circles and beyond. The
whole issue of the use of the whip has been hotly debated
over the years – more often than not by those who are
ignorant of what it takes to ride a racehorse – and the
introduction of new guidelines in 1993 concentrated on
the number of times jockeys could use the whip in the
closing stages of a race, and how they make use of it.

No-one wants to see a horse hit unnecessarily, but
as far as Flat racing is concerned little harm is done
by sensible use of the stick. Nowadays whips have
to be so short that they cannot do much damage,
and with most Flat jockeys weighing in at around 8

stone, the whole business centres on little men using little whips. Good riders only use a whip when they feel its use is needed and justified, and all horses are different: some will go as soon as you give them a tap, some need a few smacks until they can be persuaded to put their best foot forward, and some do not need the whip at all. We also have to remember that horses are bred and trained to run as fast as they can – and if it takes a few taps with the whip to make them do what they were bred for, so be it.

College Chapel was the sort of horse who needed average encouragement from the whip, but even that was not enough to get him to follow up his Royal Ascot victory in the July Cup at Newmarket, where he had no answer to the scorching speed of 33–1 outsider Hamas. Vincent's colt then went across to Deauville, where he won the Prix Maurice de Gheest by a length from Danakal before ending the season by finishing third behind Lochsong in the Nunthorpe and fourth to Wolfhound in the Sprint Cup at Haydock. At his peak I have to rate College Chapel among the best sprinters I rode, and at Ascot he gave Vincent and me a truly golden moment.

My total number of winners in Britain in 1993 showed an improvement on 1992 – up to thirty-nine – but in any event it was not the simple riding of winners which was making this period so enjoyable: rather, it was the ability to choose where and when I rode, and generally to approach race-riding in a much more relaxed frame of mind than when I was going round year after year chasing championships.

It was in that frame of my mind that I went to Tralee in August during the Rose of Tralee festival and rode a winner for the Aga Khan, and the following month returned to Ireland for a wonderful dinner arranged by Finbarr Slattery at which I was presented with a book commemorating my visit to Killarney in July 1991.

* * *

One of the most noticeable changes in the racing world during the five years I was out of the saddle was the expansion in the role of jockeys' agents. On my return I found that virtually all riders – not only the top few – were employing agents to book their rides, and I had to consider whether to follow suit. I decided against having a full-time agent, as it would not be fair on whoever it might be if I were not inclined to ride all over the place. However, I did need some back-up in the general area of organizing my riding life, and as soon as I came back to race-riding knew that I would have to find somebody to help. Anna Ludlow had become a close friend over the previous few years, and I asked her to take on the role.

Although from a family of musicians, she had turned her back on a life in the orchestra in favour of working with horses, and had moved to Newmarket in 1974 to pursue this interest. After working for some time at a veterinary practice and then handling the insurance business at Susan's bloodstock agency, Anna had founded a small company which showed visitors around Newmarket – gallops, yards, studs, the National Horseracing Museum, and so on. But she was growing tired of that and starting to look for a fresh challenge, and the opportunity to assist me provided just such a new opening: apart from booking rides, she acted as a general assistant in the day-to-day arrangements which the modern jockey has to make (especially one who travels extensively).

Over the years we had become very close, and on 28 September 1993 our son Jamie – nine weeks premature and weighing in at a very tiny 3 pounds 10 ounces – was born. This did not escape the attention of the tabloid press, but in spite of plenty of reports to the contrary my relationship with the rest of my family managed to survive.

Jamie lives with Anna near Newmarket but I spend as much time with him as I can. He is a regular visitor to Florizel, where he loves splashing about in the swimming pool, and at every opportunity goes to play with Maureen and William's children Sam and Mary-Anne. Many of his father's passions seem to have been passed on to him: he loves horses, wanting to kiss them if he can get close enough, but his main obsession in life around the time of his second birthday is cars, and he has a strong liking for raspberries, chocolate and ice-cream.

While it is far too soon to know whether Jamie will have any lasting inclination towards horses, and perpetuate the Piggott name in the saddle, the achievements of both Maureen and Tracy have been a source of continuing satisfaction to me – not least because both have ridden winners!

After learning the eventing ropes from Alison Oliver, who had trained Princess Anne to Olympic standard, Maureen made a name for herself in three-day events before continuing back trouble finally forced her to retire from competition in 1986. Her first eventing horse was Barney, on whom she competed for the first time at Badminton in 1981. That same year she received sponsorship from Cathay Pacific, and won a two-day event at Amberley and a three-day event at Bramham on her new mare Asian Princess – on whom she rode in the gold medal-winning team of young riders at the European Championships in Germany. In 1982 Maureen finished twelfth at Badminton on Hong Kong Discoverer, and would have been closer to the winner but for a technical fault.

Like her father, Maureen has ridden round the Derby course – in a ladies' race for charity in 1985, where the Princess Royal was among her opponents – and unlike him she has also tackled the Grand National course at Aintree, with commentator Richard Pitman, who so nearly won the National on Crisp in 1973.

Tracy too had her moment of glory in the saddle when winning the ladies' race at Leopardstown in 1988, and has travelled the globe building up her racing experience.

After leaving school at sixteen she went to Australia and New Zealand, then worked for a bloodstock agency and on the insurance side of Susan's business before going off to the USA, where she rode track work at such exotic locations as Santa Anita, Hollywood Park, Belmont Park, Keeneland, Gulfstream Park and Hialeah. She subsequently moved to Ireland, where for two years she was assistant trainer to Tommy Stack, and in 1989 joined RTE, for whom she has become an established part of the team presenting racing, and in 1994 started covering show jumping as well.

In December 1993 I went down to Argentina to ride at San Isidro, just north of Buenos Aires, and in the New Year warmed up for the 1994 Flat season in Dubai, Singapore, Hong Kong and Macao. Knowing that there wasn't too much for me to ride, I did not get into action in Britain until well into April, and had a quiet season, with only nineteen domestic winners.

At the July Meeting at Goodwood, however, I hit the headlines for the wrong reason. I was riding the favourite Coffee 'N Cream for Richard Hannon in a five-furlong nursery – a handicap for two-year-olds. For some reason the horse seemed to jump through the girth as the stalls opened, and as we hurtled down the five-furlong course at Goodwood I could feel the saddle slipping back towards his quarters. I knew the saddle was going to come off – it was just a matter of when! We kept the partnership intact until, inside the final furlong, I felt the saddle move again, and as I tried to get in front of it and keep my balance it slid round, shooting me out the side door.

As so often, the fall looked a great deal worse than it felt to me. I was not knocked out, though I felt a little stunned, but when at the hospital the doctor asked me what day it was I just couldn't remember: I thought that it must be Saturday so offered that as the answer. Unfortunately it was Thursday, and I was given the statutory seven days off to allow my head to clear.

A 58-year-old man falling off a galloping horse was not everyone's idea of sport, and after this fall – which felt fairly minor to me – there were the inevitable calls that I should give up riding and not risk one fall too many. The press have to write about something, and it did not particularly bother me that some journalists took this line, though I knew that nothing that was written would ever influence me. When you ride in races you expect to have falls, whether you are fifty-eight or eighteen, and while you can accept that fact of racing life the prospect of falling off simply does not enter your calculations.

I made a quick recovery and was soon back in action. My last winner of 1994 was Palacegate Jack on 5 October at Haydock Park (back where it all started over forty-six years ago), and – having ridden at only three meetings in between – my last ride came on Mr Confusion in the November Handicap at Doncaster on 5 November: my fifty-ninth birthday. I did not know it at the time, but that was my last ride in Britain.

There was still, however, plenty for me to do abroad, and in January 1995 I set off to ride in Bombay, Singapore and Australia – a tour I so enjoyed that I delayed my return for a month, getting back to Britain at the end of April. This delay triggered speculation that I would not be riding again, at least not on the domestic circuit. The simple fact was that after a fairly intensive overseas tour of duty I was not ready to plunge straight back into riding in Britain, so had not applied for a new licence.

As the months went by I found myself less and less inclined to make that application, despite various offers to return to the saddle. Susan had decided not to reapply for her trainer's licence (she sent out her last runner from Eve Lodge at the end of August) so one source of rides would not be available, and in any case I was experiencing difficulty getting the weight off. In the circumstances, I decided it was sensible to end all further conjecture.

This time there was to be no great retirement hullabaloo, with memorabilia and an emotional afternoon of farewell to the racing public – just an announcement in September 1995 that I would not be back.

As I said at the beginning of this book, you can't retire twice.

The riding record
compiled by Phillip Jones

DOMESTIC CAREER WINS
Flat

Year	Wins	Year	Wins	Year	Wins
1948	1	1963	175	1978	97
1949	6	1964	140*	1979	77
1950	52	1965	160*	1980	156
1951	51	1966	191*	1981	179*
1952	79	1967	117*	1982	188*
1953	41	1968	139*	1983	150
1954	42	1969	163*	1984	100
1955	103	1970	162*	1985	34
1956	129	1971	162*	1986–89	-
1957	122	1972	103	1990	3
1958	83	1973	129	1991	48
1959	142	1974	143	1992	35
1960	170*	1975	113	1993	39
1961	164	1976	87	1994	19
1962	96	1977	103		

* Champion Jockey		Total	4493

Hurdles

Season	Wins	Season	Wins	Season	Wins
1953/54	9	1955/56	-	1957/58	2
1954/55	1	1956/57	6	1958/59	2
				Total	20

1951	Zucchero	K Cundell	unpl
1952	Gay Time	N Cannon	2nd
1953	Prince Charlemagne	T Carey	unpl
1954	**Never Say Die**	J Lawson	won
1955	Windsor Sun	S McGrath (IRE)	unpl
1956	Affiliation Order	Mrs H J Houghton	unpl
1957	**Crepello**	N Murless	won
1958	Boccaccio	N Murless	unpl
1959	Carnoustie	N Murless	unpl
1960	**St Paddy**	N Murless	won
1961-62	–		
1963	Corpora	E Fellows (FR)	unpl
1964	Sweet Moss	N Murless	unpl
1965	Meadow Court	P Prendergast (IRE)	2nd
1966	Right Noble	MV O'Brien (IRE)	unpl
1967	Ribocco	RFJ Houghton	2nd
1968	**Sir Ivor**	MV O'Brien (IRE)	won
1969	Ribofilio	RFJ Houghton	unpl
1970	**Nijinsky**	MV O'Brien (IRE)	won
1971	The Parson	N Murless	unpl
1972	**Roberto**	MV O'Brien (IRE)	won
1973	Cavo Doro	MV O'Brien (IRE)	2nd
1974	Arthurian	H Cecil	unpl
1975	Bruni	HR Price	unpl
1976	**Empery**	M Zilber (FR)	won
1977	**The Minstrel**	MV O'Brien (IRE)	won
1978	Inkerman	MV O'Brien (IRE)	unpl
1979	Milford	WR Hern	unpl
1980	Monteverdi	MV O'Brien (IRE)	unpl

1981	Shotgun	C Thornton	4th
1982	–		
1983	**Teenoso**	G Wragg	won
1984	Alphabatim	G Harwood	unpl
1985	Theatrical	D Weld (IRE)	unpl
1986-90	–		
1991	Hokusai	H Cecil	unpl
1992	Rodrigo de Triano	P Chapple-Hyam	unpl
1993	Fatherland	MV O'Brien (IRE)	unpl
1994	Khamaseen	J Dunlop	unpl

Rides: 36; wins: 9; runner-up: 4

ENGLISH CLASSIC WINS

1000 Guineas	(2)	
1970	Humble Duty	P Walwyn
1981	Fairy Footsteps	H Cecil
2000 Guineas	(5)	
1957	Crepello	N Murless
1968	Sir Ivor	MV O'Brien (IRE)
1970	Nijinsky	MV O'Brien (IRE)
1985	Shadeed	M Stoute
1992	Rodrigo de Triano	P Chapple-Hyam
Derby	(9)	
1954	Never Say Die	J Lawson
1957	Crepello	N Murless
1960	St Paddy	N Murless
1968	Sir Ivor	MV O'Brien (IRE)
1970	Nijinsky	MV O'Brien (IRE)
1972	Roberto	MV O'Brien (IRE)

1976	Empery	M Zilber (FR)
1977	The Minstrel	MV O'Brien (IRE)
1983	Teenoso	G Wragg

Oaks (6)

1957	Carrozza	N Murless
1959	Petite Etoile	N Murless
1966	Valoris	MV O'Brien (IRE)
1975	Juliette Marny	J Tree
1981	Blue Wind	D Weld (IRE)
1984	Circus Plume	J Dunlop

St Leger (8)

1960	St Paddy	N Murless
1961	Aurelius	N Murless
1967	Ribocco	RF Johnson Houghton
1968	Ribero	RF Johnson Houghton
1970	Nijinsky	MV O'Brien (IRE)
1971	Athens Wood	H Thomson Jones
1972	Boucher	MV O'Brien (IRE)
1984	Commanche Run	L Cumani

FRENCH CLASSIC WINS

Poule d'Essai des Pouliches (2)

1964	Rajput Princess	C Bartholomew
1982	River Lady	F Boutin

Prix du Jockey-Club (1)

1972	Hard To Beat	R Carver

Prix de Diane (3)

1980	Mrs Penny	I Balding (GB)
1981	Madam Gay	P Kelleway (GB)

1985	Lypharita	A Fabre

Prix Royal-Oak (1)

1981	Ardross	H Cecil (GB)

IRISH CLASSIC WINS

Irish 1000 Guineas (2)

1971	Favoletta	H Wragg (GB)
1979	Godetia	MV O'Brien

Irish 2000 Guineas (3)

1970	Decies	B van Cutsem (GB)
1978	Jaazeiro	MV O'Brien
1992	Rodrigo de Triano	P Chapple-Hyam (GB)

Irish Derby (5)

1965	Meadow Court	P Prendergast
1967	Ribocco	RF Johnson Houghton (GB)
1968	Ribero	RF Johnson Houghton (GB)
1977	The Minstrel	MV O'Brien
1981	Shergar	M Stoute (GB)

Irish Oaks (3)

1970	Santa Tina	C Millbank (FR)
1975	Juliette Marny	J Tree (GB)
1979	Godetia	MV O'Brien

Irish St Leger (3)

1967	Dan Kano	J Lenehan
1975	Caucasus	MV O'Brien
1976	Meneval	MV O'Brien

TRAINERS OF PIGGOTT'S ENGLISH CLASSIC WINNERS

MV O'Brien (IRE) (9)

Valoris	(1966 Oaks)
Sir Ivor	(1968 2000 Guineas; Derby)
Nijinsky	(1970 2000 Guineas; Derby; St Leger)
Roberto	(1972 Derby)
Boucher	(1972 St Leger)
The Minstrel	(1977 Derby)

N Murless (7)

Crepello	(1957 2000 Guineas; Derby)
Carrozza	(1957 Oaks)
Petite Etoile	(1959 Oaks)
St Paddy	(1960 Derby; St Leger)
Aurelius	(1961 St Leger)

RF Johnson Houghton (2)

Ribocco	(1967 St Leger)
Ribero	(1968 St Leger)

J Lawson (1)

Never Say Die	(1954 Derby)

P Walwyn (1)

Humble Duty	(1970 1000 Guineas)

H Thomson Jones (1)

Athens Wood	(1971 St Leger)

J Tree (1)

Juliette Marny	(1975 Oaks)

M Zilber (FR) (1)

Empery	(1976 Derby)

H Cecil (1)

Fairy Footsteps	(1981 1000 Guineas)

D Weld (IRE) (1)

Blue Wind	(1981 Oaks)
G Wragg (1)	
Teenoso	(1983 Derby)
J Dunlop (1)	
Circus Plume	(1984 Oaks)
L Cumani (1)	
Commanche Run	(1984 St Leger)
M Stoute (1)	
Shadeed	(1985 2000 Guineas)
P Chapple-Hyam (1)	
Rodrigo de Triano	(1992 2000 Guineas)

ROYAL ASCOT WINS

1952	Malka's Boy	Wokingham Stakes	W Nightingall
1953	Absolve	Gold Vase	V Smyth
1956	Pharsalia	Queen Mary Stakes	H Cottrill
	Court Command	Kind Edward VII Stakes	N Murless
1957	Abelia	Queen Mary Stakes	N Murless
	Zarathustra	Gold Cup	Sir C Boyd-Rochfort
	Arctic Explorer	King Edward VII Stakes	N Murless
	Right Boy	King's Stand Stakes	W Dutton
1958	Right Boy	Cork and Orrery Stakes	W Dutton
	Gladness	Gold Cup	MV O'Brien (IRE)
	Carnoustie	Windsor Castle Stakes	N Murless
1959	Right Boy	Cork and Orrery Stakes	P Rohan
	Pindari	King Edward VII Stakes	N Murless
1960	Tin Whistle	Cork and Orrery Stakes	P Rohan
	New Move	Chesham Stakes	P Walwyn
	Sunny Way	King George V Stakes	N Murless
	Firestreak	Rous Memorial Stakes	P Nelson
1961	Favorita	Jersey Stakes	N Murless

1961	Aiming High	Coronation Stakes	N Murless
(*cont.*)	Abermaid	New Stakes	H Wragg
	Pandofell	Gold Cup	F Maxwell
	Aurelius	King Edward VII Stakes	N Murless
	Petite Etoile	Rous Memorial Stakes	N Murless
	St Paddy	Hardwicke Stakes	N Murless
1963	The Creditor	Jersey Stakes	N Murless
	Spaniards Close	Royal Hunt Cup	F Winter
	Raccolto	Bessborough Stakes	S Hall
	El Gallo	Cork and Orrery Stakes	N Murless
	Twilight Alley	Gold Cup	N Murless
	Majority Rule	King's Stand Stakes	W O'Gorman
1964	Roan Rocket	St James's Palace Stakes	G Todd
	Young Christopher	Jersey Stakes	F Maxwell
1965	Young Emperor	Coventry Stakes	P Prendergast (IRE)
	Casabianca	Royal Hunt Cup	N Murless
	Bracey Bridge	Ribblesdale Stakes	N Murless
	Tin King	New Stakes	RF Johnson Houghton
	Fighting Charlie	Gold Cup	F Maxwell
	Swift Harmony	Chesham Stakes	E Reavey
	Brave Knight	King George V Stakes	W Nightingall
	Sweet Moss	Rous Memorial Stakes	N Murless
1966	Falcon	New Stakes	RF Johnson Houghton
	Marcus Brutus	King George V Stakes	S Hall
	On Your Mark	Windsor Castle Stakes	F Armstrong
1967	Polmak	Bessborough Stakes	F Armstrong
1968	Petingo	St James's Palace Stakes	F Armstrong
	Mountain Call	Cork and Orrery Stakes	B van Cutsem
	Ribofilio	Chesham Stakes	RF Johnson Houghton
1969	Lexicon	Ascot Stakes	HR Price
	Kamundu	Royal Hunt Cup	F Carr
1970	Karabas	Hardwicke Stakes	B van Cutsem
	Welsh Saint	Cork and Orrery Stakes	MV O'Brien (IRE)
	Swing Easy	New Stakes	J Tree

1971	Meadow Mint	Chesham Stakes	F Armstrong
	Hickleton	Queen Alexandra Stakes	B Hills
	Swing Easy	King's Stand Stakes	J Tree
1972	Sparkler	Queen Anne Stakes	F Armstrong
	Calve	Coronation Stakes	P Prendergast (IRE)
1973	Gift Card	Prince of Wales's Stakes	A Penna (FR)
	Thatch	St James's Palace Stakes	MV O'Brien (IRE)
	Abergwaun	King's Stand Stakes	MV O'Brien (IRE)
1974	Lisadell	Coronation Stakes	MV O'Brien (IRE)
	Saritamer	Cork and Orrery Stakes	MV O'Brien (IRE)
	Ginnies Pet	Wokingham Stakes	J Sutcliffe
	Relay Race	Hardwicke Stakes	H Cecil
1975	Galway Bay	Coventry Stakes	I Balding
	Gallina	Ribblesdale Stakes	MV O'Brien (IRE)
	Gay Fandango	Jersey Stakes	MV O'Brien (IRE)
	Roussalka	Coronation Stakes	H Cecil
	Blood Royal	Queen's Vase	MV O'Brien (IRE)
	Faliraki	Norfolk Stakes	M O'Toole (IRE)
	Sagaro	Gold Cup	F Boutin (FR)
	Boone's Cabin	Wokingham Stakes	MV O'Brien (IRE)
1976	Anne's Pretender	Prince of Wales's Stakes	HR Price
	Jumping Hill	Royal Hunt Cup	N Murless
	General Ironside	Queen's Vase	H Cecil
	Sagaro	Gold Cup	F Boutin (FR)
1977	Solinus	Coventry Stakes	MV O'Brien (IRE)
	Amaranda	Queen Mary Stakes	H Wragg
	Emboss	Norfolk Stakes	R Boss
	Sagaro	Gold Cup	F Boutin (FR)
	Meneval	Hardwicke Stakes	MV O'Brien (IRE)
	Godswalk	King's Stand Stakes	MV O'Brien (IRE)
	John Cherry	Queen Alexandra Stakes	H Thomson Jones
1978	Jaazeiro	St James's Palace Stakes	MV O'Brien (IRE)
	Billion	Bessborough Stakes	J Dunlop
	Solinus	King's Stand Stakes	MV O'Brien (IRE)

1979	Baptism	Queen Anne Stakes	J Tree
	Crimson Beau	Prince of Wales's Stakes	P Cole
	Thatching	Cork and Orrery Stakes	MV O'Brien (IRE)
	Le Moss	Gold Cup	H Cecil
	Star Way	Chesham Stakes	P Kelleway
	Sea Chimes	King George V Stakes	J Dunlop
1980	Hard Fought	Jersey Stakes	M Stoute
1981	Belmont Bay	Queen Anne Stakes	H Cecil
	Strigida	Ribblesdale Stakes	H Cecil
	Rasa Penang	Jersey Stakes	R Armstrong
	Ardross	Gold Cup	H Cecil
	Cajun	Chesham Stakes	H Cecil
1982	Mr Fluorocarbon	Queen Anne Stakes	H Cecil
	Chalon	Coronation Stakes	H Cecil
	Evzon	Queen's Vase	C Brittain
	Ardross	Gold Cup	H Cecil
	Right Dancer	Chesham Stakes	P Kelleway
	Critique	Hardwicke Stakes	H Cecil
1983	Precocious	Norfolk Stakes	H Cecil
	Defecting Dancer	Windsor Castle Stakes	H Cecil
1984	Trojan Fen	Queen Anne Stakes	H Cecil
	Magic Mirror	Norfolk Stakes	MV O'Brien (IRE)
1985	Bairn	St James's Palace Stakes	L Cumani
	Jupiter Island	Hardwicke Stakes	C Brittain
	Never So Bold	King's Stand Stakes	R Armstrong
1991	Saddlers' Hall	King Edward VII Stakes	M Stoute
1992	Niche	Norfolk Stakes	R Hannon
1993	College Chapel	Cork and Orrery Stakes	MV O'Brien (IRE)

OTHER BIG RACE WINS

1951	Mystery IX	Eclipse Stakes	P Carter (FR)
1953	Zucchero	Coronation Cup	W Payne
1955	Darius	Eclipse Stakes	H Wragg
1956	Crepello	Dewhurst Stakes	N Murless

1957	Arctic Explorer	Eclipse Stakes	N Murless
	Vigo	July Cup	W Dutton
1958	Right Boy	July Cup	W Dutton
1959	Nagami	Coronation Cup	H Wragg
	Right Boy	July Cup	P Rohan
	Petite Etoile	Champion Stakes	N Murless
1960	Petite Etoile	Coronation Cup	N Murless
	Tin Whistle	July Cup	P Rohan
1961	Petite Etoile	Coronation Cup	N Murless
	St Paddy	Eclipse Stakes	N Murless
1962	Follow Suit	Dewhurst Stakes	N Murless
1963	The Creditor	Queen Elizabeth II Stakes	N Murless
1964	Linacre	Queen Elizabeth II St	P Prendergast (IRE)
1965	Meadow Court	K George VI & Q Elizabeth St	P.Prendergast (IRE)
1966	Pieces of Eight	Eclipse Stakes	MV O'Brien (IRE)
	Aunt Edith	K George VI & Q Elizabeth St	N Murless
	Hill Rise	Queen Elizabeth II Stakes	N Murless
	Pieces of Eight	Champion Stakes	MV O'Brien (IRE)
	Ribocco	Observer Gold Cup	RF Johnson Houghton
1968	Sir Ivor	Champion Stakes	MV O'Brien (IRE)
	Sir Ivor	Washington DC Int St(USA)	MV O'Brien (IRE)
	Ribofilio	Dewhurst Stakes	RF Johnson Houghton
1969	Park Top	Coronation Cup	B van Cutsem
	Wolver Hollow	Eclipse Stakes	H Cecil
	Park Top	K George VI & Q Elizabeth St	B van Cutsem
	Karabas	Washington DC Int St(USA)	B vanCutsem (GB)
	Nijinsky	Dewhurst Stakes	MV O'Brien (IRE)
1970	Nijinsky	K George VI & Q Elizabeth St	MV O'Brien (IRE)
1971	Crowned Prince	Dewhurst Stakes	B van Cutsem
1972	Noble Decree	Observer Gold Cup	B van Cutsem
1973	Roberto	Coronation Cup	MV O'Brien (IRE)
	Thatch	July Cup	MV O'Brien (IRE)
	Rheingold	Prix de l'Arc de Triomphe	B Hills (GB)

1973	Cellini	Dewhurst Stakes	MV O'Brien (IRE)
(*cont*)	Apalachee	Observer Gold Cup	MV O'Brien (IRE)
1974	Saritamer	July Cup	MV O'Brien (IRE)
	Dahlia	K George VI & Q Elizabeth St	M Zilber (FR)
	Dahlia	Benson & Hedges Gold Cup[2]	M Zilber (FR)
	Giacometti	Champion Stakes	HR Price
1975	Dahlia	Benson & Hedges Gold Cup[2]	M Zilber (FR)
1976	Quiet Fling	Coronation Cup	J Tree
	The Minstrel	Dewhurst Stakes	MV O'Brien (IRE)
1977	Artaius	Eclipse Stakes	MV O'Brien (IRE)
	The Minstrel	K George VI & Q Elizabeth St	MV O'Brien (IRE)
	Alleged	Prix de l'Arc de Triomphe	MV O'Brien (IRE)
	Try My Best	Dewhurst Stakes	MV O'Brien (IRE)
1978	Solinus	July Cup	MV O'Brien (IRE)
	Hawaiian Sound	Benson & Hedges Gold Cup[2]	B Hills
	Alleged	Prix de l'Arc de Triomphe	MV O'Brien (IRE)
1979	Thatching	July Cup	MV O'Brien (IRE)
	Monteverdi	Dewhurst Stakes	MV O'Brien (IRE)
1980	Sea Chimes	Coronation Cup	J Dunlop
	Moorestyle	July Cup	R Armstrong
	Argument	Washington DC Int St (USA)	M Zilber (FR)
1981	To-Agori-Mou	Queen Elizabeth II Stakes	G Harwood
1982	Diesis	Dewhurst Stakes	H Cecil
	Dunbeath	William Hill Futurity Stakes[1]	H Cecil
1983	Be My Native	Coronation Cup	R Armstrong
1984	Teenoso	K George VI & Q Elizabeth St	G Wragg
	Lanfranco	William Hill Futurity Stakes[1]	H Cecil
1985	Commanche Run	Benson & Hedges Gold Cup[2]	L Cumani
	Commanche Run	Irish Champion Stakes	L Cumani (GB)
1990	Royal Academy	Breeders' Cup Mile (USA)	MV O'Brien (IRE)
1992	Mr Brooks	July Cup	R Hannon
	Rodrigo de Triano	International Stakes	P Chapple-Hyam
	Rodrigo de Triano	Champion Stakes	P Chapple-Hyam

[1]now Racing Post Trophy

[2]now International Stakes

COUNTRIES IN WHICH WINNERS ARE RIDDEN
(apart from Great Britain)

Europe:	Austria; Belgium; Denmark; France; Germany; Greece; Ireland; Italy; Jersey; Norway; Slovakia; Spain; Sweden; Turkey
Americas:	Argentina; Brazil; Canada; Chile; Jamaica; Trinidad; United States
Asia-Pacific:	Australia; Hong Kong; India; Macau; Malaysia; New Zealand; Singapore
Middle East-Africa:	Bahrain; Dubi; Kenya; South Africa; Zimbabwe

THE HISTORICAL RECORD
Winningmost jockeys on the Flat in Great Britain, as at 10 September 1995

Career total	NAME (riding years)	Best Season
4,870	Sir Gordon Richards (1921–54)	269 (1947)
4,493	LESTER PIGGOTT (1948–94)	191 (1966)
3,755	Willie Carson(1962–)	187 (1990)
3,663	Pat Eddery (1969–)	209 (1990)
3,111	Doug Smith (1932–67)	173 (1947)
2,810	Joe Mercer (1950–85)	164 (1979)
2,748	Fred Archer (1870–86)	246 (1885)
2,593	Edward Hilde (1951–93)	137 (1974)
2,587	George Fordham (1851–83)	166 (1862)
2,312	Eph Smith (1930–65)	144 (1947)

Index

338

344